Microcomputers for Adult Learning

Potentials and Perils

Edited by David G. Guculette

Follett Publishing Company
Chicago, Illinois

Atlanta, Georgia • Dallas, Texas
Sacramento, California • Warrensburg, Missouri
Flemington, New Jersey

Library of Congress Cataloging in Publication Data

Main entry under title:

Microcomputers for adult learning.

Includes bibliographies.
1. Adult education—Computer assisted instruction—Addresses, essays, lectures. 2. Microcomputers—Addresses, essays, lectures. I. Gueulette, David.
LC5219.M47 1982 374′.02 82-16074
ISBN 0-695-81667-5

First Printing

Contents

Acknowledgments

I wish to thank the authors who so generously and creatively gave content to this collection. Special thanks also are extended to Zoraini Wati M. Abas, who prepared the Glossary; Vicke Heins, who helped with the preparation of articles; and A. Jean Lesher, who inspired this effort.

David G. Gueulette

Foreword

When Charles Bubbage invented the "Difference Engine" in 1821—considered to be the first computer—I doubt that he realized that some 160 years later computers would play such an important role in the lives of people. Today we chuckle when we compare Bubbage's invention made up of hundreds of rods, wheels, ratchets, and gears to the modern-day computer that sits on our desk top and takes up little more room than a typewriter. Yet, many believe that this "modern-day" computer will be viewed as clumsy and incompetent in a few years.

Computers are not new to education. In the 1950s they were introduced in colleges and universities to help manipulate numbers and assist researchers with statistical computations. These early computers, consisting of hundreds of glowing tubes and yards of multi-colored wires, filled entire rooms. With the introduction of the transistor, computers decreased in size and cost and increased in capacity and ability. In education, we began to see the beginnings of computer-assisted instruction—a kind of programmed learning in which students pushed buttons in response to questions presented by the computer. Early computer-assisted instruction never caught on in education as some educators imagined it would—it was expensive, there were many "down times" during which the machine wasn't operating, and students became bored with selected, prearranged responses to questions.

Then we began to hear about the microcomputer, a free-standing, easily portable computer powerful enough to store and manipulate information and inexpensive enough to be affordable. Many businesses, and even families, began purchasing these computers. We began to see microcomputers in elementary and secondary school classrooms, and they became the subject of computer courses at colleges and universities. But business and industry were far ahead of education in the use of microcomputers—executives had them in their offices, secretaries used them instead of typewriters, accounting departments had them, parts departments used them for inventory control; they were scattered throughout firms.

Adult education only recently has begun to explore microcomputers and their application for the education of adults. This book is an early attempt to examine microcomputers from the perspective of adult education.

Within adult education, microcomputers can be viewed in at least three ways: 1) the microcomputer as an appliance may be applied to such tasks as family budgeting, check balancing, controlling home heating systems, assisting the small business owner, and providing entertainment through computer games, 2) the microcomputer as an information finder can be tied to computer banks through telephone hookups to provide a massive amount of information, and 3) the microcomputer as teacher can be used to provide simulations that offer adult learners opportunities to practice tasks more inexpensively than working with the real thing—opportunities for learning a foreign language, mathematics, writing, and a host of other skills. When tied to video machines, the microcomputer can provide an even broader range of interesting learning experiences that offer the opportunity for student feedback and response.

The field of adult education appears to have taken three positions concerning the microcomputer. The first position is represented by those adult educators who have become aware of the microcomputer and haven't decided yet what to make of it. A second group has examined the microcomputer and decided that it has no application in adult education. These adult educators offer a variety of reasons for their position, ranging from cost to the inhumane and impersonal qualities of the computer. A third group has heard about the microcomputer, has gotten excited about it, and wants to incorporate the microcomputer in every aspect of adult education from language education to education in the arts and humanities.

Each of these perspectives presents many problems. On the one hand, those of us in adult education cannot overlook the importance of microcomputers in our society. They are in business and industry, they are increasingly to be found in elementary and secondary schools, and they have just begun to appear in homes. They are not to be ignored. Yet, in my opinion, it is an error to jump on the microcomputer bandwagon without looking carefully before we leap. Some adult educators have done so in the past with other technological innovations. Some, for example, gave adult education via television far more attention than it deserved—not that television doesn't have an important role to play, it does.

Before we become seduced by the tremendous potential microcomputers seem to have for adult education, we must examine a series of questions and explore a number of potential problems that the microcomputer presents. First, we need to recognize what the microcomputer can and cannot do. It can make available almost unlimited information, particularly when tied via telephone to computer banks. It allows the learner to talk back. It can be tied to other people who have microcomputers. It can be set up in one's home. And it allows a person to work with various types of information at a selected speed.

Given all of that, what can't it do? It cannot provide real life experiences—it can come close with simulations, but a simulation is often a quantum jump from the real thing. It can't provide the warmth that is possible when a group of adults explore some topic together, work on some problem, or attempt to learn some skill. It can't provide the opportunity for learning interpersonal skills. As some have said, if all of the world were one day to consist of isolated learners hunched over microcomputers, how would we ever solve the problems of groups, states, and nations that must learn to live in the world together?

The microcomputer is a tremendous resource for information processing. It is much more difficult to think of it as a resource for ethical decision making, for developing appreciations for the arts and the humanities, for developing attitudes and feelings about what it means to be a human being.

How can we, then, take advantage of the strengths of the microcomputer in adult education and, at the same time, be cognizant of its weaknesses? Let me suggest some "what ifs."

What if we began to view the microcomputer as a source of information for adults, and thus release education from its historical primary role of transmitting information from source to learner? Is it possible thus to change the very definition of what teaching and learning is about? Is it possible to view teaching and learning as something more than transmitting information?

If the microcomputer is a ready source of unlimited information, from computer banks and from people who are willing to share their information via microcomputer exchanges, why bother to have people "learning" information as a part of educational programs? Why, for instance, have an adult education course that explains the workings of the stock market when people can obtain that information for themselves on their microcomputers? Why offer a course that summarizes recent research in food processing when those concerned can easily obtain that information for themselves, and more inexpensively too?

Taking this idea a step further, if adult education could be freed from its role of transmitting information, it could begin to spend more time on the meaning of information, on problems and issues, on ethical concerns, on matters that require human interaction such as a nation's policies toward the environment, nuclear energy, peace, and human rights.

Before becoming enthused about this application of the microcomputer, several serious problems must be explored. What will happen to those vast numbers of adults who do not have enough money to buy a microcomputer and thus do not have ready access to the information sources? Will we develop a society even more widely split between the haves and have nots?

And what about the information controllers, those who provide the information for the computer banks? How can we be assured that the information is accurate, that the information isn't slanted in a particular way, that certain information isn't being excluded, that we aren't somehow being manipulated by the information? (Of course we already face this problem with our present information sources.)

There is every indication that the microcomputer will continue to decrease in price and thus become widely available to many more people. We in adult education are already behind in examining its potentials for assisting adult learning. It is time we began a serious exploration of these potentials, albeit an informed and thoughtful exploration.

Jerold W. Apps
University of Wisconsin

David G. Gueulette

Introduction

The way to solve the conflict between human values and technological needs is not to run away from technology. That's impossible. The way to resolve the conflict is to break down the barriers of dualistic thought that prevent a real understanding of what technology is—not an exploitation of nature, but a fusion of nature and the human spirit into a new kind of creation that transcends both. When this transcendence occurs in such events as the first airplane flight across the ocean or the first footstep on the moon, a kind of public recognition of the transcendent nature of technology occurs. But this transcendence should also occur at the individual level, on a personal basis, in one's own life, in a less dramatic way. (Pirsig 1974: 261–262)

A recently completed study involving research with the Myers-Briggs Type Indicator has strong indications for CAI uses. This study, involving 3500 learners, indicates that CAI programs may favor those learners who have the ability to quietly concentrate, pay attention to details, memorize facts, and stay with a single task until its completion. Extroverts (or perceptive learners), on the other hand, may not fare so well.

If the learner craves the presence of other people, interacts well with other people, is deeply concerned with other people, the inanimate computer does not satisfy his/her preference.

In summary, the individualized concept which might result in a computer for every learner will produce inadequate educational learning performance for a large percentage of learners. (Hopmeier 1981: 16–17)

Before adult educators rush headlong into the rapidly developing area of microcomputers for instruction, it is imperative that they examine a balanced view of the potentials, perils, and practicalities of this new medium. Beset by glowing claims, inundated by sales and promotional materials on the educational applications of microcomputers, and constantly exposed to the dramatic and colorful examples of exciting teaching possibilities as found in professional and popular literature, those in decision-making positions regarding the selection of instructional delivery systems are in great need of a reference or issues text that reveals the complex and often contradictory aspects of this technology in a critical and evenhanded manner.

The themes of the articles in this anthology express the following concerns: potentials of this new teaching medium as reflected in actual and proposed learning activities; perils or problems associated with selecting, using, and misusing the technology; and recommendations or models for the appropriate implementation and use of microcomputers for the instruction of adults.

The contributors to this anthology have been drawn from the fields of adult education and instructional technology. Several of the writers are noted experts in both fields. While it is impossible to bring together a complete or even comprehensive accumulation of all the issues, practices, or prospects for this new teaching medium, the selection of topics in this text attempts to provide sufficient balanced information on instructional microcomputers so that an adult educator or administrator might make a more informed decision on how, when, and where to employ the technology.

Some of the authors have approached the task as an exercise in overcoming traditional resistance to the adoption of innovative teaching methods or media that has characterized the field of education in general and adult education in particular. Other writers consider the adult educator to be a wise and cautious leader who thoughtfully examines potential teaching tools and accepts and implements only those that can support meaningful learning approaches and beneficial social values.

The authors have tried to avoid making references to specific equipment types, software packages, or costs, except when citing an example, as these aspects of the technology change so rapidly. Suffice it to say, that equipment is becoming more readily available, more adaptable to individual needs, and easier to program and use. Software or courseware is also easier to locate and more specific to identified learner aptitudes. Costs of equipment and software are going up, but modestly, compared to other instructional technologies.

The terms used by the authors vary somewhat in that they sometimes assign different meanings to concepts, programs, or applications. This appears to be one of several problems with this emerging field. The distinctions between the structure, uses, and impact of the microcomputer are sometimes difficult to discern from the structure, uses, and impact of the large mainframe computer. Computer-Assisted Instruction (CAI) is a basic function of both computer systems and this encourages a writer to explain the instructional process as applicable to either or both systems. The problem of separating the microcomputer, with its functions and their ramifications, from the earlier and still dominant large computer is one that has yet to be resolved. Some experts have suggested that there is really little or no distinction between the two, at least in the educational end result; perhaps they are right.

The Foreword to this collection is provided by Jerold W. Apps, who develops an informative and provocative review of the development of the computer in the educational context. He discusses the three positions that seem to reflect traditional adult educators' views of computers. His main theme, however, is a call for a more creative and responsible role for adult educators in their use of technology. He has determined that the most valuable function computers can provide for educators lies in the area of information management, which can free teachers from the time-consuming drudgery of recording and retrieving data for more important activities such as personalized instruction.

W.C. Meierhenry begins "Microcomputers and Adult Education" with an investigation of serious issues related to adult learning and technology. He argues that the dilemmas facing adult educators concerning their use of methods of instruction should not prevent them from facing the problems head-on and from making reasoned choices for the best and most humane applications of microcomputers and other teaching tools.

Meierhenry's primary contribution lies in his lucid and helpful explanation of adult learning theories and how they relate to the uses of the microcomputer. His careful review of current ideas on how adults learn considers the repercussions of interfacing mechanical and isolating systems with accepted adult learning styles.

Drawing upon a considerable base of research in adult learning, Meierhenry relates these findings to the emerging knowlege on the effects of computers and allied devices. His research findings reflecting potential uses of technology for adult education support his claim that microcomputers must be used and used humanely to provide the best possible educational support services for the many adult learners who will need educational assistance in the coming years. His conclusion suggests a future in which adults will be educated with new technologies that will be directed by appropriate learning theories.

"The Development of a Unique Teaching Technology" by Hugh Garraway is a compact yet informative review of the development of the computer and computer-assisted instruction. His explanation of the emergence of the "information society" focuses on the transition of training needs from basic instruction for vocational education purposes to the management of information in a world characterized by increasing use of electronic devices and associated materials (software).

Garraway outlines the historical development of the computer and the creation of initial applications. He defines the terminology of the medium as it has evolved with the equipment and software. He also comments on the initial success of the technology and suggests that it has proven its value for adult education in business, industry, and the military.

Garraway suggests that microcomputers have many distinct advantages over the large mainframe computers. For example, the equipment can stand alone in many diverse locations and is not tied to central equipment or software. Microcomputers are easy to operate and are not limited to time-sharing or terminal restrictions. They are less expensive to buy, maintain, and operate. His comparison of the microcomputer and the mainframe computer is most important if one is trying to determine if one system is better suited to an identified need than the other. Another useful section of this article deals with the possibility of networking to share facilities and software.

The discussion on obtaining courseware by buying or producing programs will be especially helpful to the new consumer. Garraway cautions prospective users that quality instructional programs can only be developed with the aid of adequate planning. He also points out that the medium is still in the nascent stages of its development.

George Mozes describes current applications of microcomputers in the health field in "Professional Education and the

Microcomputer." He outlines the use of this technology for solving patient-management problems (PMP) by using the microcomputer for simulations. Medical educators can avoid dangerous and expensive procedures and they can compress time by using microcomputer simulations. The problem solving emphasis of PMP is a perfect task for the microcomputer, which can simulate the various data that must be considered in teaching patient-management problems.

Mozes explains how the microcomputer has been used for actual patient-management problem simulations at Michael Reese Hospital in Chicago and provides a detailed commentary on the equipment, languages, and programs used. He also puts forth the case for using this simulation strategy for continuing professional medical education for doctors and others in the field. A network of shared simulations would be advantageous to participants as they would be relieved of the necessity of producing specific programs.

Continuing medical education for practicing physicians via the microcomputer also takes the form of pre-packaged seminars on tapes and disks.

Mozes lists and evaluates several of the typical applications of the medium for continuing education for various segments of the health services. He concludes his article with a strong argument for extensive use of the technology for continuing educational experiences in other professional areas as well; the argument is based on adult learning needs. His forecast provides a useful perspective on the potential uses of the medium from one who is currently very active in the development and use of microcomputers for continuing professional education.

Dorothy H. Judd provides a comprehensive outline of professional applications of microcomputers for teaching reading and writing skills to adults in her article, "A Microcomputer Role in Adult Reading and Writing Skill Development." She constructs a sound rationale for teaching adults reading and writing that is consistent with the technical characteristics of microcomputers. For example, she notes that the medium is very patient, very consistent, and very persistent, all of which support an effective approach for teaching adults to read and write.

Judd also points out the technical requirements of the microcomputer that must be available for the best teaching environment for an adult learner. Her analysis of computers and the Language Experience Approach suggests that the technology and its language are important to this language-teaching technique. The medium and the technique match exceedingly well.

The unique ability of the microcomputer to supply highly individualized teaching also supports other reading and writing programs. Judd discusses these programs and recommends microcomputer applications. Of particular interest is the use of microcomputers by learners with learning disabilities. One of the primary strengths of the technology may well be its ability to provide specialized instructional programs and conditions for the adult learner who has some kind of learning, visual, or auditory limitations.

"Perceptions of Decision Makers Concerning Microcomputers for Adult Learning" by Carol E. Kasworm and Cheryl A. Anderson is an engaging and useful summary of the results of a survey of adult education administrators regarding the following topics:

1. Current awareness and use of microcomputers
2. Instructional staff development for using microcomputers
3. Accessibility of software and its development
4. Perceptions about adult learners and the medium
5. Financial concerns related to the technology

The survey was designed to uncover perceptions held by adult educators and administrators about the use of microcomputers for their instructional programs with the objective of trying to list common concerns. By doing so, the authors were able to make some generalizations on how, when, and where these decision makers will begin to buy microcomputer hardware and software for their respective institutions.

The important questions listed in the survey received responses from the administrators; the authors have presented the consensus or lack thereof in a manner that can serve as a helpful guide to those in similar situations who might be considering the introduction of microcomputers into adult education programs. The results are interesting and perhaps not necessarily those that might be expected.

Computer literacy and in-service training for instructional microcomputers are the main concerns of Roger Sanders in "Computer Literacy: Innovation Adoption and In-service Training." Sanders begins his plan for microcomputer in-service training and literacy development with a review of current barriers to the acceptance and use of the technology that have been cited in the literature. His evaluations of research on computers and educator attitudes set the stage for his plan to introduce the medium and to prepare staff to use it willingly and effectively.

His outline for in-service training for potential staff and faculty users is complete, clear, usable, and easily implemented. Recommendations for administrators and teachers are specific and germane to effective introduction of microcomputers into the teaching process. His in-service model is well defined and should serve as a guide to the administrator planning to venture into using this technology. The list of questions that the decision maker must answer before he or she is ready to make a commitment to using the computer will help the educator plan a successful use for the medium with the adult learner. Sanders's emphasis on adoption of change and specific planning strategies is unique and pertinent.

"Information Resources for Computer-Assisted Instruction" by John Hortin is an informative introduction to the role of this new technology in adult learning. The article provides an overview of the initial applications of computers for adult learning as reported in respected texts and journals. Research findings that have emerged as the accepted first critiques of the medium are discussed and evaluated. The many journals that consistently offer information on the instructional use of microcomputers are listed with a commentary on their respective importance to the adult education specialist. In addition to the compiled sources, Hortin provides a description of the Educational Resources Information Center (ERIC) data bank on microcomputer technology.

This article is a useful resource for the reader who needs direction in finding further information on microcomputers as reported in the literature and in research reports. The source lists and commentaries are preceded by a background discussion of technology for teaching.

"Microcomputer Software for Educational Use" by Peter West argues against the widely held notion that there is no microcomputer software on the market for adult learning. West lists many examples of adult education programs and supplies an extensive list of software directories and distributors. This helpful guide to the software resources is a good starting point for the courseware shopper.

West's comprehensive courseware evaluation model can be

applied to the problem of deciding which programs might be useful for specific instructional purposes.

"Power, Learning, and, 'Compunication,'" is the title and the theme of a critical essay by Thomas W. Heaney. Worried that the microcomputer will preempt the formal learning of its content, leaving only organized social activities and sports to the schools, Heaney argues that the concentration of information power, far beyond anything imagined by the monopolies of school systems and universities, represents an inestimable potential for either human growth or diminishment. He builds a dramatic characterization of the relationship between knowledge control and power and its subsequent impact on the schooling system. His solution to the struggle for knowledge control rests on the implementation of "liberatory education" by which participants in the learning process can contribute to and share knowledge by means of the computer. Interactive microcomputer systems and networks are, after all, possible. Networks for sharing knowledge can be created and expanded to serve great numbers of learners.

Heaney's conclusion presents a paradox. Although he cites, with pessimism, the growing structure of the corporate-directed computer knowledge system, he also believes that microcomputers can offer a basis for liberatory education and participatory research. He hopes that the technology can enhance the ability of learners in groups to comprehend the inequalities of their world, to imagine alternatives, and to design appropriate strategies to reflect on and evaluate their own actions and thus to collaborate with each other in creating the future.

"Learning in a Wired School: Home Telecommunications-Computer Centers" by David G. Gueulette is a scenario of a future in which the microcomputer will figure as the primary component of a home telecommunications center. Adults and children alike will be isolated and inert learners, knowing the world only as it is mediated by the computer and the extensive cable and satellite television delivery systems tied to it.

Gueulette documents the development of the delivery system and the allied technologies and argues that special-interest groups have much to gain from the expansion and exploitation of a profitable centralized electronic education system. He lists problems associated with equipment, software, programming, and the concept of instructional self-sufficiency. Many of the questions regarding the acquisition and application of microcomputers are examined.

Adult educators can and must influence the direction and structure of the home telecommunications center so that a humane, democratic, and pluralistic education will still be possible. The indication that education will increasingly become what the system can deliver is an ominous prospect and must be countered by educators who can develop content or curriculum specified by learner or societal needs. Gueulette argues that the cadre of technical experts who have surfaced with the new technologies should be limited in their management of the educational systems.

Alan B. Salisbury's "Fundamentals of Microcomputer Hardware and Software" is a training guide on the fundamentals of microcomputers for the adult educator. The author provides a working knowlege of equipment and programming for the novice reader. His listing of necessary vocabulary is most helpful and comprehensive. Salisbury believes that a better understanding of the specifics of computers will enable the educator to deal with the planning, selection, and implementation of the best microcomputer systems.

Salisbury has included excellent graphics to explain the structure and process of microcomputers. He describes the terms used in the medium in the context of potential instructional applications and even lays out tentative approaches to self-programmed instruction.

His comments on equipment and software selection avoid technical jargon and specific references to current items. Rather, he stresses major overall considerations for buying and using the technology. He cautions the reader to be alert to the changing state-of-the-art of microcomputers and to carefully study new systems and materials before making a commitment to one product or another.

This article is mandatory reading for anyone preparing to initiate programs for adult instruction using microcomputers. Salisbury calls for an informed consumer and provides the information that can lead to intelligent acquisition and use of the microcomputer.

References

Hopmeier, G. 1981. New study says CAI may favor introverts. *Electrical Education.* 1:16–17.

Pirsig, R. M. 1974. *Zen and the art of motorcycle maintenance: an inquiry into values.* New York: Bantam Books.

W. C. Meierhenry

Microcomputers and Adult Education

There are predictions that the use of microcomputers will revolutionize all of education including adult education. It has been suggested that the microcomputer represents the most complete technological device for instruction that has yet been developed. There can be no doubt that microcomputers have great potential for enriching and improving adult education. This article will attempt to describe some of the factors that will facilitate or retard the use of microcomputers, some of the theoretical problems that will have to be faced, and some of the possible applications of the microcomputer in adult education.

Prevailing Philosophy of Adult Education

The first problem that anyone attempting to apply a technology to adult education has to face is the highly humanistic and process-oriented dimensions of the field. Because of their humanistic philosophy, many adult educators consider technology to be in opposition to human values. As a consequence they do not view technology, such as the microcomputer, as facilitating the development of human qualities and characteristics but rather as retarding their development.

A second philosophical issue relates to whether adult education should be primarily process or product oriented. Many adult educators, and the clientele they serve, desire considerable interpersonal interaction in the learning process as well as an emphasis on how to solve problems rather than their solution. One of the reasons for such a philosophy is that some of the well-known leaders in the field of adult education had their original academic roots in sociology and/or social work. Individuals with such a background would naturally study human behavior in the light of human interactions. Technology, including the preprogrammed microcomputer, is not perceived as contributing significantly to the process of problem solving but rather to deriving the correct response to a problem.

As a consequence of these and other philosophical issues within the field of adult education, those who promote the use of microcomputers will have to deal with such issues and others if the applications of microcomputers to adult education are to be successful. The dilemma faced by one individual who tried to make the transition from the adult education model to the training model including the use of such technologies as microcomputers was indicated recently by Proulx:

> It is certainly not an easy task trying to reconcile these two approaches [adult education and instructional technology, which would include microcomputers]. Some experts on both sides have tried; others have vehemently opposed any form of rapprochement or even detente.
>
> But my concern is with the humble practitioner battered by two very different philosophies to the teaching and training of adult learners. I am talking, here, about trainers and training developers like myself.
>
> Mine is a teaching background. Feeling some of the symptoms of the generation gap syndrome, I decided several years ago to orient my professional activities toward adult teaching/training. I very naturally turned toward "the science and art of adult education." I even acquired—not without a certain amount of difficulty or discomfort—a thorough initiation into the organic model of training and development as opposed to the "mechanistic model." I even went so far as to travel (at my own expense) to Raleigh, N.C. to sit at the feet of Malcolm Knowles, father of andragogy.
>
> Educated, I found myself a job as a training developer in a large corporation. And there I encountered a rude shock. While I was organically developing instruction, others around me were marching to a "behavioral" drum. Not wanting to be out of step, I quickly enrolled in instructional technology courses and was soon drawing little boxes and writing specific objectives and criterion referenced items in classic linear fashion.
>
> So here I am a product of two approaches and finding a lot of difficulties trying to marry the two. (Proulx 1980: 3–4)

Issues in Program Development for Microcomputers

Although computer programmers typically have come from a different academic discipline (mathematics) than have individuals who developed programmed instruction (psychology), one cannot help but be aware of the striking similarity between the theoretical constructs of programs developed for the computer and the earlier developments of programmed instruction.

The learning theory that has dominated much of the programming for programmed instruction as well as microcomputers is behaviorism. As Low (1980–81) pointed out, the behavioristic theory focuses upon the intended outcomes of instruction. Thus, if the outcomes of instruction are responses, the objectives must describe these responses. As a consequence, much effort is placed on the writing of objectives according to Mager, whose definition, criteria, and procedures for developing behavioral objectives are universally accepted.

This discussion relates to that considered earlier in regard to the issue in adult education between process and product outcomes. Adult educators place great emphasis on internally derived goals or objectives for learning rather than on those imposed externally. Objectives in behavioral terms place the locus of developing objectives outside, or external to, the learner. Adult educators prefer that objectives for learning be generated and explicated internally.

Because behavioristic psychology is such an anathema to adult educators, it is evident that those responsible for developing adult programs for microcomputers will need to consider learning theories more acceptable than behaviorism if their programs are to be readily accepted by adult educators.

A major theory currently in favor is based on the cognitive view, which is an active and generative process in which the individual constructs meanings and understandings from experiences (Wildman and Burton 1981). Learning is not viewed simply as single behaviors or classes of behaviors but as being organized into memory "units" for which there are certain known characteristics.

Two areas of work in cognitive psychology that have implications for programming the microcomputer for adults are the development of information-processing models of knowledge acquisition and the use of schemata to describe the organization of knowledge (Low 1980–81). Low indicated that a basic difference between the behaviorist approach and the cognitive or information-processing approach relates to how a learning event is described and what is presumed to be important. In behavioral psychology learning is described in terms of observable responses, and these responses are presumed to be the result of stimulus situations. The behaviorist believes that even a complex learning event may be described entirely by relating sets of stimuli to responses.

In an information-processing approach events that occur internally are covert events, and they are of prime importance. As Low pointed out, these events or intellectual events are not observable. Thus it is not clear what they consist of, and the best that can be done is to model them. Low went on to suggest that such a process is not necessarily unique in psychology. Physicists, for example, followed much the same process when they tried to describe matter. Since it was postulated that matter was composed of minute particles too small to be observed directly (atoms), a visual representation of what the atom might look like was made. This model evolved from early planetary models. Later models of the atom were more mathematical than visual.

The literature suggests that any of a number of learning theories might be pursued in microcomputer programming, but that more progress would probably be made if only one theory were researched extensively rather than adopting an eclectic view. It has been suggested that humanistic psychology as well as theories ranging from the psychoanalytic to the transpersonal might be attempted in the programming of microcomputers (Wildman and Burton 1981).

It will, therefore, be necessary that programmers of microcomputers for adult learning continue to explore a variety of approaches to learning. Howe pointed out the following:

> In the 1960s many research workers envisaged that the digital computer would play a key role in education through the development and widespread use of programs which would "teach" topics drawn from a wide variety of disciplines. Reinforced by earlier work on programmed learning, the view that children "learn by being told" was much more prevalent at that time than it is today. The ready acceptance of this particular brand of educational philosophy was manifested in the subsequent implementation of computational teaching programs, which in the persuasive advertising jargon of education claimed to individualize teaching, and so facilitate learning.

> In contrast to these practitioners of computer-assisted instruction (CAI), one of several names given to this area of endeavour, there gradually emerged by the end of the decade a group of scientists who shared a very different belief about learning and thinking processes. Many of them were actively engaged in research in a comparatively new discipline called artificial intelligence (AI). The name "artificial intelligence" is not particularly apt: it does not adequately capture their aim, which is to increase understanding of such complex cognitive activities as seeing, learning, thinking and using language by constructing and testing explanations in computer-program form. The underlying assumption is that these activities are knowledge-based, and one of the chief concerns is how best to represent them in the computer. The relevance to education, and to CAI in particular, is the belief that a learner, working in a particular domain, has to build the domain-specific knowledge into an active mental data base, active in the sense that the knowledge represented in it at any time can be accessed and used as the basis for new learning. Notice that the process of constructing such a mental representation also implies creative mental activity on the part of the learner. This "learning by doing" can be sharply contrasted with "learning by being told," and subsumes activities ranging from the seeking out of relevant from irrelevant information to altering an explanation to get rid of errors or inconsistencies. In this context, the role of the teacher is to structure a domain in such a way that it facilitates the model-building activity. (Howe 1978: 114)

There is considerable discussion of artificial intelligence both in the United States and abroad. The exact elements that go into programming for artificial intelligence are not known, and the literature contains a number of approaches to the problem. Whether programming techniques for artificial intelligence will or will not be developed is not known at this point, but such a technique would represent a promising approach for microcomputer programs to be used in adult education.

If the microcomputer movement is to have any success in adult education, programmers who develop microcomputer programs for adults must be more creative and more consistent with how adult education research suggests learning takes place. The complexities of developing programs based on theories other than behaviorism are enormous, but efforts must be made if maximum benefits are to occur for adult education programs.

Implications for Adult Education

There are several different ways in which the contributions of microcomputer programs to education can be categorized.

Since the author knows of no such categorization solely applicable to adult education, several of the lists for education in general will be presented. These lists will be analyzed in terms of their relative applicability to adult education.

Kulik, Kulik, and Cohen (1980), as a result of undertaking a meta-analysis of findings of studies dealing with the effectiveness of computer-based college teaching, developed one such classification. The following categories are adapted from their examination of computer-based instruction research studies.

Tutorial

Computer presented instruction directly to students.

Managed

Computer evaluated student performance and diagnosed weaknesses; students were guided to appropriate resources.

Simulation

Students explored relationships among variables in models simulating aspects of social and physical reality.

Programming

Students programmed the computer to solve problems in the field they were studying.

Bork and Franklin (1979) recently compiled functions of the microcomputer. The classification system that follows was adapted from their more extensive discussion of each category.

Computer Programming and Problem-solving Drill and Practice

Systematic algorithmic expression of the solution of certain types of problems.

Drill and Practice

Opportunity to work problems and receive feedback.

Drill and Practice with Remediaton

In addition to drill and practice, provides for remediation.

Tutorial Programs

Dialogue between the learner and the computer program.

Testing

Test generation, administration, grading, reporting, and summarizing.

Testing with Learning

Specific immediate feedback can be offered to learners having difficulties on an interactive quiz or test.

Controllable Worlds
Generation of rich, creative manipulable environments; difficult in the real world.

Pflaumer (1979) presented yet another classification system. She proposed the following categories as instructional classifications within training as directly applicable to computer-based training.

Definitions
Teaching a term or specific language to which a meaning is attached.

Drill and Practice
Reinforces and establishes learning by repeated exercises of a particular procedure, formula applications, timed stimulus-response exercises, or other routines using this technique as a tool for learning.

Problems
Varies from simple to complex levels of difficulty and criticality that require sophisticated analysis techniques for decision making.

Testing
Variety of test forms.

Curriculum or Course Training Agenda
Managing the course curriculum via the computer for optimal training per trainee.

Resources
Presents support documents such as reference documents, charts, job or performance aids, formulas, tables, procedural directions, rules and regulations.

Records Management
Includes course scheduling, curriculum sequencing, registration, grading, and scoring of tests.

The categories discussed are not entirely consistent in the terminology used among the authors cited. Nevertheless, they are categories that adult educators are likely to find useful.

For adult learners requiring remedial tasks, the instructional procedures dealing with tutorial approaches, definitions, drill and practice, and drill and practice with remediation would seem appropriate. Such techniques might be used, for example, with learners engaged in Adult Basic Education.

Individuals involved in continuing professional education are likely to make extensive use of games and simulations and controllable worlds. A number of continuing education programs in medicine and dentistry have made extensive use of microcomputer simulation programs. The use of programs involving the solution of problems, such as diagnosis in medicine, would also appear to be appropriate for continuing professional education.

In those instances where the adult learning objective is skill development, microcomputer programs involving testing, testing with learning, provision of resources, performance recording, and timing would be useful. Individuals faced with the problem of updating of information would find such microcomputer programming approaches as definitions, solution of problems, testing and learning, and provision of resources helpful.

These examples indicate that many instructional and learning tasks in adult education could be served through properly developed programs on the microcomputer. There is considerable potential for various kinds of programming approaches to meet many of the existing adult education needs.

Factors Affecting Microcomputer Use

A number of factors will facilitate or retard the application of microcomputers in adult education. Such factors as types of adult education, level of education, reasons for enrolling in adult education programs, locations of such programs, preferred instructional methods, and reasons for dropping adult education programs, as well as their implications for possible microcomputer use will be discussed.

Types of Adult Education Programs

The most recent study on *Participation in Adult Education* (National Center for Education Statistics 1972) found that 46.5 percent of adult learners were enrolled in occupational training (vocational and technical, managerial, and professional) courses. That 25.9 percent were enrolled in general education (adult basic education, Americanization, and high school and college credit courses for credit) courses. Enrollment in personal and family living (home and family living and personal development) courses, social and recreational lessons (hobbies and handcrafts and sports lessons), and community issues (civic and public affairs, religion, and safety) followed with rates of 14.0, 12.0, and 9.8 percent respectively. It is possible that more recent figures might differ somewhat from these percentages but major differences are not likely.

The microcomputer probably would be most useful in the area of occupational training, which includes the largest number of adult learners. The microcomputer would seem to have implications for training in the sub-fields under occupational training; these include vocational and technical training, managerial training, and professional training or retraining.

The number of individuals involved in Adult Basic Education (ABE) and Americanization preparation under the heading of general education is quite small. Although there would appear to be some possibilities for using the microcomputer in remedial work, such as ABE, the actual number of such learners would be too small to represent a large potential for the use of the microcomputer.

The use of the microcomputer in presenting programs dealing with community issues, personal and family living, and social and recreational lessons would probably be limited since the very nature of these activities suggests considerable human interaction and a process approach to learning.

Thus, although not all types of adult education activities would seem amenable to presentation via microcomputer programs, it would appear that a substantial market could be developed in terms of the number of learners to be served by appropriately developed microcomputer programs.

Level of Education

The level of education attained by the current population would seem to be important in ascertaining the possible uses of the microcomputer. The proportion of individuals in the United States completing high school, one or more years of college, or college has been increasing.

A recent graphic representation of educational attainment of the population 25 years old and over, 1910–2000 (Carnegie Commission on Higher Education 1973) indicated a dramatic increase in educational levels. For example, in 1910 only 2.7 percent of the population had completed four years of college, by 1940 that percentage was still only 4.6 percent. By 1980 it was projected that 14.6 percent of those 25 years of age and older would have a college degree. Equally as dramatic is the increase in high school completion, from approximately 12 percent in 1910 to a projected 40 percent in 1980.

A 1978 study (National Center for Education Statistics 1981) reported that only 2.4 percent of those participating in adult education had less than a ninth-grade education and that 7.5 percent had achieved the ninth- to eleventh-grade level of education. In other words, 90 percent of those individuals participating in adult education activities had a high school level of education or more, including 32.7 percent of the participants who had finished four or more years of college.

It can be postulated that the more education an individual has, the more flexible and innovative the individual would be. Therefore, the higher the education level reached, the more likely that a person would be willing to use technological advances such as the microcomputer. The fact that many young people today are being exposed to microcomputers in schools and homes is an additional positive factor for the use of microcomputers. Producers of microcomputers are also undertaking strong sales campaigns. Thus, the current and future level of education of the general population is a positive factor in the possible use of microcomputers.

Reasons for Enrolling in Adult Education Programs

The reasons why individuals participate in adult education were reported in a recent study conducted by the National Center for Education Statistics (1981) for the year ending in May 1978. According to the data, most adults take courses to advance on the current job. Next in importance were personal, social, or other non-job related reasons. The third reason for taking such courses was the pursuit of general information, and the fourth to get a new job. When the percentage of adults engaged in taking adult education courses to advance in a current job (38.9%) was added to the number enrolled to get a new job (10.5%) and to other job-related reasons (3.3%), it is evident that more than 50 percent of all adult education is related to jobs and work. As suggested earlier, the microcomputer would seem to have potential for making major contributions to job preparation for adults.

Locations of Adult Education Programs

The locations of adult education courses have important implications for the use of the microcomputer, and in the study referred to previously (National Center for Education Statistics 1981) it was indicated that the location of adult education activities is related to the nature of the learning activity. For example, job-related adult education activities are likely to occur in two-year colleges or vocational technical institutes, four-year colleges or universities, vocational trade or business schools, businesses and industries, labor organizations or professional associations, or government agencies. Personal, social, or other non-job related adult education is most likely to occur in elementary schools, junior or senior high schools, two-year colleges or vocational institutes, tutorial or private instructional situations, government agencies, and private community organizations.

The potential for the use of microcomputers in relation to the locale of adult education activities would be very high since schools, colleges, and universities are likely to have microcomputers and appropriate settings in which they could be used. A community center might include a resource center with microcomputers; this would be a favorable place to conduct adult education classes requiring the use of microcomputers. Work places that are not currently making wide use of microcomputers for training certainly have the potential to do so. The home is another place for an increasing number of microcomputers in the future. Thus, the accessibility of locations for microcomputer installations is a very positive factor in their future widespread use.

Instructional Methods Preferred by Adult Learners

The Commission on Non-Traditional Study (1973) reported that most future adult learners preferred traditional methods of instruction, but there were some preferred modes of instruction that suggest potential for such individual devices as the microcomputer. For example, such approaches as individual lessons from a private teacher (7.0%) and study on my own (7.0%) represented desired methods by about one-seventh of the future adult learners. When these figures are added to the potential for use of microcomputers in correspondence courses and to their use in conjunction with such technologies as television or video cassettes, radio, records, or audio cassettes, the potential increases to about one-fifth of the future adult learners.

Although the preferred methods of future adult learners continue to be the more traditional ones of lectures, classes, on-the-job-training, conferences, and institutes, there are many individuals who would prefer a more individualized learning approach. For such individuals the microcomputer offers considerable potential. It should also be pointed out that adults (and others) tend to prefer what they know or are familiar with, thus it cannot be assumed that their preferences preclude new learning methods and technologies unfamiliar to them.

Reasons for Dropping Programs

One important question in the use of microcomputers is would they have any impact on the drop-out rate for adult education classes. In a 1978 study (National Center for Education Statistics 1981), two factors (location inconvenient and time inconvenient) accounted for slightly more than one-eighth of all drop-outs. Other adult learners reported such factors as changed residence and job and course disappointing or too demanding. These learners might have been served better through the use of the microcomputer. Some of these individuals might not have dropped out of courses.

With the use of appropriate microcomputer programs, the number of drop-outs from adult education courses might be decreased. The time and place problems could certainly be dealt with through the placement of microcomputers in the home or in community resource centers.

Adult Educator Involvement in Microcomputer Use

Because it is difficult or impossible to force adults to learn if there is no fit between their goals or objectives and those set by the instructional program in which they are engaged, it is necessary that microcomputer enthusiasts not impose their ideas as to how the technology should be used without an understanding and involvement of adult educators. The problem of innovation and diffusion is not well understood even today, and it is obvious that users will reject new ideas unless they understand and have had some opportunity to work with these ideas.

Stones (1981), a programmed instruction enthusiast, recently wrote as follows:

> The recommendations of the Joint Committee on programme standards, laudable though they may have been, presupposed a level of user sophistication that was lacking. Much more necessary was the involvement of potential users, not only in order to fit the material to the learners, but to sensitize the teachers of modes of usage and, most important, by their involvement to sensitize the would-be innovators to problems of the practitioners and take them into account in the development and later application of the innovation. (Stones 1981: 10)

Computer specialists and adult educators will have to work together in this way to learn what microcomputers can contribute to adult learning. This is true not only of the theory and rationale of the computer movement, but also of the programming aspects.

Interfacing Computers and Other Technologies

Since other authors have addressed the issue of interfacing technological developments with the microcomputer, no extensive discussion will occur here. Nevertheless, it should be pointed out that the greatest contribution and use of the microcomputer may be when it is harnessed with other technologies.

A natural relationship is that of the video-disc and the microcomputer. This would enable visual stimuli particularly to be called up either by the learner or the program. The microcomputer would enable the preprogramming of materials or the access to such materials by the learner of the desired information stored on the video-disc. The development of a system combining the video-disc and the microcomputer is only one example of the many possible combinations of technology that may serve adult learners better than any one technology alone.

Future Developments for Microcomputers

One of the individuals with a long-time association with computers is Suppes. In a recent article Suppes provided some thoughts about the future of computers:

> One of the constraints on flexible CAI [Computer-Assisted Instruction] at the present time is the restricted processing of natural language, as either input or output. Almost surely, major improvements will be made over the next 10 years and will have widespread application in CAI.

> I have already discussed our current research in audio, but I would make the prediction that, by the end of the coming decade, operational CAI will almost always deliver audio messages as well as visual information. By 1990, silent computers will be as rare in operational CAI settings as talking computers are today.
>
> Perhaps not by 1990, but by 2000, not only students but also professors of mathematical subjects should be able freely and easily to use informal mathematical proof procedures. The most advanced work will still be difficult to handle even by the year 2000 or so, but by 2050 the bulk of mathematical work of both pure and applied nature should be done at computer terminals, and a real revolution in a long academic tradition will have taken place.
>
> By the year 2020 we shall also have first-class speech recognition, and intimate dialogue between student and computer-tutor will be the standard method of CAI. (Suppes 1979: 9)

In a recent address, Duncan discussed the need for educational change and the complexities of accomplishing such changes even with computer-based instruction.

> Thus the need for a different approach to education is no longer a matter of conjecture, and these changes will put pressure on the school system at the lower levels as well. It is happening today, and educational computing specialists must begin to cope with and become a part of this new approach. . . .
>
> Bringing change into the educational system at any level is not without trauma, but change is inevitable. The changing shape of our world and the way we will deal with information, combined with microprocessor and communications advances, will put tremendous pressures on the educational community to use these technologies to solve some of the problems and challenges created by the information explosion. What is the likelihood that we as educational computing professionals will be prepared in the 1980's to help, or given to lead? To answer this question, consider a model for the development of an educated person in the coming decades. A flexible definition of an educated person is seen as driving the model, with educated people as the product. Given the changing world and the current evolution of CBE [Computer-Based Education], the only elements of the model that seem to exist today are the learners, a few hazy notions of what it means to be educated, a few research thrusts, and some hardware. Some of the very critical missing elements of the model are a clearer concept, albeit an evolving one, of what skills an educated person will need in the future, an understanding of the process whereby a learner requires and uses all kinds of information, the tools with which to assist that learning and utilization process, and the individuals with the skills to develop and use those tools. (Duncan 1980: 2–3)

Davis (1979) suggested that we have made progress but still have much work to do to effectively link computers and microcomputers to instruction. He proposed that, even though most individuals believe that the computer can be a valuable and worthwhile tool in training, many training professionals have not seen yet the fit between what they are presently doing and the things the computer can do for them. He also indicated that we have learned that the computer is not just a teaching machine but that it is not any particular kind of machine either. The computer, he said, only becomes something when we take, program, and place it in an environment and do something with it.

And so it is with the microcomputer in adult education, we have just begun to propose the more obvious and traditional uses for this technology. Microcomputers in educational settings, workplaces, or wherever they might have potential for helping adults to learn will have newer and more exciting uses in the future in addition to the more or less predictable ones of the present.

References

Bork, A., and Franklin, S. D. 1979. The role of computer systems in education. *Association for Educational Data Systems.* 13(1): 17–30.

Carnegie Commission on Higher Education. 1973. *Priorities for action: Final report.* New York: McGraw-Hill.

Commission on Non-Traditional Study. 1973. *Diversity by design.* San Francisco: Jossey-Bass Publishers.

Davis, R. 1979. The computer in performance and instruction: or, how to tell the true color of a chameleon. *National Society Programmed Instruction Journal.* November: 7–12.

Development: The aftermath of an informational processing takeover in psychology. *Journal of Instructional Development* Spring 1981, 4(3): 5–13.

Duncan, K. A. 1980. Presidential address, 1980 conference of the Association for the Development of Computer-Based Instructional Systems. *Journal of Computer-Based Instruction.* 7(1): 1–3. Excerpt on p. 24 printed by permission of the *Journal of Computer-Based Instruction.*

Howe, J. A. M. 1978. Artificial intelligence and computer-assisted learning: Ten years on. *Journal of Programmed Learning and Educational Technology.* 15(2): 114–125. Excerpt on pp. 14–15 quoted by permission of the *Journal of Programmed Learning and Educational Technology.*

Kulik, J. A.; Kulik, C.; and Cohen, P. A. 1980. Effectiveness of computer-based college teaching: a meta-analysis of findings. *Review of Educational Research.* 50(4): 525–544.

Low, W. C. 1980–81. Changes in instructional development: the aftermath of an information processing takeover in psychology. *Journal of Instructional Development.* 4(2): 10–18.

National Center for Education, United States Department of Health, Education, and Welfare, Statistics. 1972. *Participation in Adult Education* (an unpublished tabulation).

National Center for Education, United States Department of Health, Education, and Welfare. 1981. *Participation in Adult Education* (an unpublished tabulation).

Pflaumer, E. M. 1973. Getting started in CBT. *National Society for Programmed Instruction Journal.* November, pp. 3–14. Material on p. 17 adapted from the *Performance & Instruction Journal (*formerly *NSPI Journal),* published and copyrighted by the National Society for Performance and Instruction, 1126 Sixteenth St. NW, Suite 315, Washington, DC 20036, (202) 861–0777.

Proulx, R. 1980. The dialectic of andragogy and instructional technology. *National Society for Programmed Instruction Journal.* July, pp. 3–4. Excerpt on p. 12 from *Performance & Instruction Journal* (formerly *NSPI Journal),* published and copyrighted by the National Society for Performance and Instruction, 1126 Sixteenth St. NW, Suite 315, Washington, DC 20036, (202) 861–0777.

Stones, E. 1981. Programmed learning revisited: a case study. *Journal of Programmed Learning and Educational Technology.* 18(1): 1–10. Excerpt on p. 23 quoted by permission of the *Journal of Programmed Learning and Educational Technology.*

Suppes, D. 1979. Future of computers in education. *Journal of Computer-Based Instruction.* 6(1): 5–10. Excerpt on p. 24 reprinted by permission of the *Journal of Computer-Based Instruction.*

Wildman, T. M., and Burton, J. K. 1981. Integrating learning theory with instructional design. *Journal of Instructional Development.* 4(3): 5–13.

Hugh Garraway

The Development of a Unique Teaching Technology

Two hundred years ago western society was basically agrarian. A farmer could provide for a family's needs by growing crops that would be consumed by the family. Manufactured goods and items that could not be produced on the farm could be traded for with farm produce or purchased with proceeds from selling produce. Little formal education was required by farmers and craftspeople as most of their learning was accomplished through "hand-me-down" and apprenticeship techniques. The basics of reading, writing, and arithmetic were helpful but not essential for most of the careers of this agrarian society.

The industrial revolution produced mechanized implements for farming, while scientific cultivation increased crop yields. Rail transportation and refrigeration made it possible and profitable for fewer farmers on larger farms to supply the needs of many families. The children of farmers moved to the cities to take jobs in factories. The net result of this migration was the shift from an agrarian to an industrial society.

Careers in today's industrial society require specialized training, and the basic skills are essential for blue-collar workers. Management personnel need college degrees while upper echelon executives and professionals must often obtain graduate degrees, complete specialized training, or have a combination of both as a prerequisite for a position.

The Shift from Industrial to Information Society

Futurists have predicted a new societal shift toward an information society, and there seems to be evidence that we are on the threshold of this event. In an information society many of the jobs of the blue-collar work force will be taken over by computer-controlled robots.

A robot differs from a conventional assembly-line machine in that it may be programmed to perform any number of physical chores. Sensors allows a robot to make logical choices or decisions as directed by its program. These robots don't fit the *Star Wars* image, at least not yet, but their productivity and work record is already impressive. Japan is using more than forty thousand robots in its auto industry.

Another sign that the information society is just around the corner is the use of information systems to extend the effective power of the human brain. The body of knowledge needed in almost every profession is now so large that no one person can assimilate in a lifetime all of the facts in any science and learn how to use or synthesize new ideas from them. Computer data banks and information indexing and retrieval systems now allow professionals to concentrate on concepts that may be built upon facts obtained instantly from information systems. Learners in an information society will still learn some major facts in their areas of study, but, more importantly, they will learn concepts and how to obtain and intelligently use facts from information systems.

Just as the children of farmers became blue-collar workers a few years ago, the children of blue-collar workers are becoming, or at least have the opportunity to become, technicians, designers, and data managers of the information society. These new professionals and paraprofessionals, like today's doctors, lawyers, engineers, and scientists, will require constant education and retraining as expanding technologies will require updating knowledge and learning new skills and concepts. Continuous employee training is already commonplace in high technology industries. Increased enrollment in continuing education programs also suggests that many people are taking it upon themselves to enhance their knowledge in the hopes of increasing their earning power.

Another phenomenon that seems to point toward an information society is the advent of recreational learning. Increasing numbers of people are paying to learn just for the fun of it or to save money by learning do-it-yourself skills. One has only to turn on a television to verify this as ads hawk encyclopedia-like how-to volumes ranging in content from gourmet cooking to plumbing.

The same technology that is leading (or pushing) us into becoming an information society has provided us with the potential to improve—some say revolutionize—our methods of teaching and learning.

Computer-Aided Learning

Computers have been processing payroll, billing, and scientific data since the end of World War II. Computers have also been used for learning, and most educators are familiar with acronyms such as CAI (Computer-Assisted Instruction), CMI (Computer-Managed Instruction), and CAT (Computer-Assisted Testing). Throughout the remainder of this article the term Computer-Aided Learning (CAL) will be used as a generic label for the use of computers in teaching/learning.*

CAL, which was first implemented in the late 1950s by IBM to train its programmers, was expensive, very time-consuming to produce, and totally out of reach financially to other industries and learning institutions. After Russia's Sputnik success and the United States's Vanguard embarrassment at the launching pad, large federal grants were made available for instruction and educational research. Several research projects investigated the use of CAL. The results of these studies showed CAL to be instructionally effective but not cost-effective without federal support, which soon came to an end. This research also identified problems in learner-computer communications, hardware for CAL delivery, and instructional design and authoring concepts for producing CAL.

A similarity may be seen between 1960's research in CAL and the Apollo space program. By disregarding costs, it was proven that a system could be designed and made to work. The results of this research were then put on the shelf until future higher technology at a more reasonable cost could use these results

---

*CAI may be the more familiar label and is used frequently in other articles in this collection, but CAL puts more emphasis on the *learning* rather than the *instructional* side of computer use and so is closer, conceptually, to adult education goals.

and provide cost-effective systems for both research and utility purposes. Only a decade after the Apollo program, a reusable spacecraft that will bring the use of space within financial reach was developed. Similarly, advancements in microelectronics gave us the microcomputer, which is already proving to be a cost-effective instructional tool.

Computer Systems

A computer system, whether it be large or small, may be broken into two main components: hardware and software. The hardware is the collection of physical components that make up the system. The keyboards, memory chips, microprocessor chips, display screens, printers, disk and tape drives, and other devices make up the hardware of a system.

The software is the computer programs. The system can function as a whole only after instructions in the form of programs have been placed in the memory of the system. Programs "tell" the hardware what to do and allow the system to "think" for itself. In reality computers do not think, they only follow instructions, but these instructions allow them to do things such as compare responses entered by a human to data stored in a system's memory. The program may branch to different instructions based on different responses and seemingly carry on a dialogue with a human. It is important to remember that even the most "intelligent" computer system is only following a list of instructions provided by a human.

When we speak of computer technology we are usually speaking of hardware technology, but the term can also be applied to software.

Software technology has progressed greatly in forty years of electronic computing history. The first programs (instructions) were wired into the computer by setting hundreds of switches and running jumper cables to patch panels. This method of programming was soon replaced by placing instructions into memory. Programmers had to place the instructions in memory by typing long strings of ones and zeros that would be recognized as instructions by the computer. This method of programming was replaced by a new type of program called a language processing program. Language processing programs translate a set of instructions written in a programming language that contains symbols and numbers meaningful to the programmer into the strings of ones and zeros that the computer "understands." Today's programming languages are quite an improvement over the original ones. Many current languages use English words such as PRINT, READ, and ADD to instruct the computer.

Just as important as the progress in programming languages has been the advancement in the science or art of computer programming. More efficient algorithms or problem-solving techniques have been developed. Some of these techniques have contributed new knowledge to the study of human thinking; other problem-solving techniques have been derived from existing knowledge of human thinking.

Although great strides have been made in both hardware and software, the progress in hardware has been the fastest. This is probably because hardware deals with physical laws whereas programming techniques deal with philosophical concepts.

Looking at the current state of CAL, it seems to be in a transitional period somewhat analogous to that of the transportation system in the United States some sixty years ago. The large CAL systems implemented on the expensive mainframe computers of the sixties and seventies may be compared to the rail system, while the microcomputers of the eighties can be compared to the development of automobiles for personal use. The CAL software for microcomputers can be compared to roads used by these automobiles. Continuing the analogy, we are just beginning to build bridges and pave roads.

Computers in Adult Learning: Past, Present, and Near Future

Until recently CAL has been economically feasible only for the military, high-technology industries, or high-profit organizations. NASA has used CAL for years, mainly in the form of simulations. Shuttle astronauts train extensively on computer-controlled simulators that include computer-generated visual displays. Using simulators, contingency plans may be worked out for emergency situations and these may be rehearsed until a "nominal" proficiency is reached.

The United States Air Force also uses computer simulations. Its Red Flag project at Nellis Air Force Base in Nevada is probably the most sophisticated (and dangerous) simulation in the world. It involves real jet fighters painted and piloted like enemy aircraft. Regular air force fighter pilots engage in battle with "enemy" pilots and ground forces as computers track every move of both enemy and friendly forces. Optical lasers are used instead of missiles and bullets. Hits are recorded by computer. The element of danger comes from flying at near supersonic speeds almost at ground level to evade the "enemy" forces. After a simulated battle, pilots and ground crews go to a debriefing area where they may watch computer-generated displays of the exercise from all points of view. The pilots are able to see themselves as targets of ground forces and enemy aircraft and learn to better avoid becoming a casualty in a real conflict.

The marines use techniques similar to Red Flag at Camp LeJeune, North Carolina. In training, marines wear sensors that indicate a casualty when hit by a low intensity laser beam fired from a laser-equipped rifle. Referees carry small transmitting devices that send field data to a central computer location that monitors the mock encounters and gives instant feedback to commanders.

The navy uses the Time-Shared Interactive Computer Controlled Information Television (TICCIT) as a multimedia CAL device and as a weapons simulator. In a report prepared by a subcommittee of the House Committee on Science and Technology (1978), John Volk, product-line manager at Hazeltine Corporation, noted that the navy was purchasing two TICCIT systems to use for training of crewmembers for the S3-A antisubmarine warfare aircraft. A navy analysis had shown that more than $25 million could be saved by using the two TICCIT systems instead of buying special weapons system simulators.

TICCIT was developed by the Mitre Corporation and Brigham Young University. Research and development funding was provided by the National Science Foundation (NSF). Between 1970 and 1978, $5.64 million were invested by NSF in this research. TICCIT was developed as a low-cost alternative to the PLATO system, which will be discussed later. Standard television receivers and minicomputers were used to develop the TICCIT system. Learners using TICCIT are not limited to computer-generated characters or graphics since TICCIT, as its name implies, uses video material stored in banks of videotape players. With TICCIT a learner may be shown prerecorded scenes of video information mixed with computer-generated text. A learner may select what is to be seen or an instructional program might branch the learner to selected video sequences. TICCIT can provide audio along with its video portions.

The ancestor of CAL seems to be PLATO, which is the acronym for Programmed Logic for Automated Teaching Operations. PLATO was developed at the University of Illinois at Champaign-Urbana by a team under the direction of Donald Bitzer. The development cost was more than $20 million, of which $8.86 million came from NSF. PLATO is now supported and marketed by Control Data Corporation (CDC). A mainframe CDC computer is necessary for use of the PLATO system and special plazma display terminals are used to communicate with learners. Institutions wishing to use PLATO have four options: 1) to subscribe to a subscription service that allows leased access to a central computer and installation of terminals and use of courseware (instructional programs), 2) large corporations may purchase a complete system, 3) a corporation already owning a CDC mainframe computer may purchase additional hardware and software to use PLATO on its system, 4) an institution may send learners to CDC learning centers where PLATO terminals are connected with CDC mainframes. Courseware may be leased from CDC, custom written by CDC, or produced by the institution using PLATO's authoring system.

PLATO has widespread use in the business and educational world. American Airlines uses PLATO for pilot training and retraining as new aircraft and instruments are introduced. Pilots also receive mastery certification testing via PLATO. PLATO has also been used in the health-care industry. First-line plant supervisors have interacted with simulations to learn how to better solve quality-control problems in a pharmaceutical company. Several utilities companies are using PLATO simulations of mechanical, electrical, and nuclear systems to train plant operators and employees to handle normal and emergency operating procedures. As part of a program to teach basic skills to poorly educated adults, the Reading Pennsylvania Area Community College is using a PLATO-based basic skills curriculum. The school is satisfied with the results of this program and is now developing PLATO programs to enhance its industrial training curriculum.

In 1969, Dr. Ted Hoff, a young engineer at the Intel Corporation, designed the first microprocessor. A microprocessor is the central processing unit (CPU) or brain of a computer electronically printed on a small silicon chip. When a microprocessor is combined with a few other components such as memory, which is also printed onto silicon chips; a power supply; keyboard; and display device, the result is a small but powerful computer called a microcomputer. Today's microcomputers are small, relatively inexpensive, and capable of performing computing tasks that were limited to large multimillion-dollar mainframe systems fifteen years ago. A microcompuuter is portable and may be programmed to do any number of tasks.

Educators have realized the instructional potential of microcomputers and some are working to convert this potential into kinetic power. Microcomputers have been used for several years in progressive public and private school systems; for example, the Dallas Independent School System is using microcomputers in its math curriculum, and the states of Minnesota and North Carolina have set up state agencies to oversee the acquisition and use of microcomputers in education.

One of the first implementations of microcomputers for adult learning was by microcomputer manufacturing corporations that provided microcomputer-based learning materials to teach owners of microcomputers how to program and use them. The Tandy Corporation, producers of the Radio Shack TRS-80 microcomputer, has provided a wealth of high-quality instructional materials that integrate the use of workbooks, audio tapes, and CAL. This approach has been very successful for teaching programming. The learner follows a well-written, humorous workbook that instructs the learner to type programming examples into the microcomputer. In a step-by-step fashion, the instructional material leads the learner through the processes and concepts of writing simple to intermediate programs. When a customer purchases the Scripsit word processing software, a set of audio cassette turorials is included with other computer-based instructional materials. Tandy also markets a set of CAL programs to teach the BASIC programming language.

The United States Army has applied microcomputer-based instruction to adult learning in its Remote Site Instructional System project. This project, which developed to upgrade job-specific literacy skills in isolated military installations in Europe, was a joint venture by the army and Boston University. Military personnel wishing to use the system enter an area containing a microcomputer and a library of computer-based learning materials. Once a topic of study has been chosen, the proper materials are removed from the library. The computer programs are stored on diskettes as part of the learning material and the learner simply inserts the disk into the microcomputer's disk drive and turns on power to the microcomputer. The program is then automatically loaded into the computer and the learner may begin interacting with the microcomputer-based lesson. These systems have proven to be reliable, easy to use, and relatively maintenance-free. Army personnel believe that this project proves the feasibility of using learner-operated microcomputer-based instructional systems.

Of all professions, probably none requires as much continuing education as medicine. It is not surprising that physicians and other medical professionals have already begun to use microcomputers to keep up with new developments. The Milliken Communications Corporation of Saint Louis has developed a series of in-depth, computer-based seminars that keep doctors informed of new developments and help them meet special continuing education requirements. Some of the computer programs written for the Apple II computer simulate dialogue between the physician and an expert in some area of specialization. A physician interacting with one of these seminars responds to questions displayed on the screen by typing a reply on the keyboard. If sufficient knowledge of a procedure or concept is shown by the physician, the program moves to new material; otherwise the physician is led through a unit to promote familiarization with the new material. Once competency has been demonstrated in a particular area, the program displays a code on the screen that the physician writes down. The code is sent to the software publisher who verifies it and forwards the results to a medical board that certifies the physician in that particular area. Naturally, hospitals are a market for this software and associated hardware but the affordable cost makes it attractive to the individual physician as well.

The aerospace industry is built on the leading edge of technology. It is imperative that the engineers who design and build aircraft and spacecraft be informed of new developments in all of the numerous related technical areas. Even with the most current knowledge, by the time a product has been designed, built, tested, and certified, it may contain systems that are obsolete. To keep employees informed and to minimize this built-in obsolescence, the Boeing Aerospace Company maintains an inhouse employee training organization. Part of this organization is devoted to computer training. Computer personnel's skills are upgraded and other personnel are introduced to computer concepts through various learning strategies. Boeing maintains learning centers where employees may learn by attending traditional classes, view videotape lessons, and interact with CAL on large minicomputers and microcomputers. Small microcomputers may be taken home for learning programming languages, and a program is now being implemented to allow employees to take home terminals that can access Boeing's timesharing computers by telephone. Boeing is also using mini- and microcomputers to manage their total training activities.

Microcomputer-Based Delivery Systems

One fascinating aspect of the microcomputer is its versatility. Users can now think of imaginative application-dependent instructional system configurations as they are no longer bound to the concept of a mainframe computer connected to conventional data processing terminals. In the past educators have in some instances had to mold their instructional ideas to the constraints of "The Computer" if they wished to implement it as a learning tool. Although we will still choose to use conventional configurations at times, we now have the ability in most cases to mold systems to our applications.

Stand-Alone Systems

Although a microcomputer may be used with larger systems, it is capable of being a complete independent computer. All it needs is a power source, and some models are now available with battery packs. A stand-alone system might be as simple as a calculator-looking device or it might consist of a keyboard, which in most cases houses the microprocessor; memory; and other electronic components; a television display; some type of mass program storage device(s) such as a disk-drive unit or a cassette tape recorder; and perhaps a printer or graphic plotter.

With a stand-alone configuration, the learner would most probably take the responsibility for operating the system. To use the system, the learner would insert the CAL software media (diskette or cassette tape) into the appropriate storage device and turn on power to the system. The system could then load a CAL program or prompt the learner to choose a learning unit from a "menu" of displayed options. Since software for stand-alone systems is not physically tied to a system, a learner with a personal copy of a unit of CAL software would be free to go to any compatible system to work on lessons. This would be particularly attractive to learners whose life-styles or occupations require frequent relocation.

As hardware costs continue to decline, we are reaching a point where complete stand-alone systems may be purchased by individuals or provided by corporations in the same manner as company cars at a cost comparable to that of a stereo system. Since the hardware is not limited to its role as a learning device, professionals may obtain other software to extend the system's use to areas such as bookkeeping, word processing, and almost any other imaginable computing application. From a corporate, military, or learning institution standpoint it is now economically feasible to provide CAL centers in many locations. It is also feasible to construct mobile CAL units with self-contained libraries of courseware similar to bookmobiles.

The integration of CAL and conventional textbook-learning media has already been briefly discussed but its potential is worthy of further thought. Assuming that manufacturers of hardware will arrive at some degree of compatibility concerning storage formats and programming languages, we will be able to produce interactive texts or workbooks as related CAL software may be included in a sleeve inside the book. This concept implies a new approach to authoring text and poses yet another new educational frontier. Some publishers are already establishing courseware divisions to produce CAL modules to accompany conventional textbooks. Much of this software presently takes the form of interactive end-of-chapter exercises and is supplied only as a program printout that necessitates typing the program into a system and making copies for learners to use.

There are both advantages and disadvantages to CAL systems based on the stand-alone configuration. Since each system is self-contained, hardware problems would affect only one learner in contrast to mainframe systems where a problem could affect all users of the system. On mainframe systems it is difficult and expensive to provide graphic or real-time simulation capabilities to multiple users. The response time on many mainframe systems is slow for instructional purposes as CAL programs may be given low job priority. With a stand-alone system, each learner has the complete "attention" of the computer and many graphic and simulation programs may be handled with ease. The biggest disadvantage to using a stand-alone system is the requirement that each learner have a copy of the CAL software. Another disadvantage is that data such as learner scores may not be instantly sent to a central location although data may be stored on the learner's software media for later retrieval at a central location.

Clustered Microcomputer Systems

It is possible to allow a number of microcomputers to share a common mass storage device by using a cluster (sometimes called a star network) configuration. In a clustered system, each microcomputer may copy software stored in the mass storage device into its own memory. The user may then interact with the program just as he or she would on a stand-alone system. Data generated by the user or the user's program may be transferred to storage files on the mass storage device of the cluster. Other peripheral devices such as printers may also be shared by the clustered microcomputers.

A cluster configuration usually consists of a number of stand-alone systems connected to a microcomputer acting as a "host." The host is also connected to the mass storage device(s) and other shared peripherals. A set of "operating system" programs running on the host system supervises the other microcomputers' access to mass storage and other peripherals.

Timesharing Networks

In the mid-sixties it became possible for a number of users to share a single mainframe computer through a process called timesharing. In a timesharing system, each user communicates with the system through the use of a terminal. The system continuously "rotates" the users' access to the central processing unit and memory.

Theoretically, the system operates so fast that no user is aware that anyone else is using it. In actuality, there has been a tendency to add more terminals to a system as its applications grow and this has resulted in systems where users enter something and then have to wait a few seconds for the system to respond.

Early timesharing systems consisted of a mainframe computer that was directly wired to a number of terminals which were most likely to be typewriter-like teletype terminals. Today, microcomputers have taken over many of the tasks once performed by timesharing systems and the noisy old teletype terminals have been replaced by television display CRT terminals. Devices called modems allow users to call a computer on the phone and allow the computer to answer. These advances have led to commercial timesharing networks.

At first used only by businesses, timesharing networks are now being used by individuals as well. Timesharing companies such as Compuserve now offer reduced rates for computer time after normal business hours. Individuals with a terminal or microcomputer and a modem can dial into one of these networks to play games, check stock market changes as they happen, buy or list items through computerized classified ads, send electronic mail to other users, and buy or swap software to mention just a few possibilities. The networks also make it possible to access resources such as the Lockheed Information System, a bibliographic distributor. Through this system, bibliographic citations and abstracts may be obtained from publications indexed in more than seventy-five data banks. To join a network, a potential user sends in an application; an account number is issued and charges are billed through a credit card company.

The data storage and organization facilities of timesharing networks is immense. In the very near future, detailed encyclopedias and indexed data on all knowledge may be stored and searched by users. Advanced data searching programs will prompt users to enter a subject area they wish to have searched. Searches may be limited or expanded to other areas by interacting with the search program. Just as a good librarian can help locate needed information, the search program will provide almost instant access to desired facts. This capability to perform as an information system will put the answer to almost any factual question at the fingertips of the information society.

Combined Systems

Another possible system configuration is to use both microcomputers and timesharing networks. In such a system, centralized libraries of CAL modules could be maintained. Learners who wished to interact with a module could call the network and have copies of the software transmitted over the phone lines to the microcomputer. If desired, the software could be interacted with immediately or it could be stored on the learner's software media for later use. Likewise, information generated by the learner could be transmitted to a central file in the network's facilities. This sounds like a complicated process for the learner, but isn't. The computer software can initiate all of these activities without the learner's knowledge.

Interactive Videodisc Systems

The videodisc was conceived as a television playback distribution medium principally for entertainment programming. The technology that evolved to make this concept a reality has produced an instrument that has great educational potential when combined with microcomputer technology.

A videodisc looks like a phonograph record and is "played" like one. Instead of the continuous spiraled groove of a phonograph record, the videodisc uses concentric circles holding data that are translated into pictures and sound by a laser and mirror suspended above the disk. Information to reproduce 54,000 screens (which corresponds to thirty minutes of television pictures when shown at the rate of thirty screens per second) can be stored on a single videodisc. Each of the pictures on a videodisc may be referenced by its address on the disk (the circle in which it is stored) and the laser/mirror pickup may be positioned to show any picture. For motion to occur on the screen as in normal television, the pickup simply scans and shows thirty pictures a second. For slow motion it scans and shows fewer pictures and for still pictures it hovers over one. In addition to audio and video information, the videodisc may also contain computer programs. When combined with a microcomputer, which may load a computer program from the videodisc, the player can provide random access to any single picture or group of pictures within thousandths of a second. The result of this is an interactive learning device with all of the advantages of CAL and instructional television. This combination allows us to think of instructional television in completely different terms since it is no longer just a linear medium but has the same branching and random access capabilities as the computer.

At the present time only a few prototype interactive videodisc systems exist but as commercial players are now being introduced it should not be too long before a standard for interactive devices is set. When the interactive models do arrive, we will see a new species of learning software. The Time-Life learning picture book concept will undoubtedly be applied. Video volumes such as "Interactive Plumbing" should become available. As fuel costs, inflation, and international terrorism make travel more difficult, we will learn about the seven wonders of the world through videodisc-based surrogate travel. On a surrogate tour, the tourist would sit before a screen and insert the videodisc of the destination. On the disc would be stored scenes of every street for the area. By choosing a street and dictating turns at intersections, the tourist could travel to all points within the geographic confines of the videodisc. Using photomicroscopy, the human body could be stored on videodisc so that medical learners might take an "Incredible Voyage."

Obtaining Software

There are basically three ways to obtain software for computer-based adult learning. The easiest and fastest way is to purchase or lease commercial courseware such as the Milliken series for physicians. Control Data Corporation offers a number of CAL packages aimed at the adult learner through its PLATO system, but use of these packages requires access to a PLATO system or learning center, which is definitely not a microcomputer configuration. Science Research Assosiates (SRA), which is an IBM related organization, has recently reached an agreement with the Atari corporation to produce and market CAL software for Atari microcomputers, but their present activity is directed towards elementary and secondary school students.

The CONDUIT organization evaluates, documents, and distributes instructional software produced by institutions of higher education and individuals. Originally set up to process mainframe-oriented CAL software, CONDUIT is now offering microcomputer versions of many of its packages. Although much of CONDUIT's software was designed to be integrated into the university curriculum, many packages could be used on microcomputers outside the university environment.

Several software distribution companies such as Creative Computing Software and Instant Software offer microcomputer programs of all types. Some of these programs have potential as modular components in an adult learning curriculum. Krell Software offers a set of "college board" programs to provide interactive preparation for standardized tests such as the SAT, PSAT, N.M.S.Q.T., and GRE. These programs cover vocabulary, word relationships, and mathematics and provide examples and explanations of solutions to questions.

A second method of obtaining microcomputer courseware is to produce it in-house using an authoring system. An authoring system is a program or group of programs designed to guide an author through the process of creating CAL modules. The author of a CAL module interacts with the authoring system by typing in text, test questions, and answers and by selecting options from system-displayed menus of instructional strategies. The authoring system organizes and stores the information entered by the author so that it may be presented to learners as CAL modules. Good authoring systems offer enough options and versatility to allow the author a great deal of creativity in the design and authoring process. Once a CAL module has been completed, it may be duplicated for distribution to learners using stand-alone systems or it may be placed on a timesharing network or mass storage device shared by a cluster of microcomputers.

A third method of obtaining courseware is to use a programming language to write a series of programs from scratch. This approach allows access to all of the system's capabilities, including sound and detailed color graphics. Although learning to program is not necessarily hard, it takes time and a lot of planning to produce quality software. Most microcomputer-based CAL software on the market today was written in this manner, but the trend is to improve authoring systems, especially in the area of creating instructional graphics and sound. Future authoring, or development systems as they are sometimes called, should allow the potential author full access to the microcomputer's capabilities.

Cautions About Computer Use

It is relatively easy to describe numerous nifty ways we might incorporate microcomputers into adult learning. To plan and carry through on the development, implementation, and evaluation of a project is another matter. One of the pitfalls of incorporating any new technology in learning is that projects are often hastily thrown together in the hopes that technology will magically make it work. When the project fails to achieve our planned results we tend to blame the failure on the technology rather than on our lack of planning. It is not an easy task to produce quality instructional material and each advance in technology requires educators to become jacks of another trade so that we may oversee the integration of new methods of instruction into present ones and revise or discard old methods when new ones prove to be more effective.

It is important that we do not limit our concept of the

computer's role in learning to the idea of its being a vehicle for programmed instruction. Just as the wheel has extended humanity's physical mobility the computer offers us a mental tool. Since the premise of an information society implies self-motivated learning in adults, perhaps one of our first instructional objectives should be to provide some level of computer literacy in adults so that the full potential of this tool as a mental "extender" may be realized.

Reference

U.S. House Committee on Science and Technology, Subcommittee on Domestic and International Scientific Planning, Analysis, and Cooperation. 1978. 95th Congress.

George Mozes

Professional Education and the Microcomputer

In the few years since its genesis, the microcomputer has managed to touch, in one form or another, all areas of human life: work, school, home, and leisure. The question is no longer *will* the microcomputer be used, but rather *when* and to *what extent.* This article addresses these questions as they pertain to professional and adult education. Since practicing professionals are adults and most of the characteristics of adult education are intrinsic to professional education as well, these two terms will be used interchangeably even though they are not synonymous.

The first part of the article presents a short examination of adult learning from the vantage point of the microcomputer. This is followed by a case study of the work done at Michael Reese Hospital in Chicago in developing computer simulations for practicing physicians. The second part presents a review of microcomputer applications from different parts of the country. The objective of the article is to provide information on how the microcomputer is used in professional education today, and to offer a few suggestions regarding its future use.

Adult Learning and the Microcomputer

Certain characteristics of microcomputers make them well-suited for adult learning. Indeed, in some instances, characteristics of the adult learner that could not be observed using traditional teaching methods can be successfully taken into account through the use of microcomputers.

Malcolm Knowles made four basic assumptions about the characteristics of adult learners:

> These assumptions are that, as a person matures, 1.) his self-concept moves from one of being a dependent personality toward one of being a self-directing human being; 2.) he accumulates a growing reservoir of experience that becomes an increasing resource for learning; 3.) his readiness to learn becomes oriented increasingly to the developmental tasks of his social roles; and 4.) his time perspective changes from one of postponed application of knowledge to immediacy of application, and accordingly his orientation toward learning shifts from one of subject-centeredness to one of problem-centeredness. (Knowles 1970: 39)

Let us look at these assumptions from the vantage point of the microcomputer.

Self-directivity. Self-directivity means, first of all, self-diagnosis of needs for learning. Adults should be given the freedom to decide for themselves what they need to learn. Adults, who know to some extent what their needs and interests are, could certainly develop a full and competent list of these needs if properly helped.

Such inquiries into an individual's background, needs, and interests can be easily handled by the microcomputer. Simulations are well-suited to this purpose. Going through a simulation, individuals can see clearly the strengths and weaknesses of their performance. They then can use this knowledge to decide what they need to learn to increase competence.

Self-directivity also means the freedom to choose from among many learning experiences. A large number of professionals are unfortunately unable to benefit from traditional continuing education programs because of problems of scheduling. There is a need to develop programs that allow for self-direction and self-study. It is toward this goal that the microcomputer can make a significant contribution.

First, the microcomputer provides a flexible source for teaching and learning, in terms of both place and time. Professionals can use the programs at home, at work, or at any other location, at any given time, day or night. They can use a program at their own pace, interrupt it at any point, and continue from that point the next time they turn the microcomputer on.

Second, taking into account the background and characteristics of the individual, the microcomputer can provide a very large number of variations on a given program. Tailoring a program to these individual characteristics makes it more meaningful and acceptable to the professional, and increases the chances of successful completion.

Third, the microcomputer can be used as a delivery system for an entire curriculum by developing a large number of programs covering the entire range of learner needs and interests. The system can use various modes of Computer-Aided Instruction (CAI) such as tutorials, simulations, and problem solving, and employ different forms of presentation by integrating the microcomputer with audio and videotapes, slides, and, of course, printed materials. Furthermore, the same microcomputer can be used in a Computer-Managed Instruction (CMI) mode to monitor, evaluate, advise, and guide the learner. Only a system having all or most of these characteristics can provide the learning environment needed by professionals: allowing them the freedom to choose from a large selection the information or program preferred and the presentation method preferred. All this is done while providing professionals, as needed, with information, feedback, and help to make these choices.

Finally, self-directivity also means self-evaluation. Adults should be given the opportunity to see for themselves how well they are progressing toward their learning goal. One of the general characteristics of continuing education in the professions is the push for a continuous self-evaluation activity on the part of the professional. Most educators think that self-evaluation is not only a tool, but a general attitude, a way of life for the professional, and should become second nature to all professionals. The microcomputer, when requested to do so, can collect and provide a host of data regarding learning performance. Comparisons can be made between performance at the beginning and at the end of the learning sequence, or between present competencies and the required (terminal) competencies. The microcomputer can also provide constant and immediate feedback during the learning process.

The idea of letting adults decide what their needs are makes sense not only because it is part of the drive for self-directivity, but also because, as a result of this decision making, they are better motivated to learn.

Experience. Adults bring a very valuable resource into the teaching/learning process—their own experience. Programs should take this experience into consideration and should build upon it. This means less use of traditional techniques such as lecturing and more use of techniques that require learner involvement and participation—case presentations, simulations, role playing, seminars, and debates. The microcomputer can be used in the fairly difficult process of helping individuals uncover pertinent experiences and to learn from these newly uncovered experiences.

Problem-centeredness. Adults tend to view educational activities from a problem-centered vantage point mainly because they seek an immediate application of the knowledge and skills they learn, an application that is usually related to their work or life. This characteristic requires the use of those teaching/learning techniques that are action-oriented, those that emphasize problem solving. As discussed, simulations and case presentations lend themselves well to this task, and the microcomputer could make their use easier.

Evaluation of Continuing Education. Evaluation is an issue less related to the characteristics of the adult learner and more related to the way learning activities are organized. Most continuing education activities in the professions are evaluated on the basis of the time spent by the participant in that activity. Contact hours are given for each hour of activity and credit hours are calculated based on the number of contact hours and the type of activity performed. The continuing education unit (CEU) is another evaluative tool accepted by many institutions and organizations involved in continuing education; one CEU represents ten contact hours spent in an activity organized by a qualified institution.

The major problem with these methods is that attendance does not always translate into learning. In some programs, participants can walk out in the middle of an activity only to return at the end of the program to collect their certificate. Some learners, though physically present, pay very little attention to what is being presented. The existing system of rewards cannot detect these and similar abuses. But the microcomputer can! Learning with the microcomputer is interactive and requires the professional's constant and undivided attention. A special code, to be revealed only when the professional finishes the entire program, can be used as proof of completion. A few pertinent questions or a short simulation can evaluate the quantity and quality of learning accomplished. The number of credits given could vary according to the results of the evaluation, thus providing an incentive for participants to do their best.

Health Education and the Microcomputer: A Case Study

Patient-management problems or patient simulations have been used in health education for about ten years. The approach described here is new, however, in that it employs the microcomputer as the medium for presenting these simulations. The case study begins with some background information on Michael Reese Hospital since the setting played an important role in the decision to use microcomputers. Information on simulations in general and a short description of the hardware and languages used in developing patient-management problems in diabetes will also be presented.

Michael Reese Hospital and Medical Center

Michael Reese Hospital and Medical Center (MRHMC) in Chicago is a private, nonprofit institution providing a comprehensive range of general, acute, and specialty care for in-patients and out-patients. MRHMC is recognized as one of the leading medical centers in the country. The Medical Center occupies 66 acres of land, has 26 buildings, and a staff of more than 5,000.

Patient Care. Patient-care programs are supported by 1,008 beds in nearly all specialty fields of medical care and by a staff of 650 attending physicians and 1,500 nurses and nursing personnel. More than 32,000 patients are hospitalized yearly, and 163,000 visits are made to the out-patient clinics.

Research. Michael Reese is one of the few medical centers to have its own Medical Research Institute, the first to be established by a non-university hospital. The institute encompasses 23 departments and 350 scientists and support staff, all working towards one primary aim—preventing and combating disease.

Education. Teaching has long been a tradition of MRHMC. More than 300 physicians are trained here while serving as residents and fellows in a wide range of medical specialties. MRHMC also provides faculty support and facilities for training about 40 undergraduate medical students from the University of Chicago's Pritzker School of Medicine, with which it is affiliated. In addition, the Medical Center enrolls nearly 300 students in 18 allied health and clinical programs such as Cytotechnology, Medical Technology, Radiation Therapy, and others.

Michael Reese School of Health Sciences (SHS). The School

of Health Sciences (SHS) was established in 1975 to guide, coordinate, and monitor health professional training programs and to ensure the highest quality of education within these programs. SHS brings under one administration, within a formal school structure, all the undergraduate, graduate, and postgraduate programs offered on campus. Governance of the school is guided by the Academic Council, which is composed of clinical department chairmen and department directors from all medical, nursing, and allied health disciplines.

Educational Development Unit (EDU). The Educational Development Unit was established in 1976 as a special resource of SHS. Its purpose is to provide educational expertise and guidance in curriculum development and evaluation, to engage in faculty development, and to conduct educational research. The EDU faculty consists of eight health professions educators—five at the doctorate level and three at the masters level—two full-time staff at the master's level, and four support personnel. One of the objectives of the EDU is to develop techniques, methods, and tools for resolving problems in health professions education. Among the activities undertaken to satisy this objective was that of developing a series of simulations. The following paragraphs will discuss simulations in general and outline the work done by the EDU in developing a series of computer simulations.

Simulations. A simulation is a representation of reality, a way of replicating a real event, process, or condition with the purpose of providing learner interaction and experience. Flight simulators used in training prospective pilots, military maneuvers used in training troops for actual combat, and disaster drills used in preparing employees to respond quickly and properly in case of a disaster, are a few of the better known simulations.

There are four basic formats for simulations: 1) *human interaction simulations* involve role playing, bargaining, cooperation, conflict, and other activities; e.g., the disaster drill; 2) *written simulations* involve written materials to which a single person or a group must respond; e.g., the patient-management problem in the paper-and-pencil format (to be described later); 3) *board simulations* involve a game board, dice, cards, etc.; e.g., an activity in which individuals role play a person admitted to the hospital and move around the board by rolling dice and "experiencing" problems as they land on selected squares; 4) *human-machine simulations* involve interactions with a device such as a mannequin, computer, etc.; e.g., Resusci-Anne, a mannequin that responds like an actual patient and is used to teach Cardio-Pulmonary Resuscitation (CPR).

Simulations are especially useful when it is necessary to avoid dangerous or expensive phenomena or to speed up actual time. One of the major advantages of using simulations in the teaching/learning process is that they allow learners to take charge of a situation and be responsible for the outcome of their actions.

While traditional methods such as lectures or seminars are better for teaching factual information, simulations are better for problem solving and learning by discovery. For example, a traditional method should be used to teach the abnormal metabolism and the role of insulin, and a simulation should be used to develop and assess clinical skills in treating diabetic patients. The use of simulations and role playing following traditional presentations increases the likelihood of transfer of knowledge.

Patient-Management Problems

Patient-management problems (PMPs) are based on the problem-solving processes that take place in a clinical encounter, and can be used to develop and assess the diagnostic and therapeutic skills of a health professional. The PMP is a form of simulation that gives the user an opportunity to take a case history, do a physical examination, order a laboratory test, make a diagnosis, and choose an appropriate treatment. Some PMPs include all the foregoing steps, others only one or two. PMPs have a number of benefits that make them a desirable teaching/learning tool.

Safety. PMPs can provide realistic learning without endangering the life of patients. An added benefit (because of this safety) is that the health professional can try out approaches that cannot be attempted in real life because of legal or moral limitations.

Feasibility. Using PMPs, in most instances, is more feasible and economical than experimenting in real-life situations. Economy can be realized in terms of cost as well as time needed to learn.

Clarity. PMPs can focus on specific aspects of reality, weeding out any distractions that, in real life, could impede the learning process.

PMPs are a good technique when judgment and decision are

as important as, if not even more important than, the accumulation of knowledge. In the past most PMPs were the paper-and-pencil type, i.e. written simulations. The pioneering work on developing these PMPs was done by Christine McGuire and her colleagues at the University of Illinois in the early seventies. Later, they trained a number of other educators in the techniques of developing PMPs, and published a manual (McGuire, Solomon, and Bashook 1975). As a result, the number of PMPs being produced has kept increasing.

Parallel to these developments was the evolution of the computer simulation. The computer simulation was similar in format to the written simulation. But because it was available only on large mainframe computers, including the PLATO system, it never gained widespread application. Today, with the advent of the microcomputer, the situation has changed substantially.

Enter the Microcomputer

The microcomputer is the answer to the prayer of many educators and learners who believe in the advantages of Computer-Assisted Instruction, but who couldn't avail themselves of this method in the past due to the high cost of computing. Today, with an investment of less than $2,000 (and for some models less that $1,000) an individual can get a complete computer system. These inexpensive systems can do almost everything a large computer can do, and certainly everything that is needed for CAI applications.

Since microcomputer hardware and software are discussed in detail in other articles in this book, only those aspects that pertain to the case study will be touched upon here.

Hardware. Shortly after the first APPLE microcomputers appeared on the market in 1977, I decided to convince my colleagues and chief in the EDU to purchase one and to start experimenting with CAI applications in continuing medical education. By then, I had taken a twenty-hour course in the BASIC language offered by a computer programmer at the Medical Center, and I was ready to try my hand at programming the APPLE. My colleagues and chief were easily convinced. Some of them (like Philip Bashook) were familiar with computer simulations. The only question they had was *Can you do it with the APPLE?* It was decided that if I could "put *The Traveler* on the APPLE" then EDU would buy the microcomputer. (*The Traveler* is the longest simulation—39 pages—in McGuire et al.'s (1975) manual.)

After about two months and more than 140 hours of actual programming, the program was ready. All the effort and occasional frustration that come with learning on-the-job were worthwhile. The program worked well; my colleagues and chief were convinced. We bought an APPLE computer and were on our way to becoming the first institution to write PMPs for the APPLE and to use the microcomputer for continuing medical education.

The hardware we used was an APPLE II with 48K RAM (random-access memory), one disk drive, and a 9-inch black-and-white monitor. All the programs we have written to date and the ones now under development will run on this system.

Languages. The APPLE uses two "dialects" or versions of the BASIC programming language: INTEGER BASIC and FLOATING-POINT BASIC also known as APPLESOFT. Both languages are fairly easy to learn; in fact, there are few differences between them and, if one knows one of the BASIC dialects used on other computers, one could learn these two on the APPLE within hours. BASIC is not the best language for CAI applications, but it is the language best-known by a majority of microcomputer users, young and old and it is a language many individuals feel comfortable with.

PILOT is a much better language for CAI. PILOT, developed in 1968 at the University of California in San Francisco, consists of only eight basic commands, but additional commands are usually available in different dialects. Even in its most simplified eight-command form, PILOT allows the program to print information to the user, ask questions, accept the user's response, match the response to a set of acceptable responses, and provide feedback to the user while counting the number of correct and incorrect answers. One of the major advantages of PILOT is its ease of use in programming even by individuals inexperienced with computers.

Programming. Many people still think that programming a computer requires a strong background in mathematics, many specialized courses in programming, and a knowledge of electronics. Nothing could be further from reality! Although some of this knowledge would certainly be useful for professional programmers, although not *essential* even for them, none is *needed* to write successful CAI programs in BASIC, PILOT, and other authoring languages. Many health professionals have learned to program microcomputers on their own without formal courses. One successful surgeon at Michael Reese has written and published a program called *Household Finance;* it seems he is as good with the APPLE keyboard as he is with a scalpel. Thousands of other professionals have learned or are learning to program microcomputers. When the professional, i.e., the content specialist, is the one who writes the lesson or teaching unit and also to program it for the computer, there are many built-in advantages. It is my firm conviction that programming should be considered as an important skill for the professional to have along with other knowledge and skills in research, writing, and teaching.

PMPs in Diabetes Mellitus. In 1977, a Diabetes Research and Training Center Grant (one of the eight federally funded in the nation) was awarded jointly to the University of Chicago and MRHMC. The EDU's role was to identify and assess educational needs relevant to training practitioners in effective management of the diabetic patient and to design and test model curricula to effectively meet these training needs. With this objective in mind, the EDU has to date developed a half dozen PMPs; more are under development. The PMPs are designed to be part of a larger curriculum that includes formal lectures, seminars, and independent study modules. To facilitate an understanding of what a PMP is and how it is constructed, I include here a short description of one of our PMPs *(Mr. Williamson)* with a map showing all the possible routes (Fig. 1). As one can see, significant branching takes place, that is, physicians will be directed to different sections depending on the decisions they made regarding the course of treatment.

Mr. Williamson simulates the case of an adult diabetic in the early stage of development of insulin-dependent diabetes. The emphasis is on the initial adjustment in diet and insulin made by the physician.

The PMP starts with the opening scene (Frame A), which presents the case; it gives a short history, some physical findings, and a few initial laboratory data. Next, the physician can order (and obtain within a reasonable time) additional laboratory tests deemed necessary for the management of this patient. After the information has been obtained, the physician must decide whether or not the patient has diabetes, how he will be told about it, and what the basic method of treatment will be. If the method of treatment selected is not insulin therapy (Frame E), the physician is wrong, but there are opportunities to get back to insulin therapy. If the physician insists on incorrect treatment, such as diet therapy alone (Frames U and

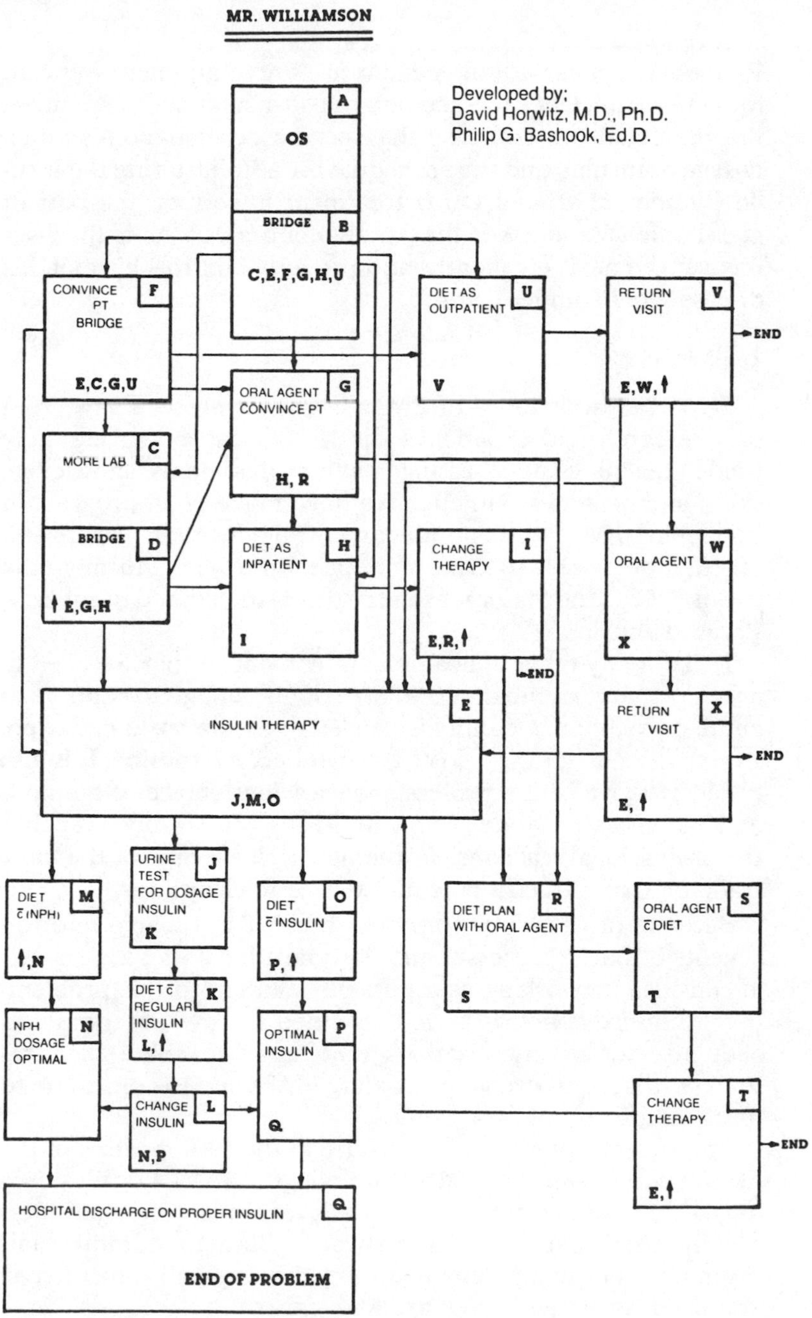

Figure 1. Map Indicating All Possible Routes Through the Simulation. (From: Patient management problems—*Mr. Williamson*, by D.L. Horwitz and P.G. Bashook. University of Chicago Diabetes Research and Training Center.)

V), the PMP ends with the patient turning to another physician for better care. Once the decision to use insulin has been made, the physician must choose the specific combination of diet, dosage of insulin, and time schedule for administering the insulin (Frames M, J, and O). If treatment is correct, the patient goes home (Frame Q). If the patient continues to take his insulin over the next few months and properly controls his diet, his disease will be under control.

The Network

Physician acceptance of PMPs is good, and we know from past research and experience that PMPs can be successfully used in teaching and assessing health professionals' knowledge, skills, and attitudes. Although we have made good progress in developing PMPs for continuing medical education, we are still far from being able to make an impact on teaching through the use of PMPs. The major reason for this is the limited number of PMPs available.

I, like many other educators, am convinced that we need to develop a large number of PMPs, perhaps enough to support an entire curriculum. Quantity is needed to assure sustained exposure to the medium and so its use can become routine. It is also needed to give health professionals a wider choice of methods and materials to study. Knowing PMPs are readily available, the professional will consider them as well as some of the more traditional resources a potential source for learning.

Because of the limited number of PMPs available and the benefits of having access to more, some educators have started to consider networking as a possible solution to this problem. In this context, a *network* can be defined as a system composed of a number of organizations that agree to share their resources, that is, to exchange existing PMPs and to contribute to the development of new ones.

At a recent exhibit of our software at the 1980 meeting of the Association of American Medical Colleges (AAMC) in Washington, DC, I asked visitors to fill out a form expressing their interest in participating in a network. Sixty-four individuals responded positively demonstrating that a significant interest and need for better access to PMPs exists.

Encouraged by this interest, we decided to take the first steps to organize such a network. A quick review of the literature confirmed our belief that networking would have many advantages and that it could indeed be a workable solution to the problem.

Advantages. Charles Tidball (1978) listed a series of advantages of networking in his *Information Technology in Health Science Education.* Although his remarks pertain to a time-sharing approach to networking (a computing technique by which many terminals at various locations can be connected to a central computer and share its facilities simultaneously), many of the advantages mentioned would also apply to the "exchange" type of networking we propose to organize.

First, networking gives CAI capabilities to institutions that do not have the money to develop their own courseware. Second, the network can develop, maintain, and distribute a very large number of programs, more than any single institution could do on its own. Third, the network can distribute developmental costs across all participating institutions. Individual institutions' shares would be relatively small, yet the aggregate amount could be larger than any single institution might be able to afford. This larger sum could be used to attempt more sophisticated or larger projects. Fourth, the network can contribute significantly, in a short time, to the enhancement of the materials by exposing them to a large number of health professionals who would then be asked to comment and make suggestions for improvement. Fifth, the network can open new channels of communication and interaction among colleagues with similar interests at various institutions. Through group involvement, they could oversee the proper utilization of the new technology in all participating institutions.

Organization. The network we propose to organize addresses itself to the problem of getting a large number of PMPs into the hands of health professionals. The network has two basic functions: development and dissemination.

1. *Development.* The network will coordinate, help and encourage participating institutions to develop as many PMPs as feasible by: a) organizing workshops to teach how to create PMPs for microcomputers; b) determining standards for software and documentation to ensure maximum compatibility; c) circulating a newsletter reporting on network activities and information from participating institutions; d) purchasing existing PMPs (written and other forms) and adapting them for the microcomputer; e) offering a number of incentives to institutions that create PMPs; and f) collecting membership fees from participating institutions and using some of the money to develop software.

2. *Dissemination.* The network will disseminate PMPs by: a) offering PMPs on a two-for-one exchange rate, that is, two free PMPs for each PMP contributed by an institution; b) selling PMPs at a reasonable price; c) setting up ongoing selection and evaluation procedures to ensure that only quality PMPs are added to the collection and that PMPs in the network are periodically updated.

We have submitted a proposal to two granting agencies for money to start the network. We are convinced that the network will be basically self-supporting once it becomes operational and that it will play an important role in propagating PMPs as a valuable tool in continuing education of professionals.

Other Microcomputer Applications in Health Education

So far this article has dealt with only one application of the microcomputer in professional education; in order to gain some appreciation of what is being done in the field as a whole, the reader should become aware of other uses as well. Eight applications from various areas will be described. The number is not impressive. In some professional fields—law, for example—there are virtually no applications for the practicing professional. In other areas, such as engineering, there are a few programs, but none that are truly educational. There are also fields in which a number of applications have been successfully implemented.

Encephalon

The *Encephalon* program was written by Gordon Banks (a former Michael Reese resident) using the PASCAL language and the high-resolution graphics capabilities of the APPLE computer. The program is basically a simulation in that it presents seven patients or cases and expects the user to diagnose their conditions. The program presents a short history for each case and then allows the user to examine the patient. Available exams are: general physical, motor, sensory, cerebellar reflexes, mental status, and cranial nerves. When the user asks for any of these exams, he or she is provided with a text describing major findings relevant to the case. Three other exams—optic nerve, ocular motility, and vestibular functions—are simulated by examining an animated representation of each patient's face.

When the user thinks that he/she has gathered enough data to make a diagnosis, or when all the exams have been made, the user exits the program and makes the diagnosis by choosing from a list of possibilities. The program will then present the author's diagnosis and the reasons for making it. One of the advantages of this simulation is that it makes possible demonstrations of syndromes that are infrequent in actual practice. *Encephalon* costs $50.00 and is available from Gordon Banks, 707 Countryside Drive, McKees Rocks, PA 15136.

Continuing Medical Education

Milliken Communications Corporation is the first—and to date the only—commercial firm to develop CAI programs for practicing physicians. The programs are designed to run on the APPLE microcomputer, but Milliken also offers a dial-up package that allows access to these programs from any computer terminal equipped with a modem.

Milliken works with specialists from around the country and trains them to write CAI materials. The authors use a program driver called QUEST based on the MUMPS language. Their product is revised by programming and education specialists and reviewed by an Editorial Board. These programs are called *seminars* and each lasts about forty-five minutes. A physician can interrupt the seminar at any point, and return to it at a later date; the program will start from the place it was halted. At the end of the program, the physician is provided with an "end code." Sending this code to Milliken proves that the physician completed the program and is entitled to receive Category I credit. (This credit system was established by the American Medical Association for participation in continuing medical education activities.)

Most of the Milliken programs are of the linear type. The computer presents a concept and asks the physician a question that requires recall, inference, or judgment. Physicians respond by typing their answers in their own words—a definite advantage over the multiple-choice format presented in most other programs. The computer then presents the next concept. Provisions are made to give those who cannot answer a question some basic information for review. Seminars are available in Medicine (22), Surgery (25), Psychiatry (9), and Urology (5). Most seminars have two or three diskettes; each diskette costs

$22.00. For more information contact: Bodie Marx, Milliken Communication Corporation, 1100 Research Blvd., St. Louis, MO 62132.

Continuing Nursing Education

The Staff Development Department at Talmadge Memorial Hospital in Augusta, GA, is working on a CAI study course to assess and develop licensed nurses' competence in drug therapy. The project consists of five units of study: drug therapy for cardiovascular and central nervous systems, anti-infective drugs, hormonal drugs, and drugs for common medical disorders. Each unit will use a variety of instructional strategies, including drill and practice, tutorial, and patient-management problems, with the APPLE microcomputer playing a key role. It will take about one hour at the terminal to complete each unit.

Having this course available on microcomputer will offer a number of advantages such as making instruction available when needed by an individual nurse, providing individualized instruction, absolving nurse educators from repetitive teaching tasks, and offering access to quality courseware to other institutions throughout the state.

One interesting aspect of this project is that the units are being authored using a system that continuously prompts the instructor and therefore allows the creation of courseware without knowledge of programming. The system is written in PASCAL for the APPLE microcomputer and makes provision for a wide variety of instructional strategies (Pogue 1981).

A similar effort is being undertaken at Texas Woman's University, where a series of nursing simulations has been designed to provide problem-solving experience in medication administration. The simulations cover medication problems in psychiatric nursing, obstetrical nursing, and medical-surgical nursing. The problems have been designed to take the user from the beginning to the end of each simulation by including such nursing functions as regulating IV drip rates, charting, reporting to team members, etc. The programs run on an APPLE with 48K and two disk drives (Villiers 1981).

Clinical Simulation Writer

One of the obstacles to a wider use of computer simulations is the insufficient number of well-developed programs. This is partly because writing a simulation is time-consuming and difficult for the physician or content specialist. George Bass (1981) recognized this fact and is now working on a program that will greatly simplify the task of the content specialist.

Bass's idea is to use the task environment exercise (TEE) to identify physicians' decisions in diagnostic problem solving. The TEE is a structured interview designed to elicit from physicians data on the context of the clinical problem, their data-gathering techniques, and the step-by-step decisions and actions used to diagnose and treat the patient. Bass plans to eliminate the need for an interviewer and to let the APPLE microcomputer do the job. The content specialist will only have to type in the response to the questions presented by the microcomputer. These responses will be stored and later formatted by the computer into a clinical simulation to be presented to users.

The TEE is a structured interview that has been already successfully used with pediatric cardiologists. Bass believes that its computerized form will yield similar results.

Health Awareness Programs

Ellis and Raines (1981) reported on a series of CAI programs intended to teach various preventive health concepts to increase public awareness of good health habits. These programs were written with the inexperienced user in mind; instructions and guidance are given throughout the programs.

Four programs are presently available in the package. *Coronary Risk* collects data from the user on age, sex, smoking habits, blood pressure, etc., and then calculates the risk for coronary heart disease. *Exercise Weight* collects data on age, sex, frame, height, etc., and then determines the desirable body weight. The computer also asks the user about daily activities including work, sleep, sports, etc., and calculates the total energy expenditures. The program can offer specific advice on various diets and allows the user to select the number of calories to be consumed daily and the duration of diet. *Lifestyle* surveys various habits of the users and graphically portrays the relative hazard due to each habit. *Life Expectancy* examines twelve of the user's personal characteristics and shows the effect of each on life expectancy.

These programs were evaluated by 420 volunteers who had no background in computers, but who considered CAI instruction in health-related material as being helpful to them.

The programs run on a 32K APPLE with one disk drive and

a monitor. They are written in APPLESOFT and come on one floppy disk. The programs cost $85.00 and can be ordered from: Biomedical Graphics Dept., Room B-192, Phillips-Wangensteen Bldg., 516 Delaware St. S.E., University of Minnesota, Minneapolis, MN 55455 (Ellis 1981).

Information Retrieval

Dr. Peter R. Hulick (1981), a radiation oncologist, has written two programs for storing and retrieving information on medical literature articles. The first program, *Journal Entry, Edit, and Review,* is used to index an article and to assign to it up to eight subject headings chosen from a list of 86 categories. The list is tailored for radiation oncology, but could be adapted for use in other fields as well. Besides subject headings, each journal article is identified as to title, name of journal, principal author, year of publication, the disk record (same number as that given to the actual filed document), the number of retrieval categories employed, and the date on which stored. Up to 1,500 journal articles can be indexed on a single mini-floppy disk.

The second program, *Journal Search,* is a companion program to *Journal Entry, Edit, and Review* used to retrieve the journal articles stored by using the first program. The search can be made by subject heading on the occurrence of one or more headings in the same article. The program can also print out a listing of all subject headings and a listing of all articles on the disk by record number.

The programs, written in BASIC to run on the TEKTRONIX 4051, are easily adaptable to any microcomputer. Documentation and program listing is available from the author free of charge by sending a request to P.O. Box 2026, Lynchburg, VA 24501.

Teaching Search Strategies

Although learning how to search on-line in various data bases can be very expensive, hands-on experience with the system is a must. Realizing the need for this kind of experience, the Central Information Service (CIS) of the University of London developed a series of computer simulations for the PET microcomputer.

Program #1, an interactive simulation of the DIALOG command language, is intended to teach librarians and other individuals without experience in searching the Lockheed data bases. All the major commands are covered (Vickery 1980). Program #2, also designed for the inexperienced users, teaches how to design searches, i.e., the basic concepts of search strategy. The program introduces Boolean logic, some advanced techniques for planning searches, and building and modifying strategies (Search Strategy 1980). Program #3 introduces the structure and characteristics of the Medline data base and teaches the basic commands needed for simple searches (Vickery, Batten, and King 1981).

All three programs are interactive, simulating very closely the encounter one would have with the real data base. It takes several sessions to go through each program, and supportive material is available in the form of a booklet. The user must follow precisely the commands and strategies suggested by the program, but the examples and exercises used are simple, clear, and direct, a fact that will undoubtedly be appreciated by inexperienced users. Training librarians and other users on a microcomputer as opposed to on-line in the real data base could save substantial amounts of money.

Teaching Quantitative Research Skills

The Newberry Library in Chicago has been involved for some time in teaching historians the quantitative research skills needed to handle quantifiable data from censuses, election returns, tax records, and other sources. The summer institutes conducted by the Newberry were designed in the past around large computers, but this is changing now. Richard Jensen and Janice Reiff are in the process of developing two program packages that will accomplish the same things on microcomputers while eliminating some of the drawbacks of the mainframes.

Census Coder is the first package. It allows historians to take samples of individuals and families from the census, to code the information into variables and files, and then to analyze the files using data-base management and statistical programs already available. The program allows keyboard entry of data, prompts the historian for necessary information, contains a full coding system, and performs validity checks automatically upon data entry. All this results in a clean file on a floppy disk that can be copied and analyzed immediately.

The second package is called *Table Analyzer* and permits the historian to analyze historical tables. Programs in this package include *Segregation,* which computes the index of dissimilarity that measures how intermingled or segregated two groups are; *Decomposition of Rates,* which finds the factors that trigger changes in rates (e.g., birth rates) in a division of population (e.g., rural); and *Life Table,* which constructs a life table that shows life expectancy at each age from given historical rates of mortality.

The authors plan to make the packages available for several microcomputers. They are convinced that the microcomputer will not only ease the task of training professional historians to do quantitative research, but will also foster a wider application of these research skills than that presently afforded by large computers (Reiff 1981).

Other Related Applications

Most of the existing programs are in areas other than education. The following list describes some of the program areas.

1. Entertainment: games, picture-drawing programs, music-generating programs, etc.
2. Household: programs that regulate the temperature throughout the house, monitor the telephone, store and calculate recipes, etc.
3. Office/business: programs that balance the checkbook, figure out income tax, write and format letters and manuscripts, etc.
4. Information retrieval: programs that access Dow Jones, United Press International, Community Bulletin Board System, etc.

Many of these applications have some educational value, and a few are closely related to education. It is this latter category that will be discussed in the following sections.

Community Bulletin Board Systems (CBBS). CBBS's have emerged in the last three years as an answer to the continuing need for communications among computerists. As a result, the CBBS's orientation was exclusively towards the computer hobbyist. But this has changed significantly within the last year. New CBBS's keep surfacing and many are now dedicated to specific fields or topics such as aviation, conferencing, education, humor, medicine, and self-improvement. In fact, the orientation and content of a CBBS is constantly changing according to the interests of those who use it since they are the ones who create the content.

The CBBS is basically a centralized message communication system, allowing users to leave messages or to see existing messages. It can be accessed by any terminal or computer equipped with a modem (modulator/demodulator, a device that enables the computer to be linked to another computer via the telephone lines). The user simply dials the CBBS number, places the telephone receiver in the modem, and, when the connection is made, hits the carriage return several times. After this, the system guides the user step-by-step by displaying prompts and information on how to use the system and what it has to offer.

There are now more than 250 CBBS systems in the country, among them, some specialized ones in medicine, engineering, education, and other professions. These systems provide a valuable medium for discussion and exchange of information. Since it is generally recognized that individuals do learn through similar informal channels of communications, it stands to reason that the microcomputer and the CBBS can and should be viewed as learning resources.

Information Retrieval via Microcomputer. The formidable increases in information resulted in the expansion of on-line (computerized) data bases, which allow fast and accurate retrieval. Typical applications include literature searches and fact-finding. The number of data bases is staggering. Some larger vendors such as SDC Search Service and Lockheed Information System offer more than fifty different data bases in a wide selection of subject areas.

Accessing these data bases is a little more complicated than accessing a CBBS. The user has to establish a line of credit with the vendor, obtain an ID number and a password, and learn the fairly intricate searching techniques and commands needed to search and retrieve information. These services are also expensive, running from $30.00 to well over $100.00 for each hour one is connected and actively searching. In most instances, however, this is well worth the cost since the user can save countless hours of searching through catalogs, indexes, journals, and other printed sources by spending five or ten minutes in searching a data base.

A less expensive service to which more and more individuals are subscribing is THE SOURCE. For a one-time charge of $100.00 and connect charge of from $2.75 to $4.75 per hour in non-prime time, the user can access hundreds of programs (educational, entertainment, household) as well as some well-known data-bases—Dow Jones News Service, New York Times News Summary, United Press International.

In addition, THE SOURCE has two desirable features of electronic communication: *mail* and *chat*. Using *mail*, one can type a message at the terminal and send it to an individual by simply providing the individual's ID number. Next time the person dials-up THE SOURCE and checks the "mailbox," the message will be displayed on that person's screen. Using *chat*, one can have a conversation with another user who is connected to THE SOURCE. A few simple commands place two users in direct contact, and everything typed by one party shows up on the screen of the other; all this while paying for a local telephone call (to be connected to THE SOURCE) even though the parties can be thousands of miles apart.

Other electronic communications systems besides THE SOURCE, such as Compu Serve, are also available. These systems offer a host of services such as person-to-person mail, bulletin boards, classified ads, electronic message delivery, and product reviews.

Related to the electronic communications systems is the concept of teleconferencing. Teleconferencing is a method of communication in which participants are connected to each other through computer terminals. Many individuals can be on-line at the same time and participate in "discussion" via typing at their computer's keyboard.

The computer has become, among other things, a communications medium, and if the history of CB radio is an indication, we might witness a proliferation of the computer as a communication tool as well.

Word Processing/Text Editing. Most of us are familiar with the word-processing marvels accomplished by big computers or by very expensive machines, those dedicated systems that function only as word processors. But what some people might not know is that, with the advent of the microcomputer, the capability for word processing and text editing is within the reach of every office, school, or home. Anybody who owns a microcomputer can accomplish most, if not all, of the intricate manipulations of text that, until very recently could be done only on expensive systems. Since word processing is used to create texts such as letters, forms, reports, and manuscripts, it has a direct relationship to educational endeavors.

Word processing is the creation, editing, and printing of text material. It includes not only editing functions but also text formatting and such organization functions as right and left justification, moving paragraphs from one location to another, varying line widths, numbering pages, centering, underlining, and indenting.

Text editing is usually limited to editing functions, that is, changes made in a text to make it acceptable. These changes include inserting, replacing, or deleting words or strings of words. Some programs have a *global edit* function which is used to find multiple occurrences of a word or string of words throughout the entire text and to make whatever changes or corrections are needed in these words automatically.

Imagine the problem you might have when you discover that the typist interpreted your "CME" abbreviation as "computer-managed education" and not "continuing medical education" as you expected. Since the error occurs on six different pages, these pages must be retyped. With a word processor this presents no problem. A simple command, something like: c/computer-managed education/continuing medical education (meaning change "computer-managed education" to "continuing medical education" wherever it occurs in the text) will automatically do the job in a few seconds and the computer will be ready to print out the corrected text in its entirety.

The fact that the microcomputer can be and is put to many useful applications is a strong enticement for many to purchase a personal computer. Practice has shown that owners of microcomputers are constantly looking for new programs—for new challenges on their machine. There is no doubt that educational programs, once made available, will become part of a growing reservoir of applications along with those in entertainment, household, office, and information retrieval.

Problems in the Present and a Look at the Future in Microcomputer Use

In this article, some of the characteristics of the adult learner on which the microcomputer has direct bearing were examined. Information on how microcomputers are used in professional education was provided in the case study and in the review of applications. In the remaining paragraphs, I intend to make a few personal remarks regarding the present and future of microcomputing in professional education.

Present

Educators are still far from a widespread use of microcomputers, in spite of the fact that CAI and microcomputing have many advantages to offer. It is true that many aspects of educational computing are not new, that CAI has been with us for two decades now, but there is a major difference now in *accessibility*—microcomputers have made CAI easily accessible to a much larger population. They also allow for more privacy—a very important aspect in adult learning. Programs can be improved and updated easily, which is essential in professions where content changes rapidly. Microcomputers also offer the potential for recordkeeping and documentation for continuing education credits.

Why is it then that the microcomputer is not used on a larger scale? In my opinion, the only major reason is lack of software and, related to this, lack of incentives in academia for developing CAI programs, lack of profits for commercial enterprises, and lack of individuals with the necessary skills to author good programs. I hope that this situation will soon change.

Future

My forecast is based on the assumption that in the next few years the microcomputer will become a household appliance as popular as the stereo. If this happens, the following events are also likely to occur.

- More and more people will use their own computers to play games, to write letters, to handle business, and to communicate with others. A large number of people will work from their home, thanks to advancements in telecommunications, word processors, and computers. Learning with the computer will be viewed as a natural activity; the distinction between educational activities and leisure activities will become fuzzy.
- The usual time lag from the introduction of a technical innovation to its acceptance in the teaching/learning process will be substantially reduced in the case of the microcomputer. This is because people will soon be accustomed to having and using microcomputers at home and at work, and they will demand that schools, universities, and other institutions of learning take advantage of this new technology, too.
- As the number of people owning computers increases, so will the potential for profit in developing CAI courseware. More publishing companies will rush to tap this growing market. With pressure from publishers, faculty, students, and lay

people, universities will slowly begin to accept the authoring of CAI programs as publishing and will provide proper incentives for faculty to produce these programs.

- Educational microcomputing will gain even wider utilization when CAI programs take advantage of the videodisk technology, especially when recording on videodisks becomes cheaper and requires less sophisticated equipment.

I would like to conclude by emphasizing that the microcomputer is not a panacea; it should be considered only as one more learning resource. Since adults learn differently and there is no *one* best method to suit all, the best approach is to provide a large variety of methods and resources from which they can choose the preferred one.

References

Bass, G. M., Jr. 1981. Personal communication. May 20.

Ellis, L. B. M. 1981. Personal communication. May 12.

Ellis, L. B. M., and Raines, J. R. 1981. Health education using microcomputers: initial acceptability. *Preventive Medicine.* 10: 77–84.

Hulick, P. R. 1981. Personal communication. May 4.

Knowles, M. S. 1970. *The modern practice of adult education: Andragogy versus pedagogy.* New York: Association Press.

McGuire, C. H.; Solomon, L. M.; and Bashook, P. G. 1975. *Construction and use of written simulations.* New York: The Psychological Corporation.

Pogue, L. M. 1981. Personal communication. June 8.

Reiff, J. L. 1981. Personal communication. May 27.

Search Strategy. 1980. *CIS software series* (No. 2). London: Central Information Service, University of London.

Tidball, C. S. 1978. Health education network. In Edward C. DeLand (ed.), *Information technology in health science education.* New York: Plenum Press.

Vickery, A. 1980. Dialog with PET. *CIS Software Series* (No. 1). London: Central Information Service, University of London.

Vickery, A.; Batten, A.; and King, J. 1981. Microblaise medline and the Elhill command language. *CIS Software Series* (No. 3). London: Central Information Service, University of London.

Villiers, A. M. 1981. Personal communication. June 19.

Dorothy H. Judd

A Microcomputer Role in Adult Reading and Writing Skill Development

Evidence indicates that reading and writing are interrelated in all language development, including adult language development. One study (Grobe and Grobe 1977) demonstrated that reading skills were a correlate of writing ability. The Grobes used a sample of 186 adult learners whose ages ranged from 17 through 44. The data indicated that one frequently used basic skills reading test clearly discriminated among levels of writing ability. The Grobes went on to reason that it would be plausible to find reading skills as a correlate of writing since the capable reader will engage in more reading than will the less able reader, thus modeling his or her writing after the author models encountered. Moreover, the reader also becomes aware of the organization of reading material and will use this knowledge to better organize his or her own writing. The able reader will then organize his or her writing in terms of appropriate models.

Adults usually have sufficient verbal facility to engage in the daily activities important to their existence, even though they may not be able to read or write. From this verbal facility, they develop a rudimentary understanding of some key letter forms, their sounds, and the meanings that inhere to words formed by such letters. As adult speech patterns provide for survival or greater than survival levels of discourse with others, it is evident that these adults are creating oral patterns similar to written composition.

The Microcomputer as a Teaching/Learning Tool

Many adults who need reading and writing skills development tend to acquire a repertoire of cover-up or dissembling behaviors to mask their difficulty with reading or writing. Since the microcomputer as a teaching/learning tool is very private, very consistent, very persistent, and very patient, most learners soon discover that there is no need or way to fool the microcomputer. Skillful verbal facility cannot be used to evade the reading or writing lessons that the microcomputer has been programmed to provide.

Educators who plan to use a microcomputer to effectively develop adult reading and writing skills will find that they need both a word-processing program and an authoring-system program that fulfill the following requirements.

1. Uppercase and lowercase images visible on the screen with true descenders on the *g, j, p, q,* and *y.*
2. Printer output, upon appropriate command, that produces uppercase and lowercase letters with true descenders on *g, j, p, q,* and *y.*

The use of either a word-processing program or an authoring-system program make possible the design and writing of computer-assisted instructional (CAI) programs for reading skills development without requiring the time and expertise of a computer programmer. A curriculum designer can probably arrange the completion of a CAI program more quickly than the instructional project could be scheduled in the typical programmer environment. Thus time is saved in the initial writing of the program and also in the modification of the program content after field-testing.

In *Computer Applications in Reading,* Mason and Blanchard pointed out that:

> . . . computers have already been used to diagnose reading problems and prescribe remedial materials. . . . to generate word lists, to record words dictated by children being taught with the language experience approach, and to model the reading process. Additional uses of the computer are simulation of the informal reading inventory, test generation from an item bank, and translation of print into braille. (Mason and Blanchard 1979: 90)

The computer applications cited by Mason and Blanchard have been, in part, transformed into microcomputer uses. As Bork and Franklin (1979) emphasized, the microcomputer is, first and foremost, a computer. Although Thompson (1980) took the position that microcomputers were not a teacher substitute, D'Angelo (1979) made the point that the precise, patient courseware of the microcomputer provided a giant step toward individualized instruction that had not been possible with the current delivery system. D'Angelo went on to state that:

> 1. Microcomputer courseware provides random access to any portion of the instructional material so that the student's time is not wasted while waiting for a match between his point of instructional need and the serially presented instruction.
> 2. Microcomputer instructional use represents a level of interactivity that no teacher can match.
> 3. Unlike books or films, microcomputer courseware can be updated as the need arises. (D'Angelo 1979: 16)

Furthermore, Skinner (1968) expressed the view that machines have the energy and patience needed for simple drill and practice and that "these are all functions that should never have been served by teachers in the first place."

The successful role of the computer and microcomputer in adult basic education (ABE) was the subject of two reports presented at the National Adult Education Association national conference held at Anaheim, California, in October 1981. Dr. E. A. Johnson, Marilyn Mitchell and Jane Gregory (1981) of Seminole Community College, Sanford, Florida, reported on their experiences with using computer-assisted instruction with ABE students. The study revealed that there was overall a 90 percent efficiency level in learners gaining an average of one grade level for each twenty hours of computer-assisted instruction. The average gains in reading (using the TABE test) were 0.73 for the first twenty hours of instruction. This result translates into a gain of almost three quarters of a grade level on the average for every twenty hours of computer-assisted instruction.

Learners in the program used the PLATO system. At the time of the study, PLATO was limited to a timesharing mode provided by the Florida State Computer Center. PLATO has since become available in a microcomputer PLATO format from Control Data Corporation.

Microcomputers and the Language Experience Approach

In that component of reading instruction known as the Language Experience Approach, the creation of oral patterns and use of vocabulary is the basis for the assertion that what the learner can phrase (or write), the learner can then read. During the early twentieth century "experience charts" were commonly used with beginning readers; these charts were the forerunners of the Language Experience Approach to the teaching of reading. The early experience charts provided the primary child with reading material developed from classroom activities. In more recent years, Russell G. Stauffer, Roach Van Allen, and Dorsey Hammond have contributed to the conceptual development of this reading instruction technique. The Language Experience Approach is no longer used with just beginning readers; it is presently being used with illiterate adults and all ages in between as well.

The Language Experience Approach uses the learner's vocabulary and experiences and enables the learner to express himself or herself through incorporating speaking, listening, reading, spelling, and writing. The beginning reader of any age approaches the task of learning how to read with a wealth of linguistic, conceptual, and perceptual experiences. The richness of this experience is even greater in the adult learner than in a younger student. Use of the Language Experience Approach permits a "match" between the learner's spoken and written language patterns because the reading materials reflect the adult learner's own experiences in his or her own language (Bakalis 1976).

Thus, one of the ways the microcomputer can be utilized for the beginning reader is to use a word-processing program in a microcomputer and encourage the adult to interact with the microcomputer in terms of the Language Experience Approach. The adult with a severe reading and writing handicap will need the teacher or tutor to key in the dictated words that form the story being related. But it should not take long before the individual adult develops the ability to key in his or her story by using the microcomputer keyboard as the medium for translating his or her use of oral speech patterns into written word patterns. These word forms can then be saved on the magnetic disk or cassette tape for later print-out on the screen or on a printer. An entire anthology of the written efforts of adult learners can be readily created by engaging in serially printing the several pages of story material each learner has contributed. Individual learners should be able to relate well to their own written material and to that created in a similar fashion by others.

Even the possibility of the adult keying-in a misspelled word is controlled by optional spelling dictionary programs that are compatible with word-processing programs. In a typical case, the spelling component of the word-processing program checks every word keyed-in against a 30,000- to 50,000-word dictionary in microcomputer memory. When the learner keys in a word that differs from the dictionary word form in any letter, the microcomputer screen indicates the word in question by creating a flashing image of that word. The learner then has the option, in at least one microcomputer program, of asking the microcomputer to correct the spelling of the word automatically. The only limitation discovered in these spelling dictionary programs is that the flashing-word format occurs not only when there is a misspelled word but also when the dictionary does not have the word in its memory at all. One popular spelling dictionary program does, however, make provision for adding new words to the dictionary in memory, up to a 70,000-word limit.

Another useful appoach to adult skill development in reading and writing is the creation of a word list. In the Language Experience Approach the concept of the word list has a special meaning; the word list represents the positive emphasis of words known by the learner and that are therefore deposited in his or her "word bank."

The word-list technique has a number of variations that are amenable to microcomputer use with a word-processing program. In the case of requiring the learner to compile a word list of his or her own, the microcomputer becomes the "electronic sheet of paper" on which the words are recorded. After the words have been keyed-in by the learner, they are saved on a disk or cassette tape. The learner's word list can then be loaded into computer memory from the disk or cassette tape, recalled from computer memory, displayed on the screen, printed on the printer, changed, added to, or manipulated as may fit the requirements of the teacher and the desires of the learner. If the teacher or learner wants to add words to a word list, the words to be added are simply keyed-in on the microcomputer keyboard and "saved" on the appropriate disk or cassette tape.

Levels of Reading Competency

An adult learner's reading competency can be evaluated by using the same three reading levels commonly used with younger students. The independent level, instructional level, and frustration level of the learner are determined on the basis of performance on word lists and on graded passages using a microcomputer program. At the independent level, the learner reads fluently with excellent comprehension; at the instructional level, the learner can make maximum progress in reading primarily with teacher guidance; and, at the frustration level, the learner is unable to pronounce many of the words and/or is unable to comprehend the material satisfactorily. The reading specialist's task of administering, scoring, and analyzing the reading strengths and weaknesses of adult learners can be assisted by using an appropriate microcomputer program.

Comprehension Skills Programs

The approach that has been described has the kind of programmatic and analytic basis necessary for creating effective CAI programs that can be used to develop reading comprehension skills. Microcomputer teaching/learning opportunities for developing comprehension skills can be provided through programs that involve

1. Context clues
2. Main idea-topic sentence recognition
3. Recognition of supporting details
4. Recognition of transition words
5. Study skill development

As these skills are developed, the CAI programs can be subtly enhanced as the authoring system is used by the adult educator to provide programs that represent further challenges and opportunities for skill development.

The Cloze technique, a commonly used technique for developing comprehension through better use of context clues, is just a beginning to the effective uses of the machine for reading development. The role of the Cloze technique as a practice activity in developing the ability to use context clues as a part of increasing reading comprehension will be treated in detail in a later section of this article.

When reading specialists teach the recognition of main idea-topic sentences, they frequently employ a triangle- or diamond-shaped form to help the learner focus on the location of the topic sentence in a paragraph. The graphics capability of most microcomputers in a CAI instructional mode makes this kind of exercise an effective demonstration for both the teacher and the adult learner.

A typical practice exercise in recognizing supporting details has the learner number or otherwise identify each supporting sentence. Again, CAI program capabilities facilitate use of this exercise for both the teacher and the adult learner while preserving the integrity of the needed activity and drill. The immediacy of microcomputer feedback, which gives positive reinforcement, is of significant importance in this mode of learning. The learner is immediately aware, while his or her thought process is still freshly in mind, of the correctness of a given answer in identifying supporting detail.

In developing skill in recognizing transition words and in using transition words, the typical paper and pencil exercise calls for the learner to locate the transition words in a reading selection or to supply transition words to link two sentences. The microcomputer CAI mode can be used to provide similar exercises for the learner with immediate feedback as to the acceptability of the choice made. The microcomputer can quickly determine whether a given word is among those listed as acceptable. Not as well known is the capability of a microcomputer to accept choices that involve composition as when a transition word is used to link the thought of two sentences. The acceptable formats for sentences created by learners can be specified by the teacher in the design of the CAI exercise.

The last area for developing reading comprehension involves the development of study skills. A number of microcomputer programs that can be used for drill and for practice exercises to develop study skills are available. Examples include:

1. Test materials to help prepare learners for SAT-type examinations
2. Reading comprehension programs
3. Word-analogy programs
4. Sentence-completion programs
5. Vocabulary-building programs
6. Spelling and word-recognition programs

7. Sentence-form and parts-of-speech programs
8. Phonics programs

These programs, available for a variety of microcomputers at varying levels of sophistication, provide both an assessment of skill level and a form of practice for the adult. Use of the programs makes possible an extensive inventory of skill levels with respect to reading ability as well as a comprehensive set of available study skill practice materials. Under the supervision of a reading specialist, these program units provide microcomputer controlled input, practice opportunities in study skills, and analysis of the adult learner's reading strengths and weaknesses.

Microcomputers and the Cloze Technique

One of the desirable diagnostic techniques for use with the adult reader is the Cloze Readability Technique (Burmeister 1974). Use of the Cloze technique with a microcomputer is similar to that of the Cloze technique with the usual paper and pencil routines. The learner is presented with an opportunity to respond with a word choice to fill in a blank space in a representative passage excerpted from a book. The significance of the microcomputer approach is that by using an authoring program to create the Cloze exercise, the passage with the appropriate blank spaces is presented on the screen, the learner's word choice is keyed in on the keyboard of the microcomputer and appears on the screen in the space provided. The microcomputer using the CAI authoring system has been programmed to accept several spellings of a given word choice as an acceptable answer to that particular Cloze technique sentence. The percentage score of correct word choices, calculated by the microcomputer, provides an estimate of the learner's independent, instructional, and frustrational reading levels in relationship to the passage used in testing.

The Cloze technique is useful not only as a diagnostic tool, but also as practice in using context clues to recognize unfamiliar words. One advantage of using the microcomputer is that the learner experiences immediate feedback from a message on the screen urging him or her to try again if a particular word choice is incorrect. The microcomputer in the authoring system CAI can be programmed to accept any of several word choices (synonyms of the desired word) as an acceptable answer to that particular Cloze technique sentence. The learner thereby discovers, through trial and error, the word that will best complete the thought of the sentence. In addition, the teacher can specify the record of first-try correct choices, second-try correct choices, or other grading options when creating the exercise.

Microcomputer Use in Informal Reading Inventory

The oral mode of the informal reading inventory is seldom used by the typical reading specialist with the adult reader. The adult informal reading inventory usually involves silent reading and response to a prepared test that covers the following types of items:

> . . using parts of a book, vocabulary, comprehension, and rate. The test might also include items on reading maps, graphs, and charts, and on skimming. . . . Next, the students are directed to read a six- to eight-page selection from which the remainder of the items are drawn. (Burmeister 1974: 42)

The key to effective use of the informal reading inventory is the variety of the questions on comprehension. For example, the *Advanced Reading Inventory* (Johns 1981), includes comprehension questions incorporating questions on main idea, fact, vocabulary, inference, sequence, and evaluation. The teacher is faced with a considerable amount of work in carrying through the evaluative plan of the typical informal reading inventory. The various questions can, however, be readily keyed into a microcomputer and saved to a magnetic disk or tape that provides the facility for the testing, scoring, and analysis at any point it is required.

The usefulness of the informal reading inventory arises from its role in confirming or modifying the evaluation of reading level provided by the Cloze technique. The special advantage of the microcomputer with respect to each of these techniques is that, when programmed through use of a CAI authoring program, the microcomputer can provide a testing situation that provides immediate feedback of results to the learner and the teacher. In addition, the teacher is freed from scoring and record-keeping chores so that he or she has time for interaction with adult learners.

Microcomputer Use in Evaluating Readability Levels

One of the persistent difficulties in teaching reading skills to any adult is matching the difficulty of the reading material assigned to his or her reading ability. Until recently it was necessary to laboriously count words, syllables, sentences, and so forth of at least three passages, depending on the requirements of the particular reading evaluation format selected—Fry readability formula, Dale-Chall, etc. In addition, it was necessary to keep track of the number of sentences in each hundred-word passage selected. The greatest difficulty encountered was the risk of losing track of the count due to an interruption or for some other reason. The number of syllables, words, and sentences were then substituted into the mathematic equation or graph and an estimate of the readability level was obtained.

In a microcomputer teaching environment, three one-hundred-word passages can be keyed in through the microcomputer keyboard, an appropriate signal indicating that input is complete is keyed in, and then the microcomputer instantly displays the reading level of the passage in terms of Dale-Chall, Flesch, Fog, or Smog indices for grades four through adult. Using a microcomputer to do the syllable and word counting obviously greatly eases the burden placed on the teacher evaluating prospective reading material for the adult learner. But the use of the microcomputer is not error-free. A possible source of error to the keying-in of words in the three one-hundred-word selections is the requirement that there be only one space instead of the more common two between the period that ends a sentence and the first word of the following sentence.

Other Microcomputer Capabilities

The microcomputer can also be used to provide a substitute for the tachistoscope type of machine often employed in reading laboratories serving adults. Adult readers, like those who are younger, need to develop visual discrimination of images accurately and quickly. There are several microcomputer programs that flash a single letter or word onto the screen at predetermined intervals; the screen-image material can be changed to include several words or even an entire phrase, as the reading specialist determines is appropriate. The letters, words, or phrases used with the tachistoscope are limited to those found on the film used with the tachistoscope. On the other hand, the letters, words, or phrases used with the microcomputer may be specially selected by the reading specialist for a particular person and entered into the microcomputer program; these can be used with relative ease through the EDIT command.

The microcomputer can also be used as a substitute for a reading pacer. The internal clock of the microcomputer is used to provide a chosen speed at which the material to be read is presented. The reading material used in this microcomputer mode must be keyed in through the keyboard, representing an added burden on the teacher for this application. But offsetting this added activity is the knowledge that the material entered through the keyboard is especially suited to the reading needs and interest of the adult learner. One of the challenging formats available for several microcomputers is the "interactive fiction" program in which the basic story is interspersed with personalized references to the reader and his or her locale. The stories available include several mystery and adventure stories appropriate to adult reading and experience.

The use of the microcomputer to provide suitable opportunities for skill development in reading comprehension was discussed earlier. Even where the material to be read and comprehended is not directly read from the video screen, but from printed sources, the microcomputer can play an important role in its computer-managed instruction mode (CMI). Answers keyed in through the keyboard can be evaluated instantly for correctness with respect to the reading assigned by the teacher, and the learner can be directed to turn to another page assignment by using the branching capabilities of the microcomputer. By using the branching capability, the adult learner can be referred to new material or back to a review of earlier material that was not sufficiently mastered. Moreover, a record of the learner's understanding of a passage can be recorded for later review by the teacher by including an item analysis of the types of questions answered correctly and incorrectly. This information is important in prescribing further comprehension instruction and practice. Thus, the useful assistance of the machine in scoring and record-keeping frees the teacher for more uniquely human interaction with the adult learner.

Not yet available in microcomputer program form is a management system for keeping track of performance when using a variety of materials such as reading skill-building kits for developing comprehension, vocabulary, or word attack. These reading kit materials could be made relatively cheat-proof by removing the answer forms and answer keys from the kit and placing the correct answers in a "tamper-proof" form of memory in the microcomputer. The learner could then be made responsible for keying-in the answers through the microcomputer keyboard. In such a program, the learner would then be rewarded with immediate feedback on the video screen. A record of the learner's progress could also be recorded in microcomputer memory for later reference by the reading teacher.

Microcomputers for Readers with Learning Disabilities

Adult readers with serious learning disabilities may have great difficulty in making the transition from oral speech patterns, which provide a survival level of discourse with other people, to the written "speech" patterns common to the needs of reading and writing. A variety of survival materials have been published; these involve such things as reading labels on packages; locating references in a table of contents or in a library; interpreting forms such as employment applications, subscription forms; reading maps; and reading a sales slip or service contract (Wilson and Barnes 1974). In each of these exercises, the answer checking that otherwise eats into the teacher's schedule can be provided by a microcomputer.

In more extreme instances of reading disability, the microcomputer can be equipped with a voice that provides oral sounds of letters and words as they are keyed in through the keyboard. In the cassette mode of operation, the microcomputer can also provide the learner with a set of verbal directions for manipulating the keyboard. Both of these alternatives call for extensive preparation by the reading teacher assisting the adult learner.

One of the latest developments, the interface of video recorders and videodisc systems with microcomputers, is of significance to teachers who use the microcomputer in a tutorial mode with adults. The interface between the video unit and the microcomputer provides visual images on the video screen under the control of the microcomputer. The linear capabilities of the videodisc or the videotape for providing visual images that allow a sequential presentation of a story or pictures are thus combined with the branching capabilities of the microcomputer. The system has the important capability of branching back to material presented earlier that was not mastered. Videodisc or videotape visual images are obviously of a better quality than any microcomputer screen image. The visual images on videodisc or videotape remain under the control of the microcomputer program, and the learner keys in his or her responses through the keyboard. Although this is the current extent of the level of sophistication available with microcomputers in their CAI or CMI modes, more effective programs of high quality will probably be developed in the coming decade. Thus videodisc and videotape images controlled by a microcomputer may be important tools for facilitating individualized reading instruction for the adult who is operating at barely a survival level in reading and writing skill development.

One tool that can be employed effectively with adults who have learning disabilities is the Language Master machine or its equivalent. These devices provide opportunities for recognition of the visual symbol and sound correspondence. A microcomputer equipped with a Votrax or similar oral speech capability can serve as a substitute for the Language Master device and provide experience for the adult in the visual symbol and sound patterns that comprise oral and written speech.

Microcomputer Use in Developing Writing Skills

Educators are learning that the microcomputer constitutes a very desirable approach to the composition of written material. Today microcomputers are involved in creating traditional poetry as well as Haiku, in creating newspaper copy, and in creating final text for doctoral dissertations; they are also used in developing everyday correspondence and reports. One such use was reported by the University of California at Santa Barbara (UCSB) where Jeff Marcus, manager of the microcomputer laboratory at UCSB stated that:

> Computer-assisted writing instruction, in addition to providing drill and testing procedures, can offer methods for engaging in the composing process itself. Students can use the computer . . . for pre-writing, writing, re-writing and editing.
>
> Computers also allow students to create, store and revise their writing, allow easy access to each other's work, and allow teachers to examine the various stages in the composing process without taking the work out of the student's hands. (Schneidawind 1981: 13)

Two professors at UCSB have developed a system in which students use seventeen microcomputers to compose poetry, edit prose, and brush up on spelling.

Use in Other Parts of the World

As might be expected, the microcomputer has made its impact felt in almost every part of the Western world. The predominance of its use in business data processing is not unexpected. Next in apparent importance to the use of microcomputers in the business world is their use in scientific and mathematic programs. In education, the most extensive use of the microcomputer to augment the reading and writing skills of adults appears to be occuring in England (Bradbeer 1981) and Australia (Keay 1981), with use in France a close second (David 1981). The most widely used microcomputer on the continent is reported to be the Commodore Pct.

Bradbeer stated that one secondary school in three in England now has access to a microcomputer system of some kind. The improvement of word-processing programs and their use has been a special focus of British microcomputer development.

Keay reported that the Angle Park Computing Center in Adelaide, South Australia, has achieved outstanding results in providing a microcomputer loan system serving more than 70 schools with more than 100 educational program packages. In 1980 the Angle Park Computing Center was reported to have conducted microcomputer course work with more than 1000 teachers and 9000 students.

Summary

Research in adult language development has demonstrated that reading and writing are correlates of each other. Based on this research, a number of effective methods have been developed to improve reading and writing competency on the part of adults as well as younger students. This article has explored the role of the microcomputer in improving adult reading competency. Authorities in learning theory, as well as in computer instructional applications, agree that the use of the microcomputer is an important development in teaching and learning reading skills at all levels.

Special attention was given to the role of the microcomputer in using the Language Experience Approach, the Cloze technique, and the informal reading inventory. Each of these three major thrusts in reading education has made substantial contributions to the advancement of adult reading competency. It is encouraging that the microcomputer adds so much to adult performance in each of these three areas of reading instruction.

In addition to the contribution of microcomputers to the three major thrusts in reading education this article also addressed itself to demonstrating the utility of the microcomputer for evaluating levels of student reading competency, prescribing remediaton, and evaluating readability levels of text material. Other microcomputer capabilities applicable to developing reading and writing competency were also discussed.

This article also dealt with the contribution of the microcomputer to the instructional needs of the reader with learning disabilities. The final concern of the article was the highlighting of the limited information available about the use of microcomputers in developing reading and writing skills in other countries.

References

Bakalis, M. J. 1976. *The language experience approach to teaching reading.* Springfield, IL: Office of the Superintendent of Public Instruction.

Bork, A., and Franklin, S. 1979. Personal computers in learning. *Educational Technology.* 19: 7–12.

Bradbeer, R. 1981. London computer club a huge success. *Microcomputing.* 5: 54–58.

Burmeister, L. E. 1974. *Reading strategies for secondary school teachers.* Reading, MA: Addison-Wesley Publishing Co., pp. 41–50.

David, D. J. 1981. Portrait of a dynamic French company. *Microcomputing.* 5: 72–73.

D'Angelo, J. 1979. The microprocessor as pencil. *Association for Educational Data Systems Monitor.* 18: 14–17.

Grobe, S. F., and Grobe, C. H. 1977. Reading skills as a correlate of writing ability in college freshmen. *Reading World.* 17: 50–54.

Johns, J. L. 1981. *Advanced reading inventory: grade seven through college.* Dubuque, Iowa: Wm. C. Brown Co.

Johnson, E. A.; Mitchell, M.; and Gregory, J. 1981. Final report, Project PLATO, 1980–81. Sanford, FL: Seminole Community College. (mimeographed)

Keay, C. 1981. The micro down under. *Microcomputing.* 5: 69–70.

Mason, G. E., and Blanchard, J. S. 1979. *Computer applications in reading.* Newark, Delaware: International Reading Association.

Schneidawind, J. 1981. Univ. of Calif. micros wax poetic, brush up prose. *Management information systems.* July 15. p. 13.

Skinner, B. F. 1968. *The technology of teaching.* New York: Appleton-Century-Crofts.

Thompson, B. J. 1980. Computers in reading: a review of applicatons and implications. *Educational Technology.* 20: 38.

Wilson, R. M., and Barnes, M. M. 1974. *Survival learning materials.* York, PA: Strine Publishing Co.

Carol E. Kasworm and Cheryl A. Anderson

Perceptions of Decision Makers Concerning Microcomputers for Adult Learning

Microcomputers are dull tools. I'm not interested in an extension of that mode of systematizing little bits of information. I believe that an adult learner needs a holistic teaching-learning approach. We need to bring people into the learning picture by what they need to know for their life process; not by predetermined teaching sequences of bits of information. Rather we should present passion learning, involving the intellect and the emotion at the same time. (Rick 1981)

It is a new frontier. The present and future growth of our nation is coming from technology. It significantly influences our economic direction, it has brought significant benefits to make life easier, and the spin-offs of technology have improved our lives immensely. There are so many fantastic applications of microcomputers for the present. . . . I'm concerned about people, particularly about people who are afraid and who won't adapt to change. Will we go the way of the dodo bird? We really have to prepare ourselves for this different future. We, as adult educators, need to help people to learn to use this technology in meaningful ways. (Transier 1981).

Although there are many issues regarding the future use of microcomputers in the adult education instructional process, it is the attitude of the adult and continuing education educator towards microcomputer instruction that is of paramount concern. This key decision maker is pivotal to the acceptance or rejection of this instructional innovation.

The instructional use of microcomputers is highly supported by the key administrator's beliefs and attitudes about technology, about the relationship of this instructional strategy to the learner, and about the relationship of this learning process to the mission of the institution. To gain a vital sense of both collective as well as individual differences of administrator perspectives about microcomputer use, the authors conducted an attitudinal survey and a series of field interviews. The first phase of the study was a survey of a cross-section sample of adult educators in the state of Texas. The survey consisted of a scale regarding the administrators' attitudes toward the microcomputer and a series of questions regarding perceptions of current and future use of microcomputers for instructional purposes. Approximately 100 surveys were mailed to equal numbers of adult basic education (ABE) administrators who direct adult education cooperatives and to administrators who provide noncredit community and continuing education programs within community, junior, and senior college institutions. The second phase of the research focused on in-depth field interviews with twelve administrators in Texas who were selected to represent a balanced composite of urban and rural settings, varied program funding sources, diverse adult learner clientele groups, and a variety of program responsibilities as well as a range of from prior use to no exposure to microcomputers. Through these person-to-person interviews, administrator beliefs and perspectives on past, present, and future use of the microcomputer for instruction were gathered. This article will present both the qualitative and quantitative findings of this select group of decision makers.

Current Awareness and Use of Microcomputers

Nine out of the forty-seven administrators surveyed* indicated that their programs were currently using microcomputers. The use varied in both management (word processing,

---

*Fifty-three responses to the survey questionnaire were received; six of these responses were not included in the survey results as they came from nonadministrative personnel.

registration, data files) and instructional functions. Some programs were using the microcomputer as a topical area for course offerings, in computer science vocational education courses and in data processing; while others were using the microcomputer for math skill drill and practice, problem-solving exercises, and for counseling purposes.

All administrators participating in the field interviews had experienced some form of computer use, either through management data systems or through instructional systems. Approximately half of the adult programs had or were presently using some form of computer-assisted instruction (CAI). Two of the programs were currently using microcomputers for instructional activity.

Administrators of adult basic education programs who had previously used computer-assisted instruction reported mixed reactions and findings. Two of the programs had developed a collaborative relationship between their adult basic education program and the local school district or education service center. Primary and secondary students accessed instructional computer programs during the day, while the adult population could use them at night. Two projects, both housed in Houston, used CAI for basic math skill development at the ABE level. The Houston School District, upon evaluation of the project, was not satisfied with the results; they believed that there had not been as significant a learning outcome as with their prior experiences using regular instructors. The Region IV Education Service Center of Houston had the opposite experience; they thought that the use of CAI had been a beneficial instructional strategy. They reported that they offered the learner the choice of using the computer for math drill practice. The results noted that learners using the computer did improve in computation skills. In addition, Houston Community College Learning Center for disadvantaged students is successfully using microcomputers in their learning lab for testing, scoring of tests, and for vocabulary and comprehension skills development at the fifth-grade level and above.

At the University of Houston, Dean Lee Transier is rapidly moving his noncredit continuing education program to incorporate microcomputers as a major program focus as well as for administrative purposes. His division is developing a wide variety of courses that provide skills and knowledge on microcomputers and their use. Several of these courscs use the diskette in a self-paced, self-instructional format. The division projects such rapid growth that plans have been made to add thirteen terminals to their computer mainframe this fall for instructional purposes. As noted by Transier (1981), Houston's high technology environment has created an expanding continuing education market for both the understanding and use of microcomputers. For example, the short course in word processing has a waiting list of more than 125 people. The university's sponsorship of the annual Southwest Writer's Conference will incorporate a demonstration of word processing for the development of manuscripts.

Opinions of administrators not currently using computers for instruction were divided regarding the advisability of their programs' future involvement with microcomputers. One adult educator, who had attended the first CAI national conference, noted her judgments on the idea and the current reality of computer-assisted instruction.

> I no longer consider computers or microcomputers innovative teaching tools. They did a great deal to systematize the form of learning process. They forced teachers to give important, serious thought about the sequence of learning. However, I believe in the Friere approach, the critical teaching, holistic approach to learning. (Rick 1981)

Another administrator, Lloyd Longnion, a director of an adult education cooperative in rural Texas, is investigating the program use of microcomputers. He is seriously investigating this option because of the impact of rising travel costs on learner participation and his belief that technology does have a place in our future. Longnion is looking at microcomputers to help him maintain learner participation and outreach. Further, he believes he would have a positive success with microcomputer instruction due to his current success with a guided home study program, a series of self-instructional materials that has only a telephone contact for instructional interaction with teachers. This form of literacy learning has proven successful and has many of the same characteristics of the learning format as do microcomputers. Second, Longnion believes that we should be projecting into the future; he formulated this opinion after reading such materials as *The Futurist* and *The Third Wave*. Dr. Longnion stated, "The third-wave adult educator is one who will be able to interact in the learning setting with all the technology to encourage self-directed learning. We're right on the cutting edge. Either we move ahead or we drop the ball."

The response from those surveyed about the educational potential of microcomputers was very positive. Approximately 92.3 percent of those in ABE and 100 percent of those in the noncredit (NCE) and credit continuing education groups were in agreement that microcomputers are helpful instructional tools. There was a strong consensus that the administrators would be interested in using the microcomputer in their adult education programs (61.5% ABE; 90% NCE). There was, however, some question about whether the best use of the microcomputer was for management of information or for instruction. Fifty percent of the ABE and the noncredit group indicated that microcomputers were best used in instruction; whereas 40 percent of the noncredit continuing education group noted that management was the best use.

Most administrators interviewed believed that a microcomputer system would best be used in a multi-purpose fashion. These respondents identified the creation of a more expanded version of a learning resource center, accessible by a large number of people, to include microcomputer instruction both as a learning strategy and as an "open system of self-paced instructional programs." Several saw this system as also incorporating instructional management tasks. Vicente Meir, Coordinator of the Learning Center for Houston Community College, noted that the center's current use of microcomputers could incorporate the tasks of testing and scoring, of storing and reporting individual profiles of prior tests, of noting attendance patterns and progression of learning, and of scheduling student access to the microcomputer. Dr. Longnion believed that, with the movement of many sectors of education towards competency levels of skill and knowledge, the microcomputer would be an ideal tool to keep the reporting of competencies in the instructional program up-to-date and easily accessible. One of Dr. Transier's "futuristic notions" is to develop a data base of courses, times, locations, instructors' names, instructors' credentials, and prior course evaluations of effectiveness. This data would be on-line and accessible to all companies and institutions interested in technical training, staff development, and/or individual professional development of continuing education. Interested businesses could easily call up the information data bases and instructional software systems. Another administrator would like to see a system that would link to other educational institutions, libraries, and nearby military installations for interactive sharing of information resources.

Last, most administrators thought that inclusion of a microcomputer instruction system would also mean incorporating microcomputers into their administrative systems for both record-keeping and accounting purposes. Dr. Rick added a word of caution, "We always go too far. We get a good tool, useful for certain purposes, then we're forced into a position of having to justify it [this particularly occurs in smaller institutions and programs]. We oftentimes invent jobs for it to do."

To determine the administrators' preferred use of the microcomputer, the survey defined nine classical educational applications. They were as follows:

1. *Drill and Practice.* Provides learners with a flash-card type of stimulus-response–feedback interaction.
2. *Tutorial.* Presents textual information that is interspersed with questions. The program will branch based upon the learner's response.
3. *Problem-solving.* Learners apply principles, rules, and logic of science and mathematics to solve problems.
4. *Simulations.* Presents a model based upon reality that allows learners to suffer the consequences of their "real-life" decisions without the danger inherent in the real situations.
5. *Testing.* Provides criterion-based tests in which questions can be generated at random. Test results can be provided immediately upon completion.
6. *Computer-managed Instruction.* Learners are given diagnostic tests, and the computer provides a learning prescription based upon the test results. The prescription may or may not include computer-assisted instruction. The learner can be directed toward any type of learning situation.
7. *Information Management.* The computer is used for budgeting, inventory, scheduling, and record-keeping. The computer maintains and manipulates data files.
8. *Word Processing.* The computer is used to manipulate text for reports, papers, handouts, etc. Spelling can be corrected and the text can be reorganized without retyping.
9. *Computer Literacy.* Teaches learners about computer hardware and how to use it.

Administrators participating in the survey were asked to rank from most important to least important each of these educational applications. In composite rankings, both ABE and NCE educators noted the following: 1) problem-solving, 2) tutorial, 3) computer-managed instruction, 4) information management, 5) testing, 6) drill and practice, 7) simulations, 8) word processing, and 9) computer literacy. An interesting difference occurred when the ABE group was compared to the NCE group. As noted in Table 1, the ABE group clearly emphasized instructional uses whereas the NCE group listed management functions first and fourth in ranking.

Administrators were also asked to rank in order of importance the areas of adult education they perceived as benefiting most from the use of the microcomputer in the instructional setting. They ranked the areas as follows:

1. Basic Math and Computation Skills
2. Basic Reading Skills
3. G.E.D. Preparation
4. Vocational Education
5. Continuing Education
6. English as a Second Language
7. Community Education

In examining the current and future projected use of microcomputers, most administrators' projections were based on limited knowledge. Some of those surveyed stated that they could not rank the educational uses because they knew nothing about one or more of the subjects (38 of 47 replied to the question). However, even those with limited knowledge had opinions as to how microcomputers could best be used. When looking at the composite rankings, two relatively important uses were placed seventh and ninth; these were simulation and computer literacy.

Simulation is perhaps one of the most powerful instructional uses of the computer for it can give the learner an opportunity to manipulate the decision-making process. Learners can make "real life" decisions and suffer the consequences of those decisions and yet avoid real danger. The computer can present problem situations at random thereby compounding the difficulty of the decision, something very much a part of the real world. Computer simulations are used extensively by the armed

Table 1. ABE and NCE Ranking of Educational Applications

ABE	NCE
1. Tutorial	1. Information Management
2. Problem-solving	2. Problem-solving
3. Computer-managed Instruction	3. Simulation
4. Drill and Practice	4. Word Processing
5. Testing	5. Testing
6. Simulation	6.5 Computer-managed Instruction
	6.5 Tutorial
7. Information Management	
8. Word Processing	8. Computer Literacy
9. Computer Literacy	9. Drill and Practice

forces to train officers in decision-making skills. Certainly the adult learner could benefit from the sophisticated use of the computer.

Computer literacy is currently a very important issue in the public schools. Pressure from business and industry and from parents to increase computer literacy is being brought to bear on the school system. Both groups believe that children need to know about computer systems—how they work and how they are used. Business and industry will expect adult educators to include the study of computers as part of their vocational and continuing education programs. Many surveyed administrators indicated that every adult should have some minimal knowledge of how computers are used in society (77.1% ABE; 100% NCE). The continuing education administrators who were interviewed indicated that there was a growing interest among a certain target group of adults in learning about the computer. Despite this evident need, the surveyed administrators ranked computer literacy as being of least importance.

The failure to adopt an educational technology often stems from a lack of knowledge and understanding concerning the innovation. Although the surveyed administrators indicated that they personally were not anxious about working with a microcomputer, personal anxiety about working with a machine was cited in field interviews as interfering with its potential use. There is also a fear that the technology will replace the teacher. If the technology is used appropriately, this fear will prove to be groundless. Appropriate use of the technology requires that the *teacher* be able to match the individual learner and his or her needs with the appropriate learning setting, material, and technology. To best implement computer-assisted instruction, a teacher must, however, have training and instructional support. For example, in the Houston Area Regional Service Center there is a strong commitment to the use of microcomputers and they have recently purchased 700 APPLE microcomputers. The Educational Service Center has had success because it has provided instructional support, in-service training, and consultants to school systems. Thus, all adult educators, instructors and administrators alike, need training in the proper use of the microcomputer before they can be expected to adopt the technology as a teaching tool.

Instructional Staff Development

A key factor to adopting microcomputers in the instructional program is the issue of staff development. In the survey of administrators, approximately 40 percent of the ABE educators and 80 percent of the NCE educators thought that extensive in-service training was needed if microcomputers were to be adopted by adult educators. Specifically, 23 percent of the ABE educators and 40 percent of the NCE educators believed that many adult educators in their program would be threatened by the implementation of microcomputers in their programs. Fifty percent of the ABE educators and 70 percent of the NCE educators believed that every adult education instructor should have some minimal understanding of microcomputers and their instructional use.

Interviewed ABE educators had sharply divided opinions concerning the nature and expectations of staff development. One group of administrators believed that all administrators and teachers should receive instruction in microcomputers. Several, such as Dr. Longnion, thought one should first introduce teachers to a use of the microcomputer that meets their specific needs. For example, he suggested training them to use the microcomputer as an instructional management tool for attendance reports and learner progress reports. The second stage of training would teach them how the microcomputer could be used with their learner groups; knowledge of the varied approaches and the software currently available would be disseminated at this stage.

Other ABE administrators believed that training should be given to all full-time administrators/teachers and to selected part-time teachers. During their interviews, both Dr. Oberholtzer and Dr. Spillar questioned the current feasibility of training *all* adult basic education teachers. Due to the predominance of part-time teachers, problems of yearly 40-percent turnover of instructional staff, and limited staff development training time, they thought that it would not be appropriate to train the total staff. Further, they thought it would be more profitable to provide instruction to only those teachers who were interested and who would implement this instructional approach.

Continuing education administrators believed that microcomputer instruction would be appropriate for selected members of their program staff. However, they saw their programs hiring instructional expertise, not developing it. Their concern focused on the training of microcomputer software developers and content instructors to understand the complexity of the learner and the learning environment.

In the survey, 20 percent of ABE administrators and 40 percent of the NCE administrators believed that the use of microcomputers in their adult education programs would cause too many staff problems to make the effort worthwhile. Many administrators expressed reservations concerning the time commitment, the costs, and the eventual outcomes of the training programs. Alternatives to developing expertise on their program staffs were suggested. Adult basic education administrators believed it might be more feasible to hire part-time teachers who have expertise and who are currently involved with microcomputer instruction at the primary or secondary level. Thus, potential microcomputer instructional staff could bridge the two programs and have access to available materials and facilities without creating special training demands upon the programs. These administrators also expressed concern about teachers having expertise in diagnosing varied learning styles, specific content/skill deficiencies, and the ability to translate those inputs into appropriate instructional activities. The effective implementation of microcomputer instruction would require more in-depth understanding of the variable learning patterns of adults in relation to the instructional alternatives available.

Fifty percent of the surveyed ABE educators and 70 percent of the NCE educators thought that learning to program a microcomputer would be too time-consuming for the adult educators even though the instructional staff would eventually desire and probably need programming skills. A majority of the administrators saw part of the staff development effort as being focused on training programmers to understand and create relevant instructional programs. "First rate programmers don't understand the instructional concepts or tasks. They think in a different way" (Rick 1981). Thus, creating effective microcomputer instructional systems would require training other expert institutional resources with regard to specific adult learner characteristics and program outcomes.

One continuing education administrator suggested the addition of a microcomputer instructional design specialist to the staff. As specific programs and content were determined for viable projects for microcomputer instruction, the instructional designer and a content expert could collaborate to develop the course. This linking of content and instructional process experts would be an ideal remedy for creating a new instructional focus with quality designed microcomputer systems.

Software Design and Dissemination

The development of instructional software is well behind the development of computer hardware, and what does exist is lacking educational quality. More sophisticated programming will come as educators become more involved in the creation of such programs. Even without special programming skills, an instructor can serve as a content specialist in a cooperative effort with an instructional computer programmer in designing software suited to the particular needs of the adult learner. Some adult education programs already have programming capability. In the survey, 36 percent of the respondents indicated that their programs had the resources to design and develop their own educational software.

Integral to the concern for appropriate instructional staff was the corresponding need for appropriate instructional course software. Most interviewed administrators confessed ignorance regarding current available software that could be used in their instructional operations. In contrast, 55 percent of the administrators who responded thought that they were well aware of existing computer software that would be suitable to the instructional goals of their programs. They also indicated that the use of limited available software would not make the use of a microcomputer impractical (46.2% ABE, 40% NCE). Most interviewed administrators, however, were suspicious of current software relevance, value, and quality in instruction. Dr. Neff thought that software programs were based on gimmickry, done hastily, not thoroughly tested, and not designed for diverse adult learner instruction. Dr. Transier noted that the "problem with buying commercial projects is that it violates one of the basic tenets of adult education. You should design programs to met the specific needs. There may be some basic skills that could be generically taught. But most content and skill instruction is target-audience designed." Several administrators noted that the instructional staff should ideally learn to program in order to develop software for their instructional units. Not only would instruction be specific to the target audience needs, but the materials could be updated as appropriate.

Several administrators voiced concern about the current linear, segmented format of programs; "most computer programs are insulting to adult learners." Dr. Longnion suggested that programs be redirected toward a loose, multiple-branching format, where there would be creative participation—interaction in the learning process. More "adult-like" reinforcement strategies and feedback strategies also need to be incorporated. "Current cutesy feedback of many programs are appropriate only for ten-year-old learners. Where is the more subtle, mature, and sophisticated computer interactions for adults?" asked the administrators.

A last consideration with the custom design of instructional software is the overriding problem of legalities regarding access, distribution, royalties, copyright, and possible piracy of in-house instructional programs and of leasing or buying programs from commercial sources. One of the interesting scenarios often discussed is that, in the future, computer companies will provide equipment at minimal cost and that the profits will center on software design and marketing (Transier 1981). Adult and continuing education programs will be caught with the lack of expertise to "competitively design programs" as well as with the inability to deal with the more complex legal issue of information usage and other broader concerns of marketing instructional programs.

The future instructional value of microcomputers in adult

education will be determined by the development of appropriate software. It might be beneficial for adult education programs to form cooperatives or consortiums for the purpose of designing quality software programs. For example, the Minnesota Educational Computing Consortium has been able to provide guidelines and to set standards for software developed with elementary and secondary school systems. Commercial software is being developed by such book publishers as Scott Foresman, Borg Warner, and Scientific Research Associates. These publishers are using appropriate instructional design procedures and are field-testing products. It is not, however, enough to let publishers or programmers develop CAI on their own; they need feedback and input from those in adult education to assure that the products are indeed suited to the adult learner.

Adults as Learners with Microcomputers

Adult and continuing education administrators believe that the potential value of microcomputer instruction is highly correlated to the characteristics of the learner in relation to the nature of the instructional task. In the attitudinal survey, at least three-quarters of the ABE administrators noted agreement with statements that the microcomputer could provide more individualized instruction and would help reduce anxiety of adult learners towards computers. At least 70 percent believed that learning to use the microcomputer would not be too difficult for the typical adult learner and that the use of microcomputers would not alienate the adult learner from the instruction. Four-fifths of the surveyed adult basic educators believed that the ability to use a computer will be an important skill for adults in the future. However, in the person-to-person field interviews, opinions regarding the use of microcomputer instruction with undereducated adults were sharply divided. Spillar profiled ABE students as low persisters with inadequate motivation and self-esteem: "You can't improve self-esteem through a computer. There are no pats on the back. They need teachers who care, who can individualize instruction at the critical teaching moments, who can build the *self concept.*" Warren Haley noted that "T.L.C. is of high concern. Students need to know that someone else cares, that someone else will listen. Computers aren't humane." Administrators at Houston

Community College noted the lack of differential responsiveness of a computer to a "failure-oriented learner who requires highly-laden positive reinforcement. . . . reinforcement which is perceived by the learner as empathetic, genuine, and valid."

People have a variety of motives that initiate adult learning outcomes. In addition to these motives, most adults also bring social, interactional needs to the learning environment. "Computers cannot intervene in the self-initiated learning process, as can a human being. It is important to be where the learner is at—as opposed to being where the computer is at" (Rick 1981). Other negative concerns expressed by these administrators focused on learners being overwhelmed by a machine (a gadget); the problem of learning simple, basic skills that were not integrated; the lack of personal, problem-solving orientation in computer instructional programs; the inadequacy of "canned" instructional programs to spot learning disabilities; and the concern for developing computer skills in lieu of providing "daily life skills development." Mr. Spillar commented, "Whenever we encourage the use of an alternative, a substitute to basic reading from printed matter, we indirectly state that reading is not that important. I don't like computers to teach basic reading when the person can learn to read through the written content accessed through his life experiences."

Other ABE educators view microcomputer instruction with undereducated adults from a positive frame of reference. Arnoldo Hinojosa noted that "although undereducated adults would initially be afraid of a computer, that with a personal desire to learn, familiarity of the machine, involvement in relevant learning, and the reward of immediate positive feedback, they can gain a sense of control and enjoyment from the computer." With the systematic instructional design of microcomputer programs, specific skills and knowledge can be developed. It may well be that learning through a microcomputer instructional program could be more beneficial than certain teacher-instructed class experiences. With appropriate familiarity and the ability to use a microcomputer, an undereducated adult could possibly feel more comfortable and gain confidence by making both successful responses and having mistakes corrected via a machine rather than through a written programmed text or through an instructor. With corrective feedback and reinforcement from microcomputer instruction, the learner would be continually guided through correct and appropriate responses. This systematic corrective feedback and reinforcement may be as viable a way to strengthen self-concept as are other more traditional forms of instruction.

One ABE administrator believes that microcomputer instruction might be of special assistance in his English as a second language (ESL) program. He has a significantly diverse mix of people who range from the nonliterate to the Ph.D.-trained, that is, Ph.D.-trained in their native language. Rarely can a teacher meet the breadth of these needs in one class. The more literate, motivated ESL students could easily learn the grammatical structures and gain proficiency in English or technical English on the microcomputer.

In the attitude survey, continuing adult educators noted a consensus: microcomputer instruction would be more individualized, would help reduce anxiety of adult learners towards computers, and would not be too difficult for the typical adult learner. The educators also expressed a consensus about the future importance of being able to use computers. However, only 60 percent of the respondents thought that the use of microcomputers would *not* alienate adult learners from their instructors.

In individual field interviews, continuing educators noted that, as with any topic or instructional strategy, the adult learner group characteristics would determine the process and learning outcomes. Most of the educators thought that those occupations and professions that were currently using microcomputers would be the more likely target groups. Dr. Frank Spikes, for example, thought that there was a large probability that both content and instructional process of microcomputers would be developed for business groups, records management groups, the hotel/motel industry, and the military. He foresees significant difficulty for the use of microcomputer instruction with general enrichment and avocational courses or for traditional classic liberal arts subject matter. He thought that continuing education program success with microcomputer instruction would be directly related to the current level of awareness and use of microcomputers in the learner's professional and personal life.

The key factor to continuing educator involvement with microcomputer instruction would come from supportive evidence of a valid and reliable needs assessment. The program developers need to clearly identify the objectives of the program, which would, in part, focus on development of skill and understanding of microcomputer instruction. No adult educator would purposely select a learning strategy or tool that would create fear, anxiety, or hostility in adult learners. As noted by Dr. Hulett, all elements of the learning environment need to be carefully considered, selected, and interfaced. "Selection of the microcomputer for instruction should be the best learning tool for the learner, for the learning objectives, and for the environment."

"For the time being, we should be offering instruction both ways—trying to provide a variety of instructional options. We also need to start taking some risks in trying to harness this new technology" (Transier 1981). In ten years adult learners will probably view microcomputers as a tool similar to today's television. In addition, as costs for travel and lodging continue to rise, alternative educational delivery systems are becoming a more important consideration for continuing education programming. Microcomputer instruction offers one of the better options for learner-access instruction.

Dr. Lee Transier believes that the use of microcomputer instruction is probably linked to age-related generational changes in our society. Computers are a part of the "common world" of children; for adults, computers are becoming a part of certain sectors of life—through work, banking, grocery stores, and consumer accounts. Microcomputer instruction will gain greater acceptance, feasibility, and sophistication as each year moves closer to the twenty-first century. As our children mature into adults, continuing education strategies will also need to mature. In the interim, adults will be seeking learning experiences that will provide them with basic awareness and understanding of microcomputers in relation to specific problem-solving needs. Continuing education can provide valuable services for adults who wish to gain knowledge, skill, and confidence in microcomputer use. Competitive continuing education should carefully experiment with this learning strategy. In ten years we will have learned proven applications and outcomes; we will be ready to meet the more microcomputer-oriented desires and learning styles of the future adult learner (Transier 1981).

Financial Commitments and Concerns

All interviewed administrators noted that their major concerns were the financial and human-resource commitments to microcomputer instruction. For most ABE educators, three statements were typical of the initial discussion of financial costs. "It's hard to think of funding computers, when you can't fund classes" (Haley 1981). "With no discretionary monies and, at best, a steady state budget, I'd rather place my instructional monies with teachers. You get more mileage out of them" (Oberholtzer 1981). "You're just spinning your wheels, wasting your time, when it is out of reach. We are trying to survive, keeping our heads just barely above water. Each year we are having to cut back the number of teachers, cutting back our programs with an increasing number of adults requesting our assistance" (Wood 1981). However, one administrator noted, "We use the cost factor as a refuge for our naiveté. We currently expend significant man hours by repeating certain instructional activities as a routine—when a microcomputer could be much more appropriate in this instance" (Longnion 1981).

Many of the ABE administrators interviewed indicated that, even if they had the funding, they would not seriously contemplate investment in a microcomputer system without substantial proof of its value. This evidence, both in the form of supportive research and learner success stories, would support an administrative commitment. Second, the microcomputer system would have to have a high level of use in the instructional program or be of a miltipurpose nature to assist in other areas or departments. "It is hard to justify an investment without its continuous usage" (Neff 1981). Most of the interviewed administrators were critical about the current level of relevant microcomputer courseware available. From prior experiences with CAI, educational television, and other instructional technological devices, they expressed the opinion that they would only consider a "proven product."

The NCE administrators predominately viewed their commitment in terms of collaborative sharing of equipment, software, and instructors with their academic institution or in terms of a leasing arrangement with computer companies. Thus, financial costs would be part of the total feasibility analysis for a specific workshop or short-course program. One vocal advocate, Dr. Transier (1981), noted, "Microcomputers aren't always cost effective. I believe it goes back to the human factor of instruction. It may be cheaper and more flexible to have an instructor, but you might learn twice as much from a microcomputer. How do you measure those kinds of things? Right now, the technology is probably more expensive. But I believe we have to invest in it—to do experimentation. We need to put money into it now or we'll never get anywhere with it."

One of the major decision points in relation to a microcomputer system's cost effectiveness was the "relevant lifespan of a system or a specific software package." Dr. Frank Spikes expressed concern about buying a total hardware and software system and in six months discovering that it had become obsolete. Between the suspicion of "planned obsolescence" and the awareness of exponential technological innovation in the computer industry, most administrators did not view themselves as making a capital investment in a microcomputer system. "I refuse to buy any technology—because it changes so fast it becomes outdated. In two years you're stuck with it" (Transier 1981).

As administrators discussed their preference for leasing, several key factors were discussed. One significant concern was the compatibility of the microcomputer system with the larger institutional computer system or other linking program systems. Costs would be lessened by joint cooperative agreements between programs and departments. Many ABE administrators thought that it would be most feasible to establish collaborative arrangements between a school district or education service centers and their particular programs. Several practical concerns as regards access to learners at their own remote sites were raised regarding current microcomputer models. A number of administrators thought that "portability" was a key feature for practical, convenient usage. Whether in a continuing education or adult basic education location, the course, the instructor, and, in this case, the microcomputer must have the capability to go where the learner is. Further concerns focused on security and storage of equipment and software. Could a multitude of instructors and sites have the ability to conveniently carry the machine, have access to hookups, be able to schedule it across sites and instructors, and be able to store it without its being stolen or damaged?

The financial concerns of the interviewed administrators were not supported by the surveyed administrators. Sixty percent of the NCE administrators believed that the combined uses of the microcomputer were appealing because of the low cost. The surveyed administrators indicated that they would be willing to purchase a microcomputer of their own (55% of the ABE group and 59% of the noncredit continuing education group). It is, however, evident from the statements made by those interviewed that opinions of microcomputers are based on past experiences with large computer systems. Small computer systems such as a Radio Shack TRS-80 or an Apple, which cost between $850 and $3,000, represent a one-time expenditure. Administrators choosing to lease microcomputers would spend more in a year's time than they would if they purchased the equipment.

Some interviewers expressed concern about the portability of the equipment as well as compatibility with larger computer systems. Microcomputers are highly portable units. The computer and keyboard can be carried in a brief-case-type of carrier. The display device can be any television set. The computer can also be used as an intelligent terminal, meaning it can be hooked up through phone modem into any large computer system. Thus, with a single purchase, one can have a stand-alone computer and terminal. Some administrators also questioned the lifespan of the system, fearing obsolescence. But many systems are designed for expandibility; users can add memory, auxiliary storage, and printers as needed. This capability would allow for the addition of new technological devices to the basic microcomputer system.

Summary

This article presented both qualitative and quantitative perspectives of a selected group of ABE and NCE administrators in Texas. Perceptions of value, commitment, and implementation to microcomputer instruction differed widely and were highly dependent upon type of program, adult learner clientele, program financial support, prior exposure to computer instruction, and personal beliefs regarding program innovations. As noted in the beginning quotes to this article, the use of microcomputer instruction is both a cognitive and an affective issue for decision makers. Personal bias regarding the nature of the learning process appears to influence these perceptions as much as does the potential value of the microcomputer as an effective instructional mode for adults.

References

The following adult educators were interviewed in 1981 and cited in this article. All interviews were tape recorded.

Mr. Warren Haley, Coordinator of Adult Education, Harris County.

Mr. Arnoldo Hinojosa, Adult Education Coop Director for gion IV, Houston, Texas.

Dr. Sarah Hulett, Director of Continuing Education, Trinity University.

Dr. Lloyd Longnion, Director of Adult Education, Comal County.

Dr. Vicente Meir, Coordinator of the Learning Center, Houston Community College.

Dr. Monroe Neff, Dean of Adult and Continuing Education, Houston Community College.

Dr. Dwight Oberholtzer, Supervisor of Adult Education, Houston Community College.

Dr. Zelda Rick, Director of Community Resource Development, College of the Mainland.

Mr. Bill Spillar, Director of Adult Education, Galveston County.

Dr. Frank Spikes, Associate Dean for Continuing Education, St. Mary's University.

Dr. Lee Transier, Dean of Continuing Education, University of Houston.

Ms. Betty Wood, Director of Adult Education, Harris County.

Roger L. Sanders

Computer Literacy: Innovation Adoption and In-service Training

Rapid advances in microcomputer technology have brought the capabilities of sophisticated computer technology within the reach of small businesses, individuals, and educational agencies. Decreasing costs along with the small size and increased capabilities of microcomputers have provided for an accelerated incorporation of computer technology into the economy and society. "In the last two decades, computers have worked their way into almost every segment of human endeavor, and there is some evidence to show that the future impact will be an accelerated extension of the immediate past" (McIsaac 1979: 11). The purchase of microcomputers for home use was estimated at 500,000 units for mid-1981; in 1982 purchases of microcomputers by educational agencies are expected to exceed 100,000 units. Considering the increasing availability of personal computers, increased purchases for education, and existing timesharing systems, it is entirely possible that more than 25 percent of all classroom students will have access to some type of computer technology by the mid-1980s (Diem 1981). The computer revolution is undoubtedly in progress and advancing rapidly.

The Need for Computer Literacy

Even as these fast-paced developments in computer technology occur, a simultaneous gap between educators' increased need for an awareness of microcomputers and their actual knowledge of this technology is developing. Molnar predicts computer illiteracy will be the next great crisis in education and suggests that "a student who graduates without being exposed to computers has had an incomplete education"(Molnar 1978: 16). Educators need to develop 1) an increased awareness level concerning computer technology in education and society, 2) minimal skills needed to operate a microcomputer in relation to the instructional program, and 3) more positive attitudes toward microcomputers including reducing their fears of computer technology.

If students and adult learners are to be exposed to computer technology in their formal education experience, it is imperative that a systematic process be developed to first train public school and adult educators in this technology.

One of the major problems contributing to the computer literacy crisis is the lack of training programs for educators (Dickerson and Pritchard 1981). Today's educator must obtain a working knowledge of microcomputer technology, and it is toward this identified need that educational agencies must focus their training programs. Local educational agencies can best develop training programs that provide a general awareness of computer technology and that meet the specific needs of a particular instructional program.

Report on Recent Studies

Although research dealing with computer-assisted instruction (CAI), such as the Stanford studies (Atkinson 1968), were undertaken in the mid-1960s, it has been only since 1978 that attention has focused upon the need to develop computer literacy in educators. Only since the mid-1970s, have technological advances made possible low priced and easily operated microcomputers. With this increased availability, it became evident that attention must be directed toward developing computer literacy on the part of educators and the citizenry as a whole. Arthur Luehrmann focused upon the computer as a new and fundamental technology "worthy of study on its own" (Taylor 1980: 6). Luehrmann, Director of Computer Research at the Lawrence Hall of Science at Berkeley, emphasized the importance of microcomputer technology in testimony before the House Committee on Science and Technology by stating the following:

1. The United States is the world leader in manufacturing microelectronic hardware.

2. That technology makes it possible today to deliver powerful personal computers to millions of individuals.

3. The biggest single impediment to the further growth of this industry is the fact that the vast majority of Americans are uneducated in the use of a computer.

4. To carry out the educational task ahead will require a substantial investment in research, development, planning, and delivery.

5. The private sector is not organized to make significant investments in the education of the public. (Taylor 1980: 136)

Scholars recognized the future implications of computer technology even before the development of the microcomputer. Donald Michael (1968) anticipated the growing separation between people working with computers and the rest of society. He stated that "ignorance of computers will render people as functionally illiterate as ignorance of reading, writing, and arithmetic" (Molnar 1978: 16).

Educators are now recognizing the emerging need to use computer technology and develop computer literacy. It is estimated that in 1980 the use of computer technology for instructional purposes has expanded to include approximately 50 percent of the nation's educational agencies.

While microcomputers are rapidly appearing on the educational scene, several studies define the need for training educators in this technology. In 1979 Stevens (1980) surveyed Nebraska educators on their knowledge and attitudes toward computers. A vast majority of them, about 90 percent, agreed that people need to be aware of the societal role of computers, and more than 70 percent thought their students should be able to demonstrate an understanding of computers. While these educators recognized the need for teaching about computers, an overwhelming 90 percent of them did not believe they were qualified to teach computer literacy. Student teachers also indicated a lack of training in this area; more than 94 percent agreeing that they were not qualified to teach computer literacy. While educators demonstrated a general awareness of computer applications, they scored only at the 50 percent level on a computer software and hardware literacy questionnaire.

Most educators did not have a working knowledge of computer software and hardware. Teachers also showed a high anxiety level, with only 30 percent indicating that they felt at ease around computers. In focusing on the need for teacher training in microcomputers: 1) more than 80 percent of the teachers surveyed indicated they did not know how to use a computer, 2) 88 percent indicated that their training to use computers in the classroom was inadequate, and 3) more than 50 percent specified a need for training.

Educators face many problems in applying computer technology to the instructional process. Dickerson and Pritchard (1981) focused on three major public school concerns that could also be applied to adult education programs. These concerns are as follows:

1. The lack of sophisticated training programs dealing with computer literacy
2. The restricted ability of public schools to develop new programs or radically change methods
3. The short-term planning of budgets and program development by public schools

Sixty percent of the respondents in a survey of Florida's school administrators indicated that computers were used for instructional purposes, but less than 40 percent provided formal training for teachers in the instructional use of computers. A direct correlation also was found between the size of the school district and use of computers. The larger the enrollment, the more likely it was that the school system used computers for instruction, provided training programs for teachers, and expected increased instructional use of computers both in the classroom and in the home. None of the districts with the smallest enrollment (0–2,000) used computers, whereas all of the largest districts (more than 25,000) did. Dickerson and Pritchard (1981) also discovered that more than 80 percent of the Florida administrators surveyed expected to be using computers for instruction by the mid-1980s. While this showed a positive movement toward computer technology, it did present a serious problem. As these researchers pointed out, "At the present time, the dichotomy between the sophistication of the technology and the sophistication of the training would seem to be increasing: computers are much easier to mass produce than trained teachers" (Dickerson and Pritchard 1981: 13).

Other descriptive studies pointed to the same theme of advancing technology and lagging teacher training. Dennis (1977) surveyed 686 Illinois administrators and found that: 1) 71 percent saw a need for computer science teachers, 2) 55 percent saw a need for state certification in computer science, and 3) 82 percent thought that some computer science background would be valuable for any teacher. Baker (1976) surveyed 78 superintendents in 50 states about their preferences concerning computer science and teacher training. Respondents indicated a need for a computer science department in their educational agencies and indicated that every educator should be trained in the basic uses of computers.

The Minnesota Educational Computing Consortium (MECC) conducted the most extensive field study regarding computer literacy in educational institutions; more than 6,800 educators were involved. In surveying Minnesota educators (MECC 1980), MECC analyzed the perceptions of educators about computers. Respondents strongly supported the need for general, minimal computer literacy, with 90 percent agreeing that all students should have some minimal understanding of computers. An even larger number of teachers, 93 percent, agreed that students should learn about the role computers play in our society. Educators also viewed the computer as a versatile instructional tool, with 93 percent agreeing that "computers can be a useful instructional aid in many subject areas other than mathematics." Regarding the adequacy of teachers' training, 44 percent of all teachers disagreed with the statement "my training has adequately equipped me to make decisions about using computers in my teaching."

A review of the literature reveals three major themes regarding computer technology and public education.

1. The rapid advance of computer technology is reflected in the increasing availability of microcomputers for both business and personal use.
2. As the application of microcomputer technology becomes more prevalent, the need for computer literacy increases.
3. Educators are inadequately trained in computers and are not computer literate themselves. They must be trained to deal with computer technology and with the microcomputer specifically.

Factors Affecting Innovation Adoption

The literature focuses upon the problem of computer literacy, but few studies have dealt with training programs that help educators reach needed minimum competencies; the MECC (1980) study was the only one to address this problem. The literature does, however, provide some direction in terms of implementing change in education and in adopting innovations.

Martellaro (1980), who analyzed the process of incorporating microcomputers into a curriculum, identified several attributes that affect the adoption of innovations.

1. *Relative advantage:* the degree to which an innovation is perceived as being better than the idea it supersedes.
2. *Complexity:* the more complex the innovation is perceived to be, the slower the rate of adoption.
3. *Trialability:* the ability to experiment with the innovation; if the innovation can be tried before adoption, the rate of adoption will increase.
4. *Observability:* the visibility of the results to people not immediately involved with the innovation. If results cannot be easily seen by others, the innovation is less likely to spread.
5. *Compatibility:* the degree to which the innovation fits in with the values, experiences, and needs of the adopter.

Before computers will become well-established in the educational arena, positive perceptions must be developed in each of these areas.

Adoption of an innovation is an "individual process" that relies upon a "chain reaction process" whereby "the number of adopters in each unit of time increases in proportion to the number that has already accepted the new practice" (Carlson 1965: 7). Carlson also noted that innovations must be viewed in perspective with the informal school social system as well as in relation to the formal organization. He discussed relative advantage, compatability, complexity, divisibility, and communicability as the factors that must be dealt with in the successful adoption of innovation; "high relative advantage, high compatibility, high divisibility, and high communicability are advantageous to the diffusion of an innovation, but high complexity is not" (Carlson 1965: 71).

The Process of Innovation

Recognizing the factors influencing the adoption of innovation as complex interrelationships dependent upon individual and organizational characteristics, the question becomes *What is the process of innovation?* Havelock (1973), who identified innovation as "any change which represents something new to the people being changed" (p. 4), focused upon the process of moving from education the way it is now to education the way we would like it to be. He proposed a six-step process for change: 1) building a relationship between the change agent and teachers, 2) diagnosing the problem to be solved in specific terms, 3) acquiring resources to support the problem-solving process, 4) choosing the solution that best fits the situation, 5) gaining acceptance of the solution or innovation, and 6) stabilizing the innovation and insuring self-renewal of the innovation. It would be the responsibility of the change agent, a person who "facilitates planned change," to orchestrate the adoption process in three broad steps: 1) preplanning, 2) adoption procedures, and 3) maintenance of the innovation to ensure integration into the total system. Havelock provided a comprehensive and detailed guide for the change agent—involvement, solid planning, and follow through were the critical issues that must be incorporated into the change process.

Burns (1969) identified twenty-two considerations that would contribute to increased teacher involvement. Of these, the following are particularly applicable to teacher training and microcomputers.

1. Work initially with a small, select staff.
2. Provide a library of reference material relating to the problem.
3. Set definite time limits—it is too easy to delay and procrastinate when time is open-ended.
4. Do not rush the project.
5. Sequentially assign short-term goals and short-term time limits; this is preferrable to complex goals and long-term time limits.
6. Train a staff through face-to-face communication rather than a more formal academic approach.
7. Encourage communication between staff members; get all the feedback possible.

8. Be flexible.
9. Encourage production of instructional materials.
10. Provide for resource persons who can assist teachers in the teaching environment.

In designing the process of implementation of an innovation, special consideration must be given to the method of delivery and techniques used in the staff development process. Bishop (1976) categorized such techniques into the following five strategies of implementation.

1. *Media.* Surround participants with relevant materials—books, films, etc. "The existence and availability of these items provide a reference base as evidence of intent, alternative ideas, and modes of sharing" (Bishop 1976: 56). When used alone, this approach lacks direction and task definition; share ideas and resources.
2. *Process or organization.* Establish a process or create an organizational unit to do the work. Standing committees or special groups should be established to be responsible for the project. There must be a conscious effort to integrate the innovation into the system, otherwise gains may disappear along with the leadership emphasizing the innovation. This approach is effective when human relations outcomes are sought and when "results are viewed in terms of skills to be learned, commitments to be made, and perceptions to be strengthened" (Bishop 1976: 57).
3. *Information.* Provide a continuous flow of research and data. It is assumed that if people are informed and know the objective, reasons, and the substance, the desired consequences will occur. This one-way information flow has a low impact when used alone.
4. *Facilities and resources.* Develop a facility that will enhance the function or task to be achieved. Establish an environmental situation that calls for the continuous need for activities. Availability, flexibility, and scheduling are considerations that must be addressed.
5. *Personnel.* Select a person to perform the desired task and make him or her responsible for its execution. "It may be more productive to train and use teacher leadership, to have certain functions performed by teaching rather than supervi-

> sory or administrative personnel" (Bishop 1976: 58). It is short-sighted to always import competence since this deprives local professionals from gaining experience and competence in the areas of concern. However, never to involve outside persons as consultants sometimes leads to futile attempts at innovation adoption.

While no strategy will stand alone in the effective implementation of change, Havelock's process of planned change and Bishop's strategies can be combined to develop an effective plan of action.

Bishop also provided a comprehensive checklist that can be used to appraise both the plan of action and the implementation process.

1. Administration and board support must be evident.
2. Rationale and objectives must be clear.
3. Professional staff members must know how to participate and relate to the program. A participatory approach allowing for various levels and degrees of involvement should be provided.
4. There must be adequacy, quality, and coordination in the materials to be used.
5. Relevance and realism for professionals is necessary. This relates to certification, status, attention, time, income, and especially to the tasks for which a staff member is accountable.
6. A reasonable plan for the achievement of the desired objectives is essential; it must include short- and long-range goals, time frames, expectations, and processes for modification.
7. Leadership and role responsibilities should be defined for all staff members. Leadership should be determined on the basis of competency and accountability.
8. Communication flow and feedback must be a part of the process.
9. Time is essential for change—time for development and accommodation, time within the priority hours of activity. If the innovation is an add-on scheduled to occur only during "off" hours or days, all of the above elements are negated.

10. Support and modification must be observable in all aspects of the innovation process. It must be recognized that a single change or thrust toward an innovation will be rejected or overpowered by the routine.

In-service Education

In-service education typically plays a major role in the retraining of practicing educators. Diem (1981) identified an in-service approach for increasing teacher knowledge of computer technology as the best answer to solving the immediate problem of computer illiteracy.

The literature, however, provides very little information on in-service education dealing with microcomputers. In fact, "the literature contains little that is readily and dependably usable by the practicing school administrator in the task of administrating for change" (Schmieder 1974: 53). In consideration of this lack of material, it is necessary to examine the theoretical framework of developing effective in-service programs. Hentschel (1977) provided a conceptual framework for applying change theory to in-service education by presenting four concepts: 1) the change agent can create an attitude favorable toward change within the organization, 2) change efforts must be directed toward needs teachers believe important, 3) continued input and support must be given to teachers, and 4) teachers must perceive that rewards will result from adopting the innovation. Hentschel also pointed out that teachers should know what specific change is desired, that involvement in the change process is essential, that a free flow of communication facilitates adoption, and that a trial use of the innovation enhances the chance of adoption of the innovation.

In support of this involvement strategy, Muller (1975) proposed that "perhaps the most important element of all in planning workshops is to assure as much active involvement of the participants in the learning process as possible" (p. 19). Houmes (1974) also emphasized this involvement process and encouraged specificity of goals and purposes, active participant involvement, and continuous follow-up.

In-service Training Model

The growing concern over computer literacy is evident in the literature. Several studies have indicated that educators do not possess the needed minimum computer literacy knowledge and skills necessary to incorporate computer technology into the instructional process nor to prepare learners for the emerging microcomputer technology. But before an in-service training program can be planned, a clear focus must be developed as to the specific uses of microcomputer technology in relation to the instructional program. Educators should identify the specific function that microcomputers will serve—for computer-assisted instruction (CAI), teaching programming, developing computer literacy and awareness, or for other functions. Specificity of purpose is of prime importance, with teacher involvement playing a major role in identifying the specific uses of microcomputers to meet specific instructional needs. Throughout the process of identifying the function these computers will serve, a core group of interested educators will emerge. It is with this group that in-service training should begin. Once this group is trained, a diffusion network can be established to train other educators within the system.

Since studies indicate that a majority of educators have little if any computer literacy, consideration must be given to addressing the basic aspects of computer technology. Areas of computer literacy that should be included in in-service training include microcomputer hardware, software, programming, applications of computers, the societal impact of computers, and attitudes and values of individuals toward computers. In-service training should increase the awareness level of educators about computers in general as well as develop their operational understanding and skills in dealing with microcomputers specifically.

Minimum Computer Literacy Competencies

The following objectives are aimed at developing minimum computer literacy competencies. Participating educators should be able to demonstrate mastery of these objectives.

Microcomputer hardware

1. Will be able to identify the components of a microcomputer system
2. Will demonstrate an understanding of the function of these components

3. Will be able to operate a microcomputer in relation to its use in the instructional program

Microcomputer software

1. Will be able to identify the types of computer software
2. Will be able to identify evaluative criteria used in assessing software quality
3. Will become aware of the software available within the local educational agency

Microcomputer programming

1. Will become aware of the need for using a language understood by the computer and be able to identify one computer language
2. Will be able to write a simple computer program

Applications of computers

1. Will become aware of the diverse use of computers in everyday life
2. Will become aware of the applications of the microcomputer as an educational tool

Impact of computers on society

1. Will become aware of the effect of applying computer technology in society
2. Will be able to identify positive and negative results of the impact of computers

Individual attitudes toward computers

1. Will demonstrate attitudes that reflect a lack of fear, anxiety, or intimidation related to computers
2. Will value increased communication and the availability of information through computers
3. Will feel confident about the ability to operate a microcomputer

The computer literacy competencies outlined are designed to increase educators' general awareness levels about computers and to develop specific operational skills needed to use microcomputers in education.

The checklist on the next page highlights considerations that must be weighed when educators plan to incorporate microcomputers into the instructional process.

1. Identify the specific function that a microcomputer will serve. For example, teaching problem solving using computer-assisted instruction.
2. Involvement of educators in determining the instructional use of computers is of prime importance. Teachers, administrators, and curriculum specialists should be involved in identifying instructional needs.
3. Prepare short- and long-term plans within achievable time limits.
4. Let the function the microcomputer is to serve dictate the particular equipment to be purchased. First identify the software to be used and then purchase the hardware accordingly.
5. Identify a core group of interested educators who will participate in a diffusion process of teaching others. Once these people are trained they can help others incorporate the technology into their instruction.
6. Work with a small group initially. Success with a few will enhance the chances of expansion.
7. Provide adequate resource material to support the instructional needs.
8. Allow for two-way communication and a sharing of ideas.
9. Implement a training program that meets the needs of participating educators. Work with small groups, allow for hands-on opportunities, and encourage experimentation. Initially people may feel more comfortable working in pairs.
10. Continually evaluate the use of microcomputers in the instructional program and allow for modification of plans as needed. Be flexible, but keep a clear focus on instructional objectives.

Conclusion

The application of theories of change and innovation implementation must be called upon to develop programs that will meet the immediate need to incorporate microcomputers into the educational arena and to retrain educators in this emerging technology. Well-planned programs must be developed; they must provide for teacher involvement and for follow-up support services to help ensure the adoption of this innovation within schools. The task of retraining educators is not a small undertaking, but one that must be accomplished. The need for computer literacy is fast becoming a reality while the ability of educational agencies to provide programs to meet learner needs in this area is far from a reality. Educators must become more knowledgeable in the area of computer literacy.

References

Atkinson, R. C. 1968. Computerized instruction and the learning process. *American Psychologist.* 23: 225–239.

Baker, J. 1976. *Computers in the curriculum, fastback no. 82.* Bloomington, IN: Phi Delta Kappa Educational Foundation.

Bishop, L. J. 1976. *Staff development and instructional improvement.* Boston: Allyn & Bacon.

Burns, R. W. 1969. Suggestions for involving teachers in innovation. *Educational Technology.* 9: 27–28.

Carlson, R. O. 1965. *Adoption of educational innovations.* Eugene, OR: Center for the Advanced Study of Educational Administration, University of Oregon.

Dennis, J.; Dillhung, C.; and Muiznieks, J. 1977. Computer activities in secondary schools in Illinois. *Illinois Series on Educational Application of Computers No. 24.* Urbana, IL: University of Illinois.

Dickerson, L., and Pritchard. 1981. Microcomputers and education: planning for the coming revolution in the classroom. *Educational Technology.* January: 7–12.

Diem, R. A. 1981. Developing computer education skills: an inservice training program. *Educational Technology.* February: 30–32.

Havelock, R. G. 1973. *The change agent's guide to innovation in education.* Englewood Cliffs, NJ: Educational Technology Publications.

Hentschel, D. 1977. Change theory applied to inservice education. *Planning and Changing.* 8: 103–114.

Houmes, G. 1974. Revitalizing inservice training for change. *Educational Technology.* 14: 33–34.

Luehrmann, A. 1980. Computer illiteracy—a national crisis and a solution for it. *BYTE.* July.

McIsaac, D. 1979. Impact of personal computing on education. *AEDS Journal.* 13: 7–15.

Martellaro, H. 1980. Computer countdown. *Creative Computing.* 6: 98.

Michael, D. N. 1968. *The unprepared society: planning for a precarious future.* New York: Basic Books.

Minnesota Educational Computing Consortium (MECC). 1980. *A study of computer use and literacy in science education, 1978–1980.* St. Paul, MN: MECC.

Molnar, A. 1978. The next great crisis in American education: computer literacy. *AEDS Journal.* 12: 11–20.

Muller, M. T., and Edwards, A. M. 1975. *The use of workshops for orienting educators on computer-based instructional techniques.* Austin, TX: Texas University.

Schmieder, A. 1974. *Literature searches of major issues on educational reform.* Washington, DC: ERIC Clearinghouse on Teacher Education.

Stevens, D. J. 1980. How educators perceive computers in the classroom. *AEDS Journal.* 13: 221–223.

Taylor, R. P. 1980. *The computer in the school: tutor, tool, tutee.* New York: Teachers College Press.

John A. Hortin

Information Resources for Computer-Assisted Instruction

Some writers have described microcomputer technology as the beginning of a new age for society. Many proponents of computer-assisted instruction (CAI) and telecommunications view this technology as the greatest discovery since fire or the wheel. Their fervor is reminiscent of a scene in Stanley Kubrick's *2001: A Space Odyssey* in which one of the ape-like humans picks up a large bone and inadvertently discovers that it can be used as a weapon. Raising the bone over his head, he sends it crashing down onto the remaining bones on the ground. The camera angle, the music, the action, and the gleam in the eye of this creature work together to make the viewer identify with him and his thrill of discovery. At the same time, the viewer recognizes the weapon's potential for destruction, because this accidental discovery not only helps the creature defend the precious water hole from other wandering, rival tribes but also gives him great power over his fellows.

Can the microcomputer with a national or multinational hookup through telephone lines or satellites be viewed in a similar way? Is it the beginning of some highly centralized system for controlling how people learn, what they learn, and what they do? Some answer *no,* though alarmists may cite Orwell's *1984,* Huxley's *Brave New World,* Skinner's *Walden II,* and Goodman's *Compulsory Miseducation* in regard to the dangerous effects of technology. This is not to say that there are no legitimate concerns in regard to the ethical use of microcomputers and technology in general, but educators have always tended to shy away from any new technology, no matter what the circumstances. Postman (1979) made a good case for education's role being one of "thermostatic activity" that slows down change in our society when the mass media culture of society is pushing for and welcoming change.

Although the state-of-the-art for education and the microcomputer is still in its infancy, business and industry have successfully incorporated microcomputers into their everyday worlds. And, with the high cost of transportation and energy and with a greater reliance on cost effectiveness in the everyday world, the home or personal computer will become an important aspect of daily life.

But unless proponents can show that microcomputers, telecommunications, and software are more useful and more efficient than traditional methods of teaching and learning, the potential of this technology as a revolutionary development in education may be short-lived. One needs only to look at the 1950s and 1960s to realize that proponents of television exaggerated its potential impact and usefulness for education. Television certainly had an impact, but not necessarily the impact expected. In fact, the pervasiveness of television's negative influence on children and adults is alarming (Arlen 1976, 1980; De Franco 1980; Mander 1978; Moody 1980; Newcomb 1979; Winn 1977). And television in the schools did not change education drastically; nor did it replace the teacher. One could say that the use of television in education has been somewhat of a disappointment, but perhaps it is only that we now have a more realistic view of television's limitations. The same may come to be true of the microcomputer; it is still too early to tell.

What educators need, of course, is to educate and prepare themselves so that given the choice of using or not using the microcomputer, they can make an intelligent decision. Obviously, educators need better software and much more training in computer literacy; the literature on microcomputers bears out these assertions (Atherton 1979; Blaschke 1979; Bork and Franklin 1979; Braun 1979; Floyd 1980; Folk 1978; Melmed 1980).

The exciting aspect of the microcomputer is the potential wide range of use it offers for a relatively low cost. New generations of microcomputers will provide voice recognition, speech generation, increased memory size, and network development.

We are at only the nascent stage in the development of the microcomputer for use in education and especially adult education. Articles dealing with microcomputers point out that for education the software developments have lagged behind those of hardware (Gleason 1981; Hausmann 1979; Lipson 1980; Moursund 1979). The microcomputer has been enthusiastically received in the business, industry, and, to some degree, home markets. In fact, it will probably be the success of the microcomputer in these markets that will force an acceptance of and a greater interest in the microcomputer in adult education. Educators will, after all, have to train people to use this technology as part of their basic education for mere survival in the everyday world.

Resources from Periodicals

There are many resources available for the adult educator who wishes to know more about the computer. Some periodical titles follow:

AEDS Journal
AEDS Monitor
Apple Education News
Apple Educator's Newsletter
BYTE: The Small Systems Journal
Calculators/Computers
Classroom Computer News
COMPUTE
Computer
Computer Applications
Computer Communications
Creative Computing
Computer Weekly
Dr. Dobb's Journal of Computer Calisthentics and Orthodontia
Educational Technology
80 Microcomputer
80 Software Critique
Funkschau
Instructional Innovator

Interface Age
Media Adult Learning
Micro: The 6502 Journal
Microcomputing
NIBBLE
PET: Cursor
Practical Computing
Recreational Computing
Robert Purser's Magazine
Softside: Apple
T. H. E. Journal
Teaching Computer Programming
The Computing Teacher
The Futurist

This list is incomplete; more journals, newsletters, and resources seem to appear each month. Adult educators forced to concentrate on just a few titles would find the following ones most appropriate: *AEDS Journal, BYTE, Classroom Computer News, Computer, Creative Computing, Educational Technology, Interface Age, Instructional Innovator, Media Adult Learning, Microcomputing,* and *T. H. E. Journal.* These journals would make a good combination of sources for keeping informed about hardware, software, methods, examples, and trends in the computer education world.

Other journals such as *80 Microcomputing* or *Apple Education* are designed specifically for TRS-80 or Apple users and deal with business, hobby, and home uses of the microcomputer as well as educational use. Information on computers geared exclusively to educators is difficult to find, but *Classroom Computer News* contains practical examples aimed at the educator. *Educational Technology* has had many recent articles on the computer in education; the journal also reviews microcomputer programs. *Interface Age* and *Microcomputing* are more typical of the business and home microcomputer magazines that feature a number of topics including speech synthesis, word processing, printers, programming, coding, system of the month, and hardware and software evaluations. These journals sometimes have articles on educational programs and practices that are useful. *T. H. E. Journal* (T. H. E. stands for Technological Horizons in Education) also has excellent articles but is oriented toward teachers using many types of technology, not only microcomputers. *Instructional Innovator,* published by the Association for Educational Communications and Technology, deals with all types of media, but the practical slant of the articles is worth noting. Microcomputers are currently receiving a great deal of attention and appropriate articles appear often. *Media Adult Learning,* a publication of the media section of the Adult Education Association, is the only journal that emphasizes adult education and media; it may contain articles that are of more interest to the adult educator in terms of theory, research, and practical applications.

ERIC Resources

Little has been written about adult education's use of the microcomputer. The Educational Resources Information Center (ERIC) has a national computer network that provides educational papers, presentations, and documents to educators, researchers, and administrators. Sponsored by the National Institute of Education, ERIC publishes monthly abstracts in *Resources in Education* and disseminates documents through microfiche, paper copy, and on-line systems.

A search for resources through ERIC (mid-1981) using the description items of *microcomputer, adult education, adult learning, continuing education, adult basic education, lifelong learning,* and others, elicited only one citation for microcomputers for adult education. This article, "Computing Education for the Developing Asian Countries" (1980) contained few aspects of general interest. The search did, however, produce 185 citations dealing with the microcomputer and education. These citations were divided into 18 categories as noted in Table 1. Listed in each category is the number of articles found that emphasized the topic of that particular category. Placement of the 185 citations was determined by actually reading and evaluating the article or by noting the description of the abstract on the ERIC print-out. Although some articles could have been placed in several categories, each was assigned to only one category.

Table 1 shows that 28 citations in the ERIC search treated some aspect of the microcomputer in the science or mathematics field; this figure should not come as a surprise since the computer already has been heavily used in those disciplines.

Table 1. Types of Articles Dealing with Microcomputers from ERIC

Category	Number
Hardware	23
Software	8
Practices in education	17
Higher education	5
Computer-assisted instruction	6
Computer literacy	10
Graphics	7
Library	3
Networks	8
Training (work-related)	5
Sources of information	6
Teacher education	1
Research	7
Opinion	7
Use with other media	4
Types of languages	14
Adult education	1
Practices in business or home	5
Administrative tasks	8
Basic skills	2
Science and mathematics	28
Handicapped	2
Comprehensive (most of the above)	8
Total	185

The next-largest category was hardware. A large amount of information on hardware seems to be available from educational and trade sources. It is disappointing that there are far fewer articles on software and that those that exist are intended for the microcomputer expert or hobbyist, not for the educator. Even in the ERIC sample, articles on software (8) were somewhat general and directed more toward what is wrong with current software than toward what is available and how it is used. More critical examination of software is needed as educators, microcomputer enthusiasts, and publishers are beginning to realize. In fact, British trade journals are beginning to carry evaluations and descriptions of software.

Some information on a program is usually available from the producer and is included in advertisements or short articles in the various microcomputer publications. There are also several organizations in the United States that provide systematic and perhaps more objective evaluations of software. CONDUIT, located at the University of Iowa and sponsored by the National Science Foundation, publishes *Pipeline,* which reviews software used in the higher education area. The Minnesota Educational Computing Consortium, which placed more than 1800 Apple II microcomputers in various institutions in Minnesota, is also evaluating materials. Elementary and secondary education level microcomputer software is being examined through *Microsift* (Microcomputer Software Information for Teachers), which is published in Portland, Oregon. Finally, the Michigan Association for Computer Users in Learning has the *MACUL Journal,* which also reviews software materials. It is hoped that better quality materials will be developed as the demand for them increases and as the various trade, professional, and hobbyist journals and these educational sources begin to evaluate more critically and objectively.

The category of computer languages, which had 14 citations in the ERIC search, was another relatively important topic. Practices in education had 17 citations, many of which were directed toward elementary and secondary school educators. Categories such as handicapped, sources of information, library, uses with other media, teacher education, and basic skills received few citations.

Books and Conference Proceedings

The comprehensive sources such as books and conference proceedings listed in ERIC and elsewhere are most useful for the person wanting an in-depth look at how educators are using the microcomputer. Some of these comprehensive sources deserve further description because they help explain current use of the microcomputer in education.

The comprehensive sources include the following works: *Computer-Based Education. The Best of ERIC* (Hall 1980), *Proceedings of the NECC/2–National Educational Computing Conference 1980* (Harris & Collison 1980), *Computer-Based*

Instruction: A New Decade (Association for the Development of Computer-based Instructional Systems 1980), *Guide to Microcomputers* (Frederick 1980), *Professional Development and Educational Technology* (Association for Educational Communications and Technology 1980), *A Gateway to the Use of Computers in Education* (AEDS 1980), *Educational Implications of Microelectronics and Microprocessors* (Harris 1979), *Proceedings: DISE Workshop on Microprocessors and Education* (Pittsburgh University 1976), *A General Introduction to Microcomputers* (Muiznieks 1978), and *The Microcomputer as an Interactive Instruction System in the Classroom* (Jelden 1980).

These sources provide a broad background of information. For instance, *Professional Development and Educational Technology* (Association for Educational Communications and Technology 1980), a monograph of collected papers from a three-day conference, contains such articles as Lipson's "Microcomputers Applied to Education" and Heinich's "Implications of the Expanding Use of Educational Technology in Education and Training." Heinich (1980) pointed out that the structure of education is resistant to the use of instructional technology, and he urged educators to create an environment that regards technology as useful and desirable. He foresaw the possibility of deconsolidation of our school districts and a reinvention of education as a "cottage industry" that would be based on technology.

Lautsch (1981) also predicted a decentralized condition for education. He believes that we will change from transportation-dependent educational centers to computerized, remote-delivery systems in the home. Telelecture, telenet, and telecourses are already beginning to transform universities to some degree from on-campus institutions to off-campus operations. Whether or not these systems of education will become more decentralized in terms of governance is another question. In terms of logistics, organizational structure, and location, the decentralized school may become a reality because of energy and transportation costs. The policy decisions and control of telecommunications systems could, however, still be highly centralized to maintain the operation of such vast systems efficiently. The control and operation of such a program could be in the hands of several types of groups, and this situation might not be altogether satisfactory. For example, control might be vested in the telecommunications network industries or a blue ribbon educational committee or perhaps the software developers from big business. It is certainly desirable if not essential that the long-term effects of electronic data processing communications networks be investigated before we proceed much further with their development.

Gueulette (1980) expressed concern about the future of telecommunications networks in the discussion of his concept of the "super school." The convergence of telecommunications (cable, satellite) with the microcomputer is natural since they both deal with communication and information; one system transmits that information (telecommunications) and the other stores, manipulates, and presents it (microcomputer).

Electronic data processing may transform our homes into communications centers for recreational, educational, and business operations. Thus, the home with a microcomputer could become a "super school," transmitting and receiving information from all over the world.

Lipson (1980), however, warns us about the disadvantages of a person's working alone at a computer terminal. To counter the limiting and isolating effect of working alone, Lipson had students in his program using the computer terminal work in pairs in order to stimulate dialogue, argument, and interaction. The effects of using a microcomputer in a solitary home environment must still be carefully studied and researched.

Another comprehensive source, *Computer-based Instruction: A New Decade,* is a collection of 50 papers that were presented at the Conference of the Association for the Development of Computer-based Instructional Systems (1980). The papers cover such topics as the handicapped, music instruction, home economics, basic skills, PLATO, and training. Most of the papers are practical descriptions of ongoing projects.

A Gateway to the Use of Computers in Education contains 45 papers that were referred and published by the 18th Annual Association for Educational Data Systems Convention (AEDS 1980). Computer-assisted instruction is stressed in this source. Two of the best sources of information on the microcomputer come from two related AEDS publications: the *AEDS Monitor* (Volume 18, Nos. 4, 5, and 6) and the Fall 1979 *AEDS Journal* (Volume 13, No. 1). Detailed information and thoughtful commentary on the role of the microcomputer in education can be found in these last two sources. Articles in this issue of the *AEDS Journal* include "The Role of Personal Computer Systems in Education," "Impact of Microcomputers on Educational Computer Networks," "Microcomputer Software

Development: New Strategies for a New Technology," "Impact of Personal Computing on Education," "How Do I Choose a Personal Computer?", "Selecting Microcomputers for the Classroom," and "Problems in Selecting a Microcomputer for Educational Applications."

Selected Abstracts

McIsaac (1979) believes that the effects of the microcomputer will be felt in every aspect of our lives. He made five generalizations that are pertinent for the adult educator's understanding of the microcomputer's impact.

1. We tend to underestimate the long range effects of technological developments.
2. A single technology probably does not develop independent of other technologies and inventions.
3. Developing technologies often require huge amounts of capital expended over a long period of time. This capital is often the result of military, recreation or entertainment interests.
4. Potential and developing markets for the technology are closely related to the willingness of man to invest.
5. We tend to overestimate the short range impact of new technologies. (McIsaac 1979: 11)

McIsaac (1979) also viewed the microcomputer as a problem-solving tool for students and not just a machine for drill and tutoring. With computer graphics and the ability to "see" solutions to problems via a computer terminal screen, the possibilities do seem promising. The most effective programs will be those on which the commercial companies seek the comment and advice of teachers.

McIsaac (1979) also predicted two other situations: 1) the setting up of library networks of software materials as they are made available through individual programmers, commercial vendors, teachers, and hobbyists and 2) an increase of computer drill and practice materials, some of which are already in evidence. Much of the success of any technology depends, as McIsaac says, on the amount of profit to be made, and if the videodisk, videogame, microcomputer, and cable television industries continue to grow as they have till now, we can expect a great volume of educational materials to be forthcoming.

Kehrberg (1979) warned educators against converting existing large computer software into microcomputer use; he believes that software should be designed to take advantage of the unique features of the smaller microcomputer. The first question the educator should ask is if the material to be taught is really adaptable to the computer format. Then he or she must determine if the best learning is going to take place in such a setting. Graphics and audio cassettes can readily be used with the microcomputer. Tactile experiences, like pointing the finger at the screen, are further possibilities for the microcomputer's use. For record-keeping and creating an interactive experience for the student, Kehrberg also suggested that the student who uses the microcomputer be asked to give some written responses and directions.

Thomas and McClain (1979) offered some suggestions for selecting a microcomputer. Their five-phase model contains the following steps: 1) identify the instructional problem, 2) determine instructional requirements, 3) infer computing requirements, 4) survey equipment capabilities, 5) select the computer to meet requirements. They suggested that educators identify those instructional problems that the computer helps solve, such as work in vocabulary, spelling, and mathematics, before doing anything else. The instructional requirements (item 2) should be strategies appropriate both for solving the instructional problem and using the computer. Such strategies might be drill, tutoring, problem solving, programming, simulation, testing, computer-managed instruction (CMI), data analysis, word processing, computer literacy, and information retrieval. Inferring computer requirements (item 3) involves the crucial decision as to whether the educator needs a timesharing (large) computer or a microcomputer or any computer at all.

Matthews (1979) offered some even more specific criteria for selecting a computer, ranging from cost to personnel available for programming and maintenance. Braun (1979), Ricketts and Seay (1979), Milner (1980), Joyce (1977), Tesler (1978), Nomeland (1979), Souviney (1980), Attala (1979), and Folk (1978) are other specific sources that deal with microcomputer selection, but these sources do not fit the comprehensive category.

Guide to Microcomputers (Frederick 1980) is especially useful for the novice. Frederick discussed the development of the microcomputer in education and described its many possible uses including control of home environment, home-based educational activities, access to different data bases (medical, ERIC, Psychological Abstracts, Social Sciences Citation Index, Dow-

Jones), different communication systems, estate planning, and the ability to examine, compare, and purchase goods and services from businesses and industries worldwide. Like many microcomputer proponents, Frederick predicted that the home computer will enable people to transfer money; pay bills; plan dinner menus; make theater, plane, and travel reservations; converse with people in distant cities; and educate themselves at home. Two other excellent articles on the home computer terminal are those by Vail (1980) and Cornish (1981); both appeared in *The Futurist.*

Frederick (1980) also described computer languages for microcomputers. The most common one now in use is BASIC; however, programming in BASIC is awkward. Newer, more easily programmed languages are being developed. For instance, Bell and Howell has come up with a couple of languages (GENIS I and PASS) that were designed to be self-tutoring, self-authoring languages that allow teachers to create curriculum materials through computer-assisted instruction.

Other languages include PILOT, PASCAL, LISP, FORTH, MUMPS, FORTRAN, and COBOL. COBOL, basically a business language, is used to teach programming; FORTRAN is also used to teach programming through the microcomputer and would be obviously suited to those who already know FORTRAN language. LISP, which deals with language manipulation, can also be used with a class on programming. MUMPS, as the name suggests, was developed for the medical field and provides an alternate language for computer-assisted instruction. According to Frederick (1980), a language is chosen for the microcomputer based on cost, accessibility, convenience, programming features, speed, size, and availability of existing programs written in the language.

Articles on Educational Uses of Computers

Several good sources exist that discuss current educational practices involving the microcomputer. While the ERIC search turned up only 17 citations that fit that specific category, other articles do exist. Since not much material directly related to adult education and the computer is available, some non-ERIC search articles will be presented along with the ERIC articles.

Bork and Franklin's (1979) "The Role of Personal Computer Systems in Education" compared the then current capabilities of personal computers and timesharing computers. Timesharing computers can exchange messages, maintain central records, and access central data bases (libraries), operations that personal computers cannot currently perform. Network systems that connect microcomputers to larger computers and telecommunications will, however, change this current lack of capability. Bork and Franklin also described the computer as the first technological innovation that enables the educator to work in a Socratic fashion: the computer enables the teacher, through technology, to engage a large number of students in a dialog of questioning and answering. "We cannot clone Socrates, but we can use computers to give today's large numbers of learners more of the type of learning experiences that his students had" (Bork and Franklin 1979: 24).

An article by Levin (1980), "Microcomputers: Out of the Toy Chest and into the Classroom," outlined some of the positions schools have taken on the uses of microcomputers for teaching. Specific applications of microcomputers for education are also found in articles by Bass (1980), Walters (1980), Clark and Rogers (1980), Merrill and Bennion (1979), Lucas (1980), Joiner (1980), Hull and De Sanctis (1979), and Price (1978).

In a more theoretical perspective, Moore (1980) presented a brief historical account of his research on the talking typewriter, computer-generated motion picture, and folk model theory for design of learning environments. According to another author (Keyser 1979), microcomputer programs in the classroom have generally been categorized into drill and practice, tutorial, simulation, problem solving, and computer literacy. Keyser described several innovative software programs that teach poetry, spelling, graphic simulations in science (Huntington simulations created by Braun), music instruction, and lesson writing.

Another researcher, Vanderheiden (1981), wrote about the practical applications of the microcomputer in helping the handicapped. Vanderheiden said that "it is quite clear that computer literacy will soon be a basic requirement of anyone involved in rehabilitation, particularly of individuals with severe or multiple disabilities" (Vanderheiden 1981: 61).

Other articles described programs in higher education (Sousa 1979; Jenkins and Dankert 1981; Cavin, Cavin, and Lagowski 1980; Hausmann 1979; Huntington 1980; Johnson 1980; Walters 1980), rural schools (Joiner, Silverstein, and Ross 1980; Lockard 1980), student behavior (Clark and Rogers 1980), social studies (Saltinski 1981), reading and writing (Fox, Bebel, and Parker 1980), spelling (Bejar 1981), decision making (Simmons 1979), and computer skills (Diem 1981). A number of additional articles are about computer crime, economic changes as a result of the microcomputer, employment, robots, household use of the computer, and communication (Cornish 1981; Miller 1980; Molitor 1981; Norman 1981; Simmons 1979; Vail 1980). Articles predicting future trends include Gleason's (1981) "Microcomputers in Education: The State of the Art," Souviney's (1980) "There's a Microcomputer in Your Future," Raskin and Whitney's (1981) "Perspectives on Personal Computing," Papert's (1981) "Computers and Computer Cultures," Aiken and Braun's (1980) "Into the 80's with Microcomputer-Based Learning," Mazur's (1980) "A Wave of the Future," Jay's (1981) "Computerphobia: What to Do About It," and McKinnon's (1980) "Computer Literacy and the Future: Is It Possible to Prevent the Computer from Doing Our Thinking for Us?"

Research Reports

There are problems associated with the use of the microcomputer, the lack of good software for one, but with proper incentives for producers (profit) and more careful reviewing by educators, this lack should not be a problem in the future. As far back as 1964, Paul Goodman saw a drawback to programmed instruction. He said, "In this pedagogic method it is only the programmer—the administrative decision-maker—who is to do any 'thinking' at all; the students are systematically conditioned to follow the train of others' thoughts" (Goodman 1964: 80).

In his article, "The Microprocessor as Pencil," D'Angelo (1979) provided another view; the microcomputer, he said, should be thought of as a pencil, a tool to be used only when it can serve education.

Some of the reasons people have for not using the computers are emotional ones, but emotional antipathy is not the only factor. A survey of department heads at colleges and universities conducted by CONDUIT identified the following reasons for not using computers in higher education:

Lack of training	32%
Lack of equipment	22%
Lack of funds	12%

Lack of time	12%
Lack of interest	11%
No application	10%

(Hausmann 1979: 34)

The survey results would seem to indicate that we need to make a concerted effort to train all educators to use the computer. That means that workshops, conferences, minicourses, and research with the microcomputer must be supported and adult educators encouraged to learn all they can about microcomputer use in education.

Research on computer-assisted instruction as reported by Gleason showed the following:

1. CAI can be used successfully to assist learners in attaining specified instructional objectives;
2. There appears to be a substantial savings in time (20 to 40%) required for learning as compared to "conventional" instruction;
3. Retention following CAI is at least as good as if not superior to retention following conventional instruction;
4. Students react very positively to good CAI programs; they reject poor programs. (Gleason 1981: 16)

Research conducted during the mid-1960s and more recently concurs with these conclusions (Kulik, Kulik, and Cohen: in press). Hausmann reported:

> Generally, CAI has the potential to be an effective instructional aid when measured through the results of student achievement. It appears to be more effective in tutorial and drill modes than in problem-solving and simulation and gaming modes. Tutorial and drill modes seem to be more effective for low-ability students than for middle or high-ability students. (Hausmann 1979: 36)

Programs on the microcomputer have advanced considerably beyond the drill exercises that were typical of early computer-assisted instruction. Myers (1981) discussed such advances as color table animation, stereoscopic computer graphics, and realistic display in his article, "Computer Graphics: Reaching the User." Oldknow (1980) described computer-generated film and the use of high-resolution color graphics in mathematics education. Another kind of innovative research involves microcomputer painting in which color pictures are produced on the screen and can be stored for later use (Hicks and Zibit 1978; Hicks and Zibit 1979; Kosan and Hicks 1979).

The Department of Secondary Education at the University of Illinois has available a user's manual on producing microcomputer painting (Kosan and Hicks 1979).

Conclusions

This survey of the various sources available suggests that the following conclusions can be drawn:

1. Agitation and uncertainty about the use, standardization, and future of the microcomputer in education will continue as more equipment and newer technologies are developed.
2. A more realistic and practical approach and attitude toward the microcomputer will eventually emerge. Home learning centers may develop but not in the revolutionary sense of completely changing education as we know it today.
3. Educators will remain reluctant to use the microcomputer until they receive training in its use and until software improves. More importantly, educators will have to feel a change in attitude toward technology before they accept widespread use of the microcomputer; success of the microcomputer in business will encourage this change in attitude.
4. Since the microcomputer, unlike television, can interact with students and can store data bases, its impact on education will be greater than was that of television.
5. Using the microcomputer to free teachers from the routine of drill, practice, and paper work associated with teaching is an important goal. If this goal is realized, teachers will be able to devote more time to interacting with students and developing more creative and social experiences for their students.
6. Even though research in microcomputers or computer-assisted instruction is not conclusivc, cducators will still try new methods and programs with the microcomputer.
7. Most of the materials designed for the microcomputer are locally produced. If interest in microcomputer programs grows and if profits are to be made, more commercially produced programs will come on the market. This increase will benefit elementary and secondary educators by making available to them a greater number of materials; the situ-

ation may work against adult educators. If commercial producers concentrate on materials for elementary and secondary levels because that is where the largest market is, fewer materials on the adult level will be available.

Microcomputers will not solve all the problems in education; Moursund (1979) made this point when he described 25 problem areas that computer advocates must face. The greatest problem, of course, is the lack of teacher knowledge about the computer or computer illiteracy. We must learn to use the tools of the new, electronic technology (telecommunications, microcomputers, and satellites) in order to assure that decisions, policies, and programs are not left to just an elite, powerful few. Adult education is by tradition a participatory activity that should involve all segments of society and encourage the use of the best technology that society can provide.

References

Aiken, R. M., and Braun, L. 1980. Into the 80's with microcomputer-based learning. *Computer*. 13(7): 11–16.

Arlen, M. J. 1976. *The view from Highway 1*. New York: Ballantine Books.

Arlen, M. J. 1980. *Thirty seconds*. New York: Farrar, Straus and Giroux.

Association for Educational Communications and Technology. 1980. *Professional development and educational technology*. Washington, DC: Association for Educational Communications and Technology.

Association for Educational Data Systems (AEDS). 1980. *A gateway to the use of computers in education*. Washington, DC: AEDS. (ERIC Document Reproduction Service No. ED 192 718)

Association for the Development of Computer-based Instructional Systems. 1980. *Computer-based instruction: a new decade*. Bellingham, WA: Association for the Development of Computer-based International Systems. (ERIC Document Reproduction Service No. ED 194 047)

Atherton, R. 1979. Microcomputers, secondary education and teacher training. *British Journal of Educational Technology*. 10(3): 198–216.

Attala, E. E. 1979. Mass storage media for microprocessor-based computer-assisted instructional systems. *Educational Technology*. 19(10): 53–55.

Bass, G. M. 1980. *Creativity through the microcomputer*. Norfolk, VA: National Educational Conference. (ERIC Document Reproduction Service No. ED 190 128)

Bejar, I. I. 1981. Show and spell from Radio Shack. *Creative Computing*. 7(3): 22, 24.

Blaschke, C. L. 1979. Microcomputer software development for schools: What, who, how? *Educational Technology*. 19(10): 26–28.

Bork, A., and Franklin, S. D. 1979. The role of personal computer systems in education. *AEDS Journal*. 13(1): 17–30.

Braun, L. 1979. How do I choose a personal computer? *AEDS Journal*. 13(1): 81–87.

Cavin, C. S.; Cavin, E. D.; and Lagowski, J. J. 1980. The use of microcomputers in college teaching. *Educational Technology*. 20(5): 41–43.

Clark, D. C., and Rogers, D. H. 1980. The study of student covert behaviors with the aid of microcomputers. *Educational Technology*. 20(11): 46–49.

Cornish, E. 1981. The coming of an information society. *The Futurist*. 15(2): 14–21.

D'Angelo, J. 1979. The microprocessor as pencil. *AEDS Monitor*. 18(5): 14–17.

De Franco, E. B. 1980. *TV on/off*. Santa Monica, CA: Goodyear Publishing.

Diem, R. A. 1981. Developing computer education skills: an in-service training program. *Educational Technology*. 21(2): 30–32.

Floyd, S. 1980. Designing interactive video programs. *Training and Development Journal*. 34(12): 73–77.

Folk, M. 1978. Should your school get a microcomputer? *Mathematics Teacher*. 71: 608-613.

Fox, M. S.; Bebel, D. J.; and Parker, A. C. 1980. The automated dictionary. *Computer*. 13(7): 35–48.

Frederick, F. J. 1980. *Guide to microcomputers*. Washington, DC: Association for Educational Communications and Technology.

Gleason, G. T. 1981. Microcomputers in education: the state of the art. *Educational Technology*. 21(3): 7–18.

Goodman, P. 1964. *Compulsory mis-education and the community of scholars.* New York: Vintage Books.

Gueulette, D. G. 1980. Home computers teaching machines born again. *The Learning Connection.* 1(3): 3, 10.

Hall, K. A. 1980. *Computer-based education. The best of ERIC.* Washington, DC: National Institute of Education. (ERIC Document Reproduction Service No. ED 195 288)

Harris, D., and Collison, B. (eds.). 1980. *Proceedings of NECC/2–National Educational Computing Conference 1980.* Iowa City: Iowa University. (ERIC Document Reproduction Service No. ED 194 060)

Harris, N. D. C. (ed.). 1979. *Educational implications of microelectronics and microprocessors.* Bath, England: Claverton Down. (ERIC Document Reproduction Service No. ED 190 129)

Hausmann, K. 1979. Instructional computing in higher education. *AEDS Monitor.* 18(5): 32–37.

Heinich, R. 1980. Implications of the expanding use of educational technology in education and training. In *Professional Development and Educational Technology. Proceedings of the National Conference.* Washington, DC: Association for Educational Communications and Technology, pp. 23–31.

Hicks, B., and Zibit, M. 1978. *MC painting: a new medium for art education.* Urbana, IL: Department of Secondary Education. (ERIC Document Reproduction Service No. ED 160 068)

Hicks, B., and Zibit, M. 1979. *MC painting manual: A user's guide.* Urbana, IL: Department of Secondary Education. (ERIC Document Reproduction Service No. ED 183 201)

Hull, G. L., and De Sanctis, V. 1979. How to teach adult learners on their own terms. *Audiovisual Instruction.* 24(8): 14–15.

Huntington, J. F. 1980. Microcomputers and university teaching. *Improving College and University Teaching.* 28(2): 75–77.

Jay, T. B. 1981. Computerphobia: what to do about it. *Educational Technology.* 21(1): 47–48.

Jelden, D. L. 1980. *The microcomputer as an interactive instruction system in the classroom.* Greeley CO: University of Northern Colorado. (ERIC Document Reproduction Service No. ED 194 710)

Jenkins, T. M., and Dankert, E. J. 1981. Results of a three-month PLATO trial in terms of utilization and student attitudes. *Educational Technology.* 21(3): 44–47.

Johnson, J. W. 1980. Getting from here to there: the status of instructional computing in higher education. *Technological Horizons in Education*. 7(6): 48–53, 57.

Joiner, L. M. 1980. Potential and limits of computers in schools. *Educational Leadership*. 37: 498–501.

Joiner, L. M.; Silverstein, B. J.; and Ross, J. D. 1980. Insights from a microcomputer center in a rural school district. *Educational Technology*. 20(5): 36–40.

Jordan, J. J. 1980. Computing education for the developing Asian countries. *Computer*. 13(6): 11–17.

Joyce, J. 1977. Hardware for the humanist: what you should know and why. *Computers and the Humanities*. September/October: 299.

Kehrberg, K. T. 1979. Microcomputer software development: new strategies for a new technology. *AEDS Journal*. 13(1): 103–110.

Keyser, E. L. 1979. The integration of microcomputers into the classroom or now that I've got it, what do I do with it? *AEDS Journal*. 13(1): 113–117.

Kosan, C., and Hicks B. 1979. *Instructions for microcomputer painting*. Urbana, IL: College of Education. (ERIC Document Reproduction Service No. ED 172 772)

Kulik, J. A.; Kulik, C. C.; and Cohen, P. A. in press. Effectiveness of computer based college teaching: a meta-analysis of findings. *Review of Educational Research*.

Lautsch, J. C. 1981. Computers in education: The genie is out of the bottle. *Technological Horizons in Education*. 8(2): 34–35, 39.

Levin, D. 1980. Microcomputers: out of the toy chest and into the classroom. *Executive Educator*. 2(3): 19–21.

Lipson, J. 1980. Microcomputers applied to education. In *Professional Development and Educational Technology. Proceedings of the National Conference*. Washington, DC: Association for Educational Communications and Technology, pp. 149–152.

Lockard, J. 1980. Computers blossom at a small school in Iowa. *Instructional Innovator*. 25(6): 25, 48.

Lucas, J. P. 1980. Programs for small children. *Creative Computing*. 6(3): 136–137.

McIsaac, D. N. 1979. Impact of personal computing on education. *AEDS Journal*. 13(1): 7–15.

MacKinnon, C. F. 1980. Computer literacy and the future: is it possible to prevent the computer from doing our thinking for us? *Educational Technology.* 20(12): 33–34.

Mander, J. 1978. *Four arguments for the elimination of television.* New York: Morrow Quill Paperbacks.

Matthews, J. I. 1979. Problems in selecting microcomputers for educational applications. *AEDS Journal.* 13(1): 69–79.

Mazur, K. 1980. A wave of the future. *Personal Computing.* 4(12): 35–39.

Melmed, A. S. 1980. Information technology for education: an agenda for the 80's. *Technological Horizons in Education.* 7(6): 46–47, 62.

Merrill, P., and Bennion, J. L. 1979. Videodisc technology in education: the current scene. *NSPI Journal.* 18(9): 18–19, 22–26.

Miller, I. 1980. The micros are coming. *Media and Methods.* 16(8): 32–34, 72–73.

Milner, S. D. 1980. How to make the right decisions about microcomputers. *Instructional Innovator.* 25(6): 12–19.

Molitor, G. T. 1981. The information society: the path to post-industrial growth. *The Futurist.* 15(2): 23–30.

Moody, K. 1980. *Growing up on television.* New York: Times Books.

Moore, O. K. 1980. About talking typewriters, folk models, and discontinuities: a progress report on twenty years of research, development, and application. *Educational Technology.* 20(2): 15–27.

Moursund, D. 1979. Microcomputers will not solve the computers-in-education problem. *AEDS Journal.* 13(1): 31–39.

Muiznieks, V. 1978. *A general introduction to microcomputers.* Urbana, IL: Department of Secondary Education. (ERIC Document Reproduction Service No. ED 178 054)

Myers, W. 1981. Computer graphics: reaching the user. *Computer.* 14(3): 7–14, 17.

Newcomb, H. (ed.). 1979. *Television: the critical view* (2nd ed.). New York: Oxford University Press.

Nomeland, R. 1979. Some considerations in selecting a microcomputer for school. *American Annals of the Deaf.* 124: 585–593.

Norman, C. 1981. The new industrial revolution. *The Futurist.* 15(1): 30–40, 42.

Oldknow, A. 1980. Some notes from a microcomputer workshop. *Mathematics Teaching.* June: 45–47.

Papert, S. 1981. Computers and computer cultures. *Creative Computing.* 7(3): 82, 84, 86–88, 90, 92.

Pittsburgh University, Department of Electrical Engineering. 1976. *Proceedings: DISE workshop on microprocessors and education.* Pittsburgh: Pittsburgh University. (ERIC Document Reproduction Service No. ED 182 139)

Postman, N. 1979. *Teaching as a conserving activity.* New York: Delacorte Press.

Price, C. C. 1978. Microcomputers in the classroom. *Mathematics Teacher.* 71(5): 4.

Raskin, J., and Whitney, T. 1981. Perspectives on personal computing. *Computer.* 14(1): 62–73.

Ricketts, D., and Seay, J. A. 1979. Assessing inexpensive microcomputers for classroom use: a product-oriented course to promote instructional computing literacy. *AEDS Journal.* 13(1): 89–99.

Saltinski, R. 1981. Microcomputers in social studies: an innovative technology for instruction. *Educational Technology.* 21(1): 29–32.

Simmons, W. W. 1979. The Consensor. *The Futurist.* 8(2): 91–93.

Smith, L. 1979. Microcomputers in education. *AEDS Monitor.* 18(5): 18–20.

Sousa, M. B. 1979. Computer augmented video education. *Educational Technology.* 19(2): 46–48.

Souviney, R. 1980. There's a microcomputer in your future. *Teacher.* 97(5): 52–58.

Tesler, L. 1978. Measuring time on PET and other microcomputers. *People's Computers.* March/April: 4–6.

Thomas, D. B., and McClain, D. H. 1979. Selecting microcomputers for the classroom. *AEDS Journal.* 13(1): 55–67.

Vail, H. 1980. The home computer terminal: transforming the household of tomorrow. *The Futurist.* 14(6): 52–58.

Vanderheiden, G. C. 1981. Practical applications of microcomputers to aid the handicapped. *Computer.* 14(1): 54–61.

Walters, J. P. 1980. Personal computing goes to college. *Personal Computing.* 4(8): 44–47.

Winn, M. 1977. *The plug-in drug.* New York: Bantam Books.

Peter West

Microcomputer Software for Educational Use

A computer without a program, or "software," is like a $3,000.00 stereo set without any records or tapes. (Time Magazine 1981:69)

Sales of microcomputers in the $500.00 to $10,000.00 range have already exceeded one million units. Microcomputers are expected to be one of the largest growth industries of the 1980s. There is no question that the hardware is readily available; numerous companies are designing and marketing the equipment. Reasons why more units have not yet been sold may be because the equipment has been perceived as being overly complicated and because potential buyers believe little or no software is available. Just the opposite is true though. Microcomputers are as easy to use as typewriters (although some people will argue that a typewriter is not necessarily easy to use), and software in sufficient quantities is readily available. To illustrate the proliferation of software, it has been reported that companies producing computer software are growing as fast as microcomputer manufacturers themselves. Additionally, sales of software programs, produced on cassettes or disks, is already a $265-million-a-year business and is expected to surpass $1 billion by 1985! The concern then should not be about the availability of software, but rather the *selection* of that software.

This article will provide adult educators and others with suggestions for selecting appropriate programs from the abundance of available software. Lists of software directories and of educational software distributors are included at the end of the article. Many of the distributors will be more than happy to send catalogs of their software, and the directories are excellent reference tools for locating software in specific disciplines.

Evaluating Computer Software Descriptions

One problem confronting microcomputer users is the attempt to identify suitable instructional materials, or software, by reading reviews and product abstracts. Unfortunately, a process for selecting materials based solely on a review or abstract can be somewhat risky. At times, though, such a procedure is necessary because previews of instructional materials are not always available, and previews of computer software are almost nonexistent because of the possibility of copyright violations. As a result, the educator's decision to purchase software may be entirely dependent on reviews and abstracts. But how does one decide if the software reviewed will be suitable for one's instructional needs?

Certain criteria are helpful in evaluating reviews and abstracts to determine suitability of materials (Fig. 1). These criteria might help eliminate some of the guesswork involved in selecting software by review only.

These criteria are as follows:

1. *Locate resources.* Where can one find reviews and descriptions of computer software? A variety of sources can be consulted to locate software.
   a. Software directories (see listing at the end of this article)
   b. Catalogs of software distributors (see listing at the end of this article)
   c. Journals *(Classroom Computer News,* P.O. Box 266, Cambridge, MA 02138; *Interface Age,* P.O. Box 1234, Cerritos, CA 90701; *Creative Computing,* Box 789–M, Morristown, NJ 07960; and *Purser's Magazine,* P.O. Box 466, El Dorado, CA 95623 are among the journals that include software reviews of computer programs for the adult educator). Local libraries and bookstores will also be able to provide

the names of many more journals dealing with microcomputers.

d. Conventions and professional meetings
e. Curriculum centers (colleges, schools, etc.)
f. Colleagues
g. Information agencies. (Educational Resources Information Center (ERIC), U.S. Dept. of Education, Washington, DC; Educational Products Information Exchange (EPIE), P.O. Box 620, Stony Brook, NY 11790)
h. Direct mail (This source, though haphazard, can often provide valuable information about computer software to consumers)

2. After one has identified sources for locating computer software program reviews, one must determine if appropriate programs are available. A good place to start is a *subject listing* in a directory. Such a list will normally provide a number of titles in the area of interest. Subject listings can also supply information that would seem compatible with general learner requirements in the area of interest, but they will offer little in the way of specific content information.

3. The *title* of the item will often provide more detailed information about the actual content. The title will indicate whether or not one should spend time reading the rest of the review or abstract. Some titles are not as descriptive as others though, so one should keep in mind the general subject area when considering a title.

4. After a title that appears compatible with learner requirements has been isolated, one should begin to check the review for *environmental constraints.* One needs to know if the use of the program would be affected by any of the following:
   a. Equipment/format
   b. Cost
   c. Teacher/learner skill
   d. Other

5. The name of the *publisher* might indicate something about the quality of the program. Is it a major publisher whose works are familiar? If not, the item might still be extremely useful. Excellent computer software can often be purchased from the smaller "cottage industries" consisting of individual

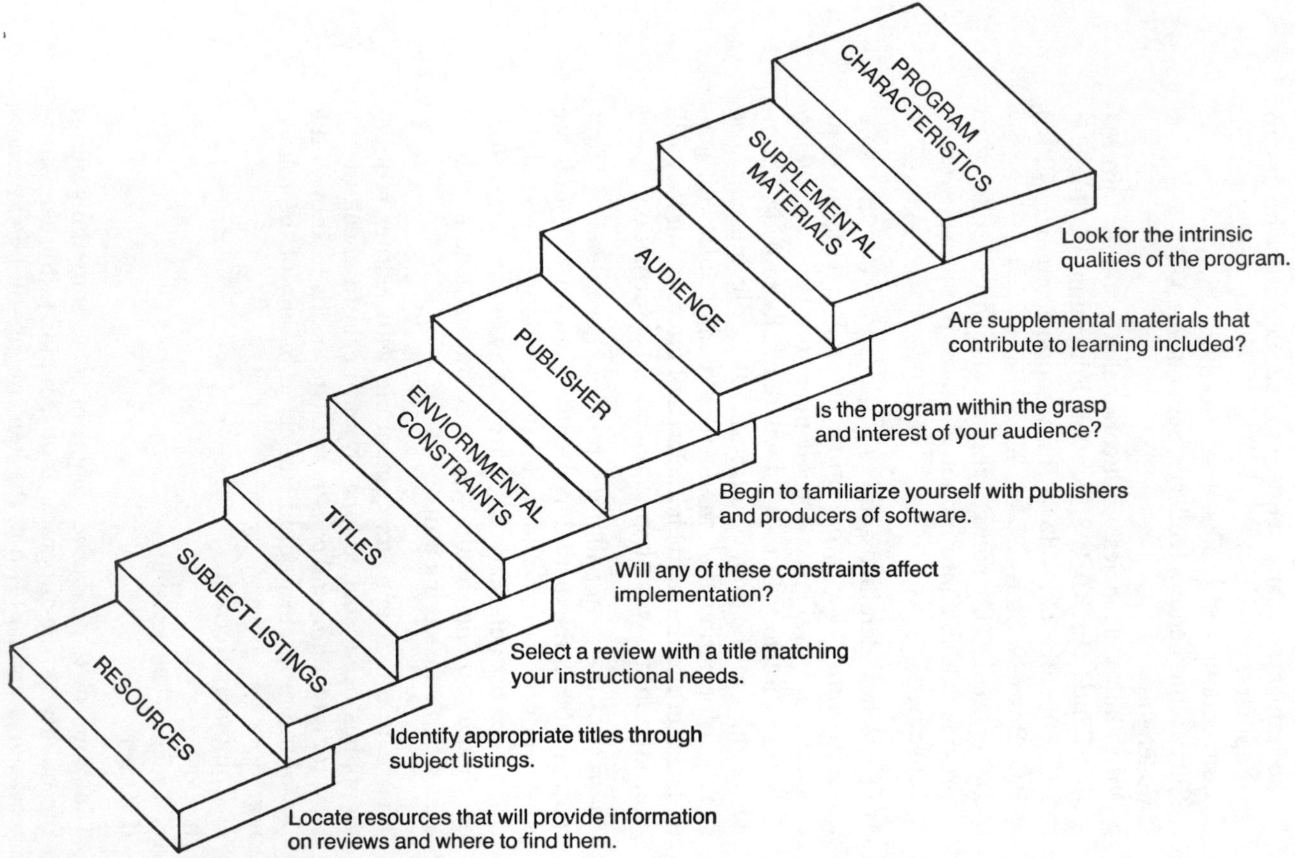

Figure 1. Finding and Analyzing Reviews and Product Abstracts for Software Suitability. (To identify suitable instructional materials through reviews and product abstracts all of these steps should be considered and followed.)

programmers and small firms. Word-of-mouth and experience is still the best way to get to know publishers and producers.

6. Does the review mention an *intended audience?* If so, can one determine if the program is within the grasp and interest of that audience, and would it be appropriate for the target audience?
7. Does the review or abstract mention supplemental materials? Does the program include a teacher's or user's guide? A guide is often an indication that thc producers have done their homework. Additionally, a guide often means that the program has some built-in quality.
8. The last step is to read the review itself noting as many *program characteristics* as possible. It's a next to impossible task to try to determine the intrinsic qualities of the program by reading a review. By developing a feel for "reading between the lines" one will begin to be able to separate the better programs from the poorer ones. Some tips for "reading between the lines":
   a. Many reviews are not written by an unbiased reviewer, but are written by the producer (i.e., the seller). One should try to ignore computer software programs that promise the moon. Instead one should look for reviews that indicate a program that has developed its topic or concept in a straightforward manner. The content of the review must demonstrate that the program meets both instructional and learner requirements.
   b. The content of the review should include information on learning objectives.

An Example Review Analyzed

The following is an example of a review of a program that might be worth purchasing for a high-interest/low-level reading program (See Fig. 1). This review contains all the necessary criteria for selecting software from reviews. The review appeared in the *K-12 MicroMedia Catalog* (Resources, Step 1). It was located in the catalog under the "Reading/vocabulary" section (Subject listing, Step 2).

Reading Comprehension: What's Different?

(2–4) Five reading comprehension programs present logical problems wherein the student must pick the one word in four that doesn't fit. Builds critical thinking skills. Excellent enrichment or for remedial work in higher grades. 32K Applesoft for Disk; 16K for Apple II; 8K PET or Atari. $16.95C/$21.95D

One can get a fairly good idea about the content of the program from the title *Reading Comprehension: What's Different?* (Title, Step 3). The program can be used with either Apple, PET, or Atari equipment, is available in either disk or cassette format, and sells for a reasonable cost (Environmental constraints, Step 4).

K-12 MicroMedia is a distributor of computer software from many different producers. This distributor makes an attempt to screen programs, and then to serve as a vehicle through which programs can be sold. Thus, although the publisher (Step 5) of this software program—Program Design Inc. (PDI)—may not be well-known, this lack of visibility should not discourage potential purchasers.

Since locating a high-interest/low-level reading program was a primary objective and since this review indicates that this item would be excellent for enrichment or remedial work (Audience, Step 6), the software continues to meet all selection criteria.

Although the review doesn't mention supplemental materials (Step 7), the program should not be discounted on this point alone. While it's true that a teacher's or user's manual is a handy guide for the instructor, many programs are self-instructional; a manual may not be necessary.

Finally, by "reading between the lines" of this product abstract, it is apparent that the program concentrates on one concept and presents that concept in a straightforward manner (Program characteristics, Step 8).

Some Last-Minute Thoughts

Educators need not think that they have to invest heavily in computer software and hardware just because everyone else is. The computer industry began to indoctrinate the public by introducing computer games. These very popular games can be found almost everywhere. But just because computer games are popular and abundant doesn't necessarily mean computers and corresponding computer software hold the key for providing adult educators with a revolutionary new teaching tool. While it's true computer software is now available in almost all disciplines, it's also true that the quality of many programs is still lacking. Software should be selected carefully after learning to "read" reviews and product abstracts with a feel for what one wants. In this way the interested educator can build an excellent collection of programs. Since software is rapidly becoming available at every level from pre-school through college and adult education it is important to develop this "feel" for reading reviews and abstracts. Experience is still the best teacher and with a little practice anyone should soon be able to identify suitable computer software programs just by reading reviews and abstracts.

Software Directories

The following directories provide information about computer software as of January 1982. (Prices are subject to change.)

Appleseed
Software Publications
6 South St.
Milford, NH 03055
Cost: Free
Software for Apple, TRS-80, Atari, and PET.

Educational Software Directory
Sterling Swift Publishing Co.
P.O. Box 188
Manchaca, TX 78652
Cost: $11.95
Software for Apple II.

Educator's Handbook and Software Directory
Vital Information, Inc.
350 Union Station
Kansas City, MO 64108
Cost: $16.95
Software for Apple. Excellent source for education.

Huntington Computing Catalogue
P.O. Box 787
Corcoran, CA 93212
Cost: Free
Programs for Apple, Atari, PET, and TRS-80.

International Microcomputer Software Directory
Imprint Software
420 South Howes St.
Fort Collins, CO 80521
Cost: Free
Lists 5,000 software packages.

K-12 Micro Media
P.O. Box 17
Valley Cottage, NY 10989
Cost: Free

Marck, Inc.
280 Linden Drive
Branford, CT 06082
Cost: Free

Opportunities for Learning, Inc.
Dept. L-4
8950 Lurline Ave.
Chatsworth, CA 91311
Cost: Free

Queue
5 Chapel Hill Drive
Fairfield, CT 06432
Cost: $8.95

Radio Shack Catalog
Radio Shack Box 17400
Fort Worth, TX 76102
Cost: $2.00
TRS-80 programs.

School Microware Directory
Dresden Associates
Dept. CCN
P.O. Box 246
Dresden, ME 04342
Cost: $25.00/yr.

Skarbeks Software Directory
11990 Dorsett Rd.
St. Louis, MO 63043
Cost: $10.00
Over 1,000 programs listed. Excellent source for education.

VanLoves 1981 Apple II/III Software Directory
Vital Information, Inc.
350 Union Station
Kansas City, MO 64108
Cost: $19.95

Educational Software Distributors

ACORN Software Products, Inc.
634 N. Carolina Ave., S.E.
Washington, DC 20003
202/544-4259

Activity Resources, Inc.
P.O. Box 4875
Hayward, CA 94540

Addison-Wesley Publishing Co.
2725 Sand Hill Rd.
Menlo Park, CA 94025
415/854-0300

Apple Cations
21650 W. Eleven Mile Rd.
Suite 103
Southfield, MI 48076
313/354-2559

Apple Computer Inc.
10260 Bandley Dr.
Cupertino, CA 94017
408/996-1010

Atari, Inc.
1272 Borregas Ave.
Sunnyvale, CA 94086
408/745-5069

ATMCO
P.O. Box 12248H
Gainesville, FL 32604

Avant-Garde Creations
P.O. Box 30161
Eugene, OR 97403
503/345-3043

Basics and Beyond Inc.
P.O. Box 10
Amawalk, NY 10501
914/962-2355

Bell & Howell
7100 N. McCormick Rd.
Chicago, IL 60645
312/262-1600

Bluebird's Computer Software
2267 23rd Street
Wyandotte, MI 48192
313/285-4455

Borg-Warner Educational Systems
600 W. University Dr.
Arlington Heights, IL 60004
800/323-7577

The Bottom Shelf
751 DeKalb Industrial Way
Atlanta, GA 30033
404/296-2003

Brain Box
601 W. 26th St.
New York, NY 10003
212/989-3573

California Software
P.O. Box 275
El Cerrito, CA 94530
415/527-8717

Charles Mann & Associates
55722 Santa Fe Trail
Yucca Valley, CA 92284
714/365-9718

Comm*Data Systems
P.O. Box 325
Milford, MI 48042
313/685-0113

COMPress
P.O. Box 102
Wentworth, NH 03282
603/764-5831

Compumax, Inc.
P.O. Box 1139
Palo Alto, CA 94301
415/321-2881

Computer Curriculum Corp.
P.O. Box 10080
Palo Alto, CA 94303
415/494-8450

Computer Information Exchange
P.O. Box 159
San Luis Rey, CA 92068
714/757-4849

Control Data Corp.
8100 34th Ave. South
P.O. Box O
Minneapolis, MN 55440
612/853-4541

Cook's Computer Co.
1905 Bailey Drive
Marchalltown, IA 50158

CourseWare Magazine
4919 N. Millbrook
Fresno, CA 93726

Creative Computing
P.O. Box 1139
Morristown, NJ 07960
800/631-8112

Education Programs
Disney Electronics
6153 Fairmont Ave.
San Diego, CA 92120
714/281-0285

Educational Activities, Inc.
1937 Grand Ave.
Baldwin, NY 11510
800/645-3739

Educational Courseware
3 Nappa Lane
Les Port, CT 06880
203/227-1438

Educational Software
Midwest
414 Rosemere Lane
Maquoketa, IA 52060
319/652-2334

Educational Software
Professionals, Ltd.
38437 Grand River
Farmington Hills, MI 48018
313/477-4470

Entelek
P.O. Box 1303
Portsmouth, NH 03801
603/436-0439

Hartley Software
P.O. Box 431
Dimondale, MI 48821
616/942-8987

Houghton Mifflin Co.
One Beacon Street
Boston, MA 02107
617/725-5000

J.L. Hammett Co., Inc.
Hammett Place
P.O. Box 545
Braintree, MA 02184
617/848-1000

Level IV Products Inc.
32461 Schoolcraft
Livonia, MI 48150
313/525-6200

McGraw-Hill
1221 Ave. of the Americas
New York, NY 10020
212/997-6194

MECC Publications
2520 Broadway Drive
St. Paul, MN 55113
612/376-1118

Micro Learningware
P.O. Box 2134
N. Mankato, MN 56001
507/625-2205

Microsoft Consumer Products
400 108th Ave., N.E.
Bellevue, WA 98004
206/454-1315

Milliken Publishing Co.
Computer Department
1100 Research Blvd.
St. Louis, MO 63132
314/991-4220

Milton-Bradley Co.
Shaker Rd.
E. Longmeadow, MA 01028
413/525-6411

Microcomputer Education
Applications Network
1030 Fifteenth St., NW
Suite 800
Washington, DC 20005

National Coordinating Center
for Curriculum Development
State University at Stony
Brook
Stony Brook, NY 11794

Prescription Learning
1301 S. Wabash Ave.
Chicago, IL 60605
312/922-0579

Quality Education Design
P.O. Box 12486
Portland, OR 97212

Radio Shack Education
Division
1600 One Tandy Center
Fort Worth, TX 76102
817/390-3832

Random House
2970 Brandywine Rd.
Suite 201
Atlanta, GA 30341

Scholastic Software
Dept. C.C.N.
22 E. Quackenbush Ave.
Dumont, NJ 07628

Science Research Associates
155 North Wacker Dr.
Chicago, IL 60606
800/621-0664

Scott, Foresman & Co.
1900 East Lake Ave.
Glenview, IL 60025
312/729-3000

Teaching Tools;
Microcomputer Services
P.O. Box 12679
Research Triangle Park, NC 27709
919/851-2374

Reference

Time. 1981. Small computer shootout. March 2, pp. 68-69.

Thomas W. Heaney

Power, Learning, and "Compunication"

> *The cultural model of a society depends on its memory, control of which largely conditions the hierarchy of power. Access to infinitely greater sources of information will entail basic changes and will affect the social structure by modifying the procedures for acquiring knowledge.* (Nora and Minc 1980: 131)

For good or ill, most of our knowledge of the world and its culture is derived from television, radio, and word-processed media that instantly replay our experiences almost before we are conscious of them. Forerunner among these media is the microcomputer, which could soon preempt formal learning of its content, leaving only organized social activities and sports to the school's curriculum.

The concentration of information power, far beyond anything imagined by the monopolies of school systems and universities, represents an inestimable potential for human growth or diminishment. Already the emergence of mass information utilities, from the data banks of the Internal Revenue Service to those of private credit institutions, would suggest that the hegemony of government, financial institutions, and corporate business is likely to remain unchallenged (Laver 1980). Since computers have represented a capital intensive technology that only the already powerful could afford, the new machines were destined to be used to accomplish the old tasks—until now. The portable and affordable microcomputer suggests some alternative scenarios that might eventually challenge the balance of information power. A redistribution of such power would have profound consequences for adult education.

Adult education, when it succeeds, results in change; this is its fundamental purpose. Most adult programs are directed to individual learners who seek to acquire new skills, master new understandings, or attain certification or a credential. Ways in which individualized learning can be enhanced through interactive computing have been discussed in previous articles in this anthology. Such human-machine interactivity is designed to integrate the learner into dominant social and economic patterns, to assist the learner in understanding these patterns and using them for personal advantage, but seldom to empower the learner to change the given order of things. Traditionally, educators are adaptive in their purposes—that is, they seek to adapt learners to the demands of jobs or to the responsibilities of citizenship. Such educators would like to believe that the unemployed and disenfranchised are personal failures who did not take advantage of their schooling. Closer scrutiny makes it clear that this is not so (Jencks 1972). There are far too many for whom adaptation to the social order would be disfunctional; only reconstruction of the social order would allow them a place and a role. Liberatory adult education has this purpose in view: to enable learners to deepen their involvement in the struggle to change their world through reflection and understanding. Such adult education is generally not pursued in formal educational institutions, but rather in community-based organizations, in unions, in civil rights and feminist groups, and wherever activists pause to reflect, evaluate, and plan.

This article will explore the possibility of microcomputers providing a tool for such liberatory education. On the surface, the possibility seems remote. Computerization has already centralized information-power on a scale never before imagined and has placed a tool for the control and manipulation of knowledge in the hands of the old and emerging megacorporations. But can this same technology be used to negotiate shifts in power and, more importantly, a decentralization of information control with open access to the public? Some analysts argue that such a redistribution of power is possible. Computers can be adapted to serve as instruments of coordination in decentralized economic structures very different from those of corporate capitalism (Bodington 1973) and are likely to increase "contact between social groups and the vulnerability of large organizations" (Nora and Minc 1980: 5). Advances in cybernetics and the continued deflation of microprocessor costs clearly have resulted in computers that are easy to operate and that are well within the budgets of most community-based organizations. But how can these computers be used and to what end? And what does their use have to do with education? Can microcomputers, linked in regional and national networks, provide a vehicle for learning that will induce and foster social change? To answer these questions we must first look at 1) the relationship between power and knowledge, 2) the role of collective, community-based, participatory research in empowering adults to change their world, and, finally, 3) the potential use of computer-based information networks in effecting a redistribution of knowledge.

The Roots and Nature of Power

There is a sense in which all education seeks to empower learners. Power, in its most elemental usage, is simply the ability to act. Successful clients of schooling are, by reason of their learning, empowered to read, empowered to operate a lathe or drill press, to speak Spanish, or to accomplish any of myriad tasks included in the school's curriculum. Such "powers" derived from traditional education are better termed "capacities" or—to use the more current neologism—"competencies." But in the world of social relationships, power is exercised in conflict over goals, decisions, strategies, and position. Power is more than mere capacity; it is capacity exercised at the cost of another's capacity to act. The exercise of power assumes competing interests. To the extent that these interests solidify and polarize, power can lead to the establishment of a powerless class, which is effectively disenfranchised from decision making in matters affecting its own welfare. Steven Lukes (1974), in *Power: A Radical View,* explored three dimensions of power. The first dimension emphasizes open and explicit conflict in decision making wherein power is established by the outcome. Power inheres in the one who, by reason of physical strength, mental acuity, or both, prevails over the opposition. Competitors lock horns; power goes to the victor.

But certainly not all power is characterized by fists and invectives. In the second dimension of power, its wielders systematically exclude potential competitors from the process of decision making. The public agenda is controlled to eliminate from discussion those issues that are potentially threatening to the interests of the powerful. This dimension of power is characterized by "the mobilization of bias" (Bachrach and Baratz 1970) by which decisions appear inevitable and irreversible. Thus the existence of conflict is obscured. Power is maintained by non-decisions, defined as

> a means by which demands for change in the existing allocation of benefits and privileges in the community can be suffocated before they are voiced, or kept covert; or killed before they gain access to the relevant decision-making arena; or, failing all of these things, maimed or destroyed in the decision-implementing stage of the policy process. (Bachrach and Baratz 1970: 44)

The capacity to enforce non-decisions by keeping an issue from ever being raised is a profound, if largely invisible, form of power. In this regard, the role of educational institutions in maintaining and stabilizing the status quo is best described in terms of what is *not* contained in the curriculum. Non-information or limited access to information is a prior condition of non-decisions—a condition for which the schools and media are primarily responsible. The university especially has been able to exercise a monopolistic hold on information-power in many areas by legitimizing only that knowledge which is derived from academic research, the canons of which neglect the ideological bias of all interpretations of reality (Hall 1980). Research by and for experts, in which an elite trained corps of researchers determine the questions to be raised, collect the data, and analyze the results, excludes the masses not only from its process and conclusions, but, more importantly, from the decisions to which research gives rise. This control and manipulation of information—this mobilization of bias—whether in academic institutions, media, or government, represents a more economical and far-reaching exercise of power than reliance on overt force or the direct imposition of will.

While the second dimension of power weakens opposition by withholding critical knowledge, the third and ultimate dimension of power eliminates opposition by the imposition of false consciousness. Here the wielder of power "influences, shapes, and determines conceptions of the necessities, possibilities, and strategies of challenge in situations of latent conflict" (Gaventa 1980: 15). Such "mind control" need not conjure up images of

1984 and *Walden Two.* The mechanisms of this dimension of power simply involve the inverse of information control. Images propagated by mass media and the process of socialization not only *exclude* data and meanings that have a high risk of unmasking conflict (as in the second dimension of power), but also *include* data and meanings that can negatively affect self-concepts and expectations regarding "realistic" modes of behavior (Lukes 1974).

Those over whom power proclaims itself in the first dimension of power are simply losers. In the second dimension of power, they are disenfranchised. Paulo Freire (1970), in his analysis of the dynamisms of power, reserves the term "oppressed" for those who are silenced by power's third dimension. The oppressed speak with a voice that is not their own. Their very consciousness is the product of a total environment created in the image and interests of the powerful—that is, the oppressors. The oppressed are not only powerless, but are reconciled to their powerlessness, perceiving it fatalistically, as a consequence of personal inadequacy or failure. This reconciliation to powerlessness inhibits self-determined action and fosters increased dependency. Dependency further precludes the development of a positive and self-affirming consciousness and thus lends to the dominant order an air of legitimacy. The ultimate product of highly unequal power relationships is a class of individuals who "cannot articulate their interests or perceive social conflict. Since they have been socialized into compliance, so to speak, they accept the definitions of political reality as offered by dominant groups, classes, or government institutions" (Mueller 1973: 9).

For our purposes, it is important to note that the principal instrument for the establishment and protection of power in its second and third dimensions is the control of knowledge. Knowledge here includes not only consciousness—self-knowledge and understandings about the world as it relates to images of one's self—but also information—that is, direct and practical knowledge of one's world. It is, in fact, the latter that precedes and informs the former. We come to know ourselves through our interaction with and reflection upon the world. And thus the control and withholding of information is a critical factor in the control of knowledge and the exercise of power. Some social theorists, in analyzing the new technologies of information control, have concluded that "knowledge, not labor, is the source of value" in all economic and social exchanges (Bell

1979: 168). Such a theory, however, confuses an attendant circumstance with the cause of value. While the lack of information can make the exercise of power impossible, the possession of knowledge does not of itself create power. It is for this reason that education cannot *of itself* empower adults to change their world. But education, or at least learning, accompanies and informs movements for social change. The role of information in such movements is critical, but not decisive.

Most highly developed societies sponsor educational systems that consciously support and maintain unequal distributions of power. In the United States, such systems extend the free market ideology of American capitalism to an educational meritocracy in which the trained mind will command a fair price on the block (Carnoy 1972). Remediation for adults whose earlier training was deficient is a compensatory response to the many persons on the bottom of the socioeconomic scale, but it cannot challenge an economic system that leaves an increasing number of persons at the bottom unemployed. An occasional Horatio Alger success story serves to maintain the credibility of the compensatory/meritocratic system by falsely increasing confidence in the ability of education to make a difference.

Many traditional programs make use of nontraditional methods to maximize their sphere of influence. These methods include electronic media, programmed instruction, computer-assisted learning, and a variety of techniques and applications of behavioral psychology. The programs employing these methods remain traditional in their purposes and in their effects. Most developments in educational hardware and technology have merely provided educators with new tools to accomplish old tasks more efficiently. The process of learning remains rooted in the same anti-critical values; only the machinery changes.

Learning for Empowerment

In contrast to traditional schooling, education for empowerment encourages learners to challenge and change social institutions, not merely to adapt themselves to institutional demands. Such education is antithetical to a pedagogy that focuses on the unique needs of individuals who are expected, one-by-one, to establish their credentials in a competitive market characterized by unequal power relationships. Education for empowerment—liberatory education—seeks to develop a pedagogy that emphasizes mutual responsibility for learning and teaching, shared critical reflection on the social order, and collaboration in action (Heaney 1982). Liberatory programs are those that facilitate the development of independent, critical, and politically aggressive makers of history, persons who have discovered the barriers to freedom and power and are not overwhelmed, and persons who, in concert with their peers, are capable of collective initiatives to begin the conquest of these barriers. Such programs can be called liberatory in that they support and complement larger struggles for liberation. This is especially evident in several Latin American and African countries where revolutionary governments could have, ironically, recreated the old traditions of schooling; instead, a new pedagogy that supports liberation has been developed, not as a *fait accompli,* but as an ongoing process and part of the task of reconstruction.

Liberation is a constant subject for redefinition. It begins as an overcoming of the immediate barriers to freedom. For the slave, liberation is the breaking of chains; for the destitute, it is a job. Yet, the victims of servitude or poverty are not freed by a broken chain or by a paycheck. The elimination of these immediate barriers enables the now liberated persons to perceive more clearly their remaining "unfreedom." On progressively more profound levels, the barriers are discovered, no longer external, but internalized and reflected in self-recriminations and socially destructive behavior. Sexist policies in employment cannot prevail if force must be used to uphold them; the social order is maintained by the control of information, even about self. "Facts" about inherent sexual differences are used to justify differentials in pay scale and power. Similarly, the strategy of the civil rights movement was to unmask racism by externalizing it—by placing it in public view so that it could be seen for the violence that it was. Emancipation had removed the chains but left minds confined. Liberatory education begins with inward reflection followed by an outward intensification of action on the world, shaping it anew into conformity with the emerging consciousness of the liberated person. This educational praxis first intensifies the learner's awareness of and sensitivity to concrete, historical situations; second, it raises questions regarding these situations—it comprehends the situation as a problem in search of a solution. Learners in this process become "critically conscious," and are empowered to challenge and change the world. This melding of reflection and action, joining education and politics, has become the focus of much discussion among adult educators, especially those who have attempted to learn from Paulo Freire and other educators politicized by revolution.

While a liberatory pedagogy emphasizes direct and immediate understanding of the world through action upon the world, it does not minimize or neglect the importance of information: data about the world, sequences in historical events, research findings, and so forth. Rather, it radically alters the role of learners in the production and use of such information. In traditional educational systems, learners are the passive recipients of information—or more frequently, non-information—as prescribed by curriculum designers and academic administrators. Higher educational institutions especially have relegated the production, validation, and eventual distribution of knowledge to experts. The deleterious consequence of such monopolistic control of knowledge has already been noted. In liberatory education, learning *is* research. The discovery and production of knowledge is the collective work of all. Several groups throughout the world, principally under the sponsorship of the International Council for Adult Education, have introduced the concept of "participatory research" in order to counter the oppressive consequences of information control by experts and technocrats. Participatory research involves the full and active participation of those persons most directly concerned with the knowledge sought—those most likely to benefit or be harmed by its dissemination. This involvement begins with the identification of questions to be asked (problem posing), the selection of appropriate methods, data gathering, collective analysis of the data, and, most importantly, the determination of the use to which the resulting knowledge will be put. Participatory research is the means by which content is generated in liberatory education and is the essential link between learning and action for social change.

The assumptions upon which participatory research are based are not so much methodological as political. That is, these assumptions are less concerned with *how* research is undertaken and more with *who* researches *what* and *for what purpose*. Techniques of participatory research are often the same as techniques of traditional empiricism, but these same techniques are always subjected to the rigors of consensus regarding their appropriate application and the questions to which they will be applied. Studies relating to the development of impoverished communities, for example, research on land use, market analysis, economic and environmental impact, or differentials in insurance rates, availability of mortgages, and expenditures of public revenues, are likely to require the same methods of inquiry as do similar studies undertaken by financial or governmental institutions (Callaway 1980). The principal difference between community-based research and research by professional researchers lies in the control exercised by the researcher over knowledge derived from research. Knowledge created by professionals can, and most likely will, be hidden from the public if research conclusions threaten the ideological or conceptual basis for a balance of power that benefits the researcher or the sponsors of research. More likely, the research questions leading to such knowledge will not be asked in the first place. Knowledge, when produced by business, industry, government, or academic institutions, becomes private property, a commodity, a wholly-owned natural resource that is used to increase the profit, prestige, or wealth of its possessors. The market value of such knowledge is guaranteed by invalidating and discrediting knowledge generated elsewhere. For example, the university maintains its hegemony by cornering the market on the "credentialing" of knowledgeable people. It does this by granting degrees and certificates only to those who have acquired their knowledge through prescribed academic courses. Universities have been reluctant to trade in "life experience," and have done so only when such experiences could be suitably translated into appropriate categories relating to the academic curriculum.

On the other hand, knowledge that results from the authentic questioning of a community of learner/activists is *not* controlled by experts and is likely to remain accessible to all and to readily inform or transform action. Liberatory education eschews the commodification of knowledge, preferring to organize the pursuit of knowledge as a cooperative venture. Just as cooperatives represent an alternative strategy for the distribution of goods, so also does liberatory education seek to create an alternative to schooling in which information presently exploited by knowledge industries is reappropriated for each person and for each community. Such educational endeavors have been labor-intensive and have, in most instances, avoided reliance on technological solutions. The relationship between information and power, as well as the strategy of liberatory education to collectivize control over information through participatory research, provides the context in which questions concerning the appropriate application of computer technology to adult education for empowerment must be raised.

"Microcompunications"

The word "compunications" was coined by Anthony Oettinger of Harvard to describe the merger of computers, telephone, and television into a new kind of digital code—"a single yet differentiated system that allows for the transmission of data or interaction between persons or computers 'speaking to' computers, through telephone lines, cables, microwave relays, or satellites" (Nora and Minc 1980: vii). The French have coined a similar term, "telematics," to describe this growing interconnection between telecommunications and computers. The potential for such a merger of technologies to be used as an instrument of information control and domination is obvious. Critics of these media find them to be tyrannous technologies without redeeming social merit (Mander 1978), while media advocates blithely and approvingly foresee a world in which humankind is superceded by machine gods of its own making (Baer 1972). The middle ground between these two extreme positions is well charted and traveled, especially by educators who have been quick to "dress up their act" with the latest in electronic gadgetry.

Technologies that enhance the prestige of the professional and that multiply the mechanisms of control available to a few wielders of power are inconsistent with liberatory education. Until recently, computers and telecommunications—especially television—have more clearly been instruments of knowledge and information control than of liberation and critical thinking. Sackman suggests that mass information utilities may soon become the ultimate embodiment of social control.

> Radio and television allowed more timely collection and dissemination of information, but these mass media were still not linked to direct social action. In real-time computing systems, however, the collection, organization, and storage of information leads directly to action, to integrated surveillance and control over the object environment. This dynamic marriage of information and control in real-time systems is a fusion of knowledge and action, and, through directed action in real time, information is expressed as power. (Sackman 1971: 247)

Despite such evident possibilities for the concentration of power, other images of the future need to be explored. Low cost and easily operated microcomputers coupled with ubiquitous and commonly accessible telephone technology forces liberatory educators to again raise the question *Can these media be convivial tools for reconstructing the social order in the hands of common, unsophisticated, and unprofessionalized people?*

Experiments with the interactive use of video have, over the past decade, been highly successful in bringing about social change on the local level (Niemi and Stephens 1979). Beginning with the efforts of the National Film Board of Canada, and more recently with the work of Communications for Change in Chicago, community-based groups have been trained in the use of portable video equipment as a tool for organizing and raising community consciousness. Groups have used video to document issues of public concern, to force accountability from elected officials and bureaucrats, to articulate and refine collective statements of position, and to force public attention on matters ignored by commercial mass media. In the efforts of these groups, "interactive" conveys two related levels of meaning. First, the process allowed persons who were previously only passive recipients of television to become producers; they *interacted* directly and critically with the medium itself. Second, and more importantly, video became a medium of communication both within and among groups; television mediated the *interaction* of people as they struggled to know what was possible and to improve the conditions of their lives.

It is clear that the advance of microcomputer technology has made interactive computing possible on the first level of meaning. No longer are computers the exclusive domain of technicians and programmers. Any person who can type, or even speak, can converse with a microcomputer, program it, play games with it, be its pupil, entrust it with maintaining personal financial records, and enjoy countless other user-initiated interactions. But can the computer be an interactive tool on the second level of meaning? Can microcomputers mediate communications within and among community-based groups and further their efforts to know the world and to use that knowledge to bring about social change?

The linkage of modem-equipped microcomputers over great distances by means of telephone lines suggests possibilities that could greatly expand the abilities of community-based organizations to communicate with each other regarding information critical to their common struggles. Significant data, now relegated to the pages of many thousands of newsletters with limited circulation, could be stored in communal data banks. National networks of organizations could gain access to such data—both to add to and to obtain information—by means of a microcomputer. Such a network is already in operation as a component of the Neighborhood Information Services Exchange (NICE) in Washington, DC. NICE provides its members with immediate access to current information on community and neighborhood development projects, funding sources, legislation affecting present and future programs, as well as summary narratives of the experiences of organizers and community developers within the network. Members pay an annual membership fee of $35, which includes this computer-based service. A toll free telephone number that allows a member-organization to connect its own microcomputer with the "collective memory" of more than 3000 members is provided. At present, members can only receive information from the data base, but NICE staffers predict that within a year there will be provision for members to enter information as well. Procedures are being developed now to permit quality checks on such member-initiated data.

The Limits of Technological Solutions

A prerequisite for the appropriate use of any technology is knowledge of its limitations. Technology cannot unequivocally provide *the* solution in situations where technology has clearly made a major contribution to the problem. The cost of technology, and the energy sources needed to drive it, has been extorted from each of us, with the highest tariffs reserved for those with the least economic and political power. The use of computers in liberatory education and participatory research is a case in point. The potential contributions of computerization are clear enough; but unless we are aware of what the computer can't do, we run the risk of losing far more ground than we can ever hope to gain.

Knowledge is never simply a matter of possessing facts. Our perceptions of the world are not simply given to us in experience; they are contextualized by our personal history, previous experiences, value systems, and ideologies. We see an aggregate of many things when we observe the world, and, from those things we see, we select what we are after, we order what we select, and ultimately arrive at a more or less consistent and coherent world (Harris 1979). The influence of our political and social values is even more apparent in our perceptions of complex relationships between persons and institutions. Our engagement in a struggle to change those relationships, to reconstruct social reality in a manner that will effect a redistribution of power, is never simply a matter of acting on the basis of *known fact*. Heuristic arguments have far greater influence on both reformist and revolutionary action than does raw data, as the polemics that surround social change will quickly attest. As Kaufmann pointed out, "to maintain his independence in the midst of increasingly complex mechanisms which must be controlled, the man of action must remain a creator, and he needs *ingenium*" (Kaufmann 1968: 35). Decisions in action are informed by a mixture of inventive intuition, logic, and factual knowledge.

Computerized networks for the exchange of information can provide two of these influences: logic and data. But even here, the rules of logical discourse and the "facts" amassed in computer memory are value-laden—tainted by judgments about the world that were either knowingly or unknowingly entered into the data base. Collaborators in action exchange information frequently and unreflectively. Interpersonal knowledge, derived from the ongoing experience of shared activity, establishes a heuristic base for assuming common ground, shared perception, and ideological conformity. Information is provided and received in an atmosphere of trust—trust not only in the facticity of the information, but in common, shared hermeneutic principles by which the meaning of facts is determined. Networks based solely on the exchange of information are unlikely to generate trust, the latter depending, as it does, on creative intuition even more than on logic. And it is only trust that could move such a network from collective knowing to collective doing. In other words, a network based solely on the exchange of information is unlikely to become a political party or a national activist organization. It is unlikely to generate power in the way that compunications have generated power in ideologically monolithic organizations such as IBM and the IRS.

Not only will computer-based information networks fail to effect a balance of power between corporate and community-based organizations, but they are also unlikely to narrow the information gap. Community groups equipped with microcomputers are playing the computer game with a stacked deck.

Community data banks can only hold on deposit that information which is already available to a member or to members of the community. Whereas, as we have already seen, the powerful maintain their power by withholding and manipulating information. While computer networks can maximize the dissemination of "leaks" in corporately guarded information, they cannot of themselves breach the protective veil that surrounds backroom deals, political payoffs, secret trusts, and the large-scale personal information systems of private credit agencies and government investigative units. What Freire has said of education is especially true of the educational potential of computer-based information networks in advanced capitalist societies.

> In a class society, the power elite necessarily determine what education will be, and therefore its objectives. The objectives will certainly not be opposed to their interests. As we have already said, it would be supremely naive to imagine that the elite would in any way promote or accept an education which stimulated the oppressed to discover the *raison d' etre* of the social structure. The most that could be expected is that the elite might permit talk of such education, and occasional experiments which could be immediately suppressed should the status quo be threatened. (Freire 1973: 8)

Information networks are likely to achieve some modest, short-term successes without encountering major opposition. Corporate and governmental organizations are even likely to support such networks, as long as the information exchanged among members of the network does not threaten the sponsor's power. It might be noted that the Neighborhood Information Services Exchange, until recent cutbacks in public spending, was federally funded by the U.S. Department of Housing and Urban Development. But the likelihood of widespread or long-term social change resulting from such networks is remote, at best. The reason for such pessimism is not based on any intrinsic limitations of microcomputers, but on the overarching limitations of technology itself. The redistribution of power is not a technical or even an educational problem, it is a political one. Just as the potential of computer-activated, two-way cable television has not been (and is unlikely to be) seriously applied to the involvement of mass populations in public policy decision making, neither is the full potential of the computer likely to be applied to the bypassing and eventual destruction of mechanisms by which unequal power is maintained.

To thus describe its limits is not to ignore or gainsay the obvious merits of microcomputers in liberatory education and participatory research. Information networks accessed by microcomputers will greatly expand the potential for peer learning among community-based organizations and might quickly eliminate the more costly and less efficient production of hard-copy educational materials and newsletters. As a component of more holistic networking efforts, drawing similarly committed community groups into collective action as well as information sharing, computers can encourage and support organization at a level previously impossible without a loss of local autonomy. Microcomputers cannot create or substitute for a movement toward social change. But they can greatly enhance the abilities of members of such a movement to comprehend the inequalities of their world, to imagine alternatives and design appropriate strategies, to reflect on and evaluate their own actions, and to collaborate with each other in creating the future.

References

Bachrach, P., and Baratz, M. S. 1970. *Power and poverty: theory and practice.* New York: Oxford University Press.

Baer, R. M. 1972. *The digital villain: notes on the numerology, parapsychology, and metaphysics of the computer.* Reading, MA: Addison-Wesley.

Bell, D. 1979. The social framework of the information society. In *The computer age: a twenty-year view.* M. L. Dertouzos and J. Moses (eds.). Cambridge, MA: The MIT Press.

Bodington, S. 1973. *Computers and socialism.* Nottingham, England: Spokesman Books.

Callaway, H. (ed.). 1980. *Case studies of participatory research.* Amersfoot, The Netherlands: Studiecentrum ncvd.

Carnoy, M. (ed.). 1972. *Schooling in a corporate society: the political economy of education in America.* New York: David McKay.

Freire, P. 1973. Education, liberation, and the church. *Study Encounter.* 38: 9.

Freire, P. 1970. *Pedagogy of the oppressed.* New York: Seabury.

Hall, B. L. 1980. Knowledge as a commodity and participatory research. *Prospects.* 9(4): 393–408.

Harris, K. 1979. *Education and knowledge: the structured misrepresentation of reality.* London: Rontledge and Kegan Paul.

Heaney, T. W. 1982. Adult learning for empowerment: toward a theory of liberatory education. Reston, VA: Latino Institute, Research Division.

Jencks, C. 1972. *Inequality: a reassessment of the effect of family and schooling in America.* New York: Basic Books.

Kaufmann, A. 1968. *The science of decision-making: an introduction to praxeology.* New York: McGraw-Hill.

Laver, M. 1980. *Computers and social change.* Cambridge, MA: Cambridge University Press.

Lukes, S. 1974. *Power: a radical view.* London: Macmillan.

Mander, J. 1978. *Four arguments for the elimination of television.* New York: Morrow.

Mueller, C. 1973. *The politics of communication: a study in the political sociology of language, socialization and legitimation.* New York: Oxford University Press.

Niemi, J., and Stephens, S. 1979. *The Rockford Interactive Media Project.* DeKalb, IL: Northern Illinois University, College of Continuing Education.

Nora, S., and Minc, A. 1980. *The computerization of society.* Cambridge, MA: The MIT Press.

Sackman, H. 1971. *Mass information utilities and social excellence.* New York: Auerbach Publishers.

David G. Gueulette

Learning in a Wired School: Home Telecommunications-Computer Centers

The current increasing use of home videocassette recorders, microcomputers, cable television, and large computers that can access and manage cable television delivery systems suggests that the home telecommunications entertainment/education business is booming and that the so-called wired nation is, in fact, the wired school. This wired school already exists. Home telecommunication centers that incorporate cablecasting via cable networks and satellites managed by computers with interactive response devices or microcomputers and video recorders coupled with software (in many cases courseware) are becoming an important factor in the lifelong education of Americans.

As Beder noted, "From a purely technical standpoint, by 1990 it will be possible to have virtually unlimited access to information in one's own home for less than $1500 in today's dollars" (Beder 1981: 4). He also noted that there will be interactive cable television with microcomputer systems that will allow the home learner to interact, communicate, and share instructional resources with immediate feedback and storage of information.

The "Teaching Machine" Approach

The computer is an integral component of the home telecommunication center. For at least the last sixty years, educators have been trying to ape the techniques of industrialists to find a way to make teaching mechanical, capitalized, and thus efficient (profitable). Evidence of serious attempts to develop a "teaching machine" can be traced to the works of Sidney L. Pressey and B. F. Skinner, early educational entrepreneurs of the 1920s and 1930s. These first "teaching machines" were clumsy and crude affairs primarily directed to testing and later to actual drill and instruction with some means for recording students' efforts.

Skinner (1968), who became the best known of these "teaching machines" pioneers, espoused behavioral management techniques based on "programs of instruction." While interest in programmed instruction persisted even to current applications for language, mathematics, and some vocational training, "teaching machines" per se have fallen by the wayside. This technology-education connection was not widely accepted.

By the 1960s, the "teaching machine" was having something of a revival in the form of the electronic computer. Called computer-based instruction (CBI) or computer-assisted instruction (CAI), this new electronic device differed from the mechanical brutes of Pressey or Skinner in mechanics and programs/software. This new, elaborate electronic information, storage, and retrieval system had the same basic instructional intent as the earlier teaching machine but incorporated much more sophisticated and rapid interaction possibilities. Although the computer had the potential for widespread use by schools and industry for training in institutions and even at home through telephone lines or cable television networks, it met with little immediate success. The initial failure of the large applications computer for CBI or CAI has been blamed on several underlying factors associated with the technology and the programs. High costs of purchase or rental of capital equipment and maintenance are most often cited as the causes for their lack of use in the primary stages of development of CAI/CBI. The dearth of proven effective and inexpensive courseware or instructional programs is also mentioned as an important factor.

By the late 1970s, however, the computer in a small and much less expensive form, the microcomputer, began a major reemergence for instruction. This renewed interest came mostly from consumers in the public sector and not from educators. The so-called "chip" or miniature electronic information storage and processing board that replaced the larger, more expensive transistor or circuit board, revolutionized the information-processing world. The chip, which was perfected in the late

1970s, encouraged the development of cheap and effective small computers. These microcomputers have become hot-selling consumer items with myriads of applications, programs, games, and information-storage facilities. Marketed under many brand names, these small, take-me-home systems consist of a tape or a disk-recording-and-playback device, a keyboard, and television-like display console. The total cost for this basic computer can be less than that of a good stereo outfit; some are priced at under $1,000.

> Bell and Howell has developed a microcomputer with excellent educational potential. The Genis I can be operated with no special knowledge of computer language—English is fine. It can be adapted to many subject areas and is designed to encourage a tutorial dialogue that responds to each student individually. The teacher can create materials to move the student to objectives with relevant information and challenges. Programs can teach concepts, skills, drill, and practice, problem solving, remedial review, discovery learning, testing and evaluation. Genis I can compute statistics on students' scores. With the use of plug-in boards, it can retrieve information on video and cassette tapes, provide printouts, imitate graphics drawn with an electric pen, generate musical scores and transfer freehand drawings to the television screen. (Kruse 1980: 6)

Like their predecessor, the large memory rapid computer, microcomputers lack the extensive instructional programs necessary to let them become truly integrated into total educational programs for individuals at schools or at home. Programs that have been developed in certain fields are exceptions. PLATO, or Programmed Logic for Automated Teaching Operations, an instructional courseware distribution system with a custom program development service, has been used to create and distribute many comprehensive instructional courses via mainframe computer and telephone lines. But there are few programs that cover substantial areas of disciplines or grade levels; programs equivalent to materials and skills covered in K–12 are very far from realization.

In sum, the present and future educational uses of the microcomputer, electronic games and toys, and television interactive systems are substantial. The electronics and delivery systems exist. All that is needed to mushroom this technology into the mainstream of the national educational arrangement are additional effective comprehensive instructional programs, increased interest, and a planned integration into the schooling/credentialing institutions.

QUBE: A Case Study of an Experiment with Home Telecommunications

QUBE is a contemporary exercise in cable/computer/satellite interactive delivery that began in Columbus, OH, on 1 December 1977. The system has received considerablc attention in the press, professional journals, and cable service advertisements. It has been cited often because of

> its unique interactive capability, which allows subscribers by means of push-button consoles in their homes, to respond directly, immediately, and individually to specific programs, information or questions delivered through thc cablc channel. Responses are recorded immediately by computer in the cable studio. QUBE's instantaneous polling techniques and audience samplings have been utilized most often, thus far in monitoring live programming. (Miller 1979: 3)

QUBE also offers extensive local origination programming, university courses, and the syndicated satellite rebroadcasting service, Home Box Office. Miller added the caution that, "Certainly, to encourage the use of cable television with unique interactive capabilities for social, educational and informational purposes appears to be an honorable as well as functional objective. However, in the rush to implement advanced technology several important issues may be easily ignored" (Miller 1979: 4). She was concerned that interactive/computer home television would not serve the societal or personal values so necessary to genuine education. "Are there means by which interactive cable television can provide help to those who wish to receive aid in the basic skills areas and, at the same time, supply that information within a context which presents possibilities of choice, growth and action to individuals?" she asked (p. 6). She did not put forth a possible answer but suggested that interactive television was a part of a large perspective that defines education as a process that is always larger, richer, and more complex than what occurs in a structured instructional program.

Critical Views of the Medium

In addition to Miller's concerns, there are other debates about the use of instructional microcomputers. Arguments for extensive implementation of microcomputers or for CAI in general are based on several educational ideals: 1) they can provide personalized instruction; 2) they provide large amounts of accurate and timely data; 3) they offer a non-threatening learning environment; and 4) their use spreads computer literacy. (Computer literacy is the knowledge that the computer is just a tool with many useful applications and limitations.) It is also argued that computers will promote an informed population that can participate in important aspects of a complex and technical world with free access to ideas and ever-increasing information.

Arguments against the widespread use of educational computers generally suggest that the machine is dehumanizing; easily controlled by a ruthless autocracy; and not appropriate for the ideal education that should be dealing with morals, ethics, values, human relations, or aesthetics. The electronic machine, the argument goes, is a threat to the best teaching, which takes place through human interaction and discovery.

Critics also cite more specific problems associated with the computer. While the electronics and delivery systems may exist, the instructional programs that make up the courseware are still scant and unproven, based on rote or highly linear modes of teaching. And it would still be very expensive, perhaps prohibitively so, to develop, test, and install complete programmed approaches to K–12 and beyond for all types of learners for all types of learning needs. It would be costly indeed to create, evaluate, and implement a complete ninth-grade curriculum with all allied activities and mediations for the varied general programs a typical ninth grader might require—academic, vocational, or art among others. Educators are quick to point out that learning theory still is not so well defined as to permit the design of a programmed system that would be useful for every kind of learning style or every learning environment. Research on computers for education yields the typical "no significant difference" from traditional modes of instruction in test cases. This research indicates that while computer education is probably just as effective as conventional teaching in specific cases, it is certainly no more effective. No results can be generalized to an entire schooling plan from such data.

The controversy about the use of computers for education continues. Whether or not computers will become a major component of the national education system probably depends more on events than on ideas or theories. Recession, political unrest, and social dynamics will have more to do with how education persists and evolves with or without technology than will new teaching devices or theories.

Future scenarios are varied and could include a high technology schooling arrangement based on capital intensive electronics and delivery systems in which the microcomputer along with home televisions and cable networks will play the key role. Or, in a world in which technology has failed because of high energy cost or lack of skilled operators, technicians, or maintenance, the microcomputer and other equipment of the "super school" may become yet more pieces of junk in the scrap heap that will include internal combustion engine automobiles, nuclear power plants, and the DC 10. Most likely the future will hold a hybrid educational system not unlike the one we have today—labor (teacher) intensive with some moderately effective and inexpensive instructional tools such as audio recordings, radio, and similar small media, perhaps even microcomputers for specialized applications.

While microcomputers and similar technologies like central, large computers with cable television hook-ups could provide twenty-four-hour, home-based, and lifelong teaching possibilities, it is probably unlikely and inappropriate that they should do so. In such a situation, isolated and inert learners would learn about the world only as it is mediated by the technology of the computer and the already too-pervasive television. A totally simulated world could encourage only imitation lives. It has been said that "the man shapes the tool and the tool shapes the man." Heaven forbid that all humanity becomes another HAL, the computer of Kubrick's *2001.*

Control of Programming for the Telematique School

Competition for the control of content or programming for home telecommunications centers will no doubt be vigorous.

> Given the enormous costs of preparing new software for telematique school systems, fewer and fewer giant suppliers may survive a competitive struggle for business, the winners increasingly holding sway over the content, selection, character, and real worth of telematique subject matter. Preschoolers may move through a lifetime of formal learning grounded in micro-electronic media (including the video home "newspaper", the TV home entertainment games, and the "Sesame Place" concept park), essentially interacting only with two or three giant purveyors of information (global corporations' subsidiaries such as Time-Life, Control Data Corporation, and so on). (Shostak 1981: 358)

While cable companies with elaborate technical delivery systems and giant software corporations apportion the educational home cable video market, local organizations such as schools, churches, and public service institutions will lose the tenuous hold they now have on cable access channels.

Problems of Cost and Servicing

Costs of personal microcomputers are nominal and seem to have stabilized in spite of inflation in comparison to the costs of other teaching media such as film projectors, tape recorders, and video recording and playback systems.

One must, however, remember that microcomputers can serve only one person at a time—at best two or three. Thus, the per-person costs of a microcomputer can be quite high for the equipment, especially if high courseware costs are figured into the capital outlay. Individual microcomputer equipment and courseware costs can be excessive compared to broadcast television courses, which can be seen by many learners and shared across a broad geographic area. Microcomputer systems are expensive—even compared to traditional media like 16mm films or filmstrips—for both initial equipment and subsequent software purchases. And, software costs for microcomputers are going up. The key strength of the microcomputer is its unique ability to provide individualized and interactive instruction; that is also its financial weakness. It is always necessary to consider if potential users will choose expensive optional electronic systems or the more traditional, less expensive public schools or educational television.

It has been customary to retain traditional instructional media in school settings; print materials and human resources are used for general educational missions. Administrators are loath to invest in "frills" *(Time* 1981*)*. In spite of glowing reports in the press, professional journals, and manufacturers' ads, microcomputers have not yet found extensive applications in the public schools. The cautionary approach of educational decision makers suggests a pervasive public apprehension regarding the large investments in new and costly instructional media.

Many questions have also arisen concerning the need for frequent and costly servicing or maintenance of microcomputer systems. Users complain that microcomputers are often in "down time," that they do not function, and that they are difficult to service. Heavy use of the equipment is necessary to reduce overall per-person costs of microcomputer instruction, and course programs often require lengthy user stays at the keyboard. Heavy use invites potential maintenance problems, as it does in any other mechanical device.

Dealers who quickly promote and sell microcomputer equipment are often tardy in responding to service requests. The state of the art of microcomputer chips and circuitry is new; it is sometimes difficult, if not impossible, to locate accessible and affordable repair personnel; especially in non-urban areas.

The replacement of basic components is sometimes mandatory, and these are the expensive items in the devices. One often hears horror stories about microcomputer breakdowns and subsequent problems including the cost of repairs.

Perhaps the most frequent and frightening service problem is the loss of program or courseware due to equipment malfunction. Microcomputers have a reputation for erasing or destroying programs on cassettes primarily, but also on disks. These programs were expensive or took time to produce; replacement and program "down time" can be disruptive and costly.

Microcomputers are elaborate, interrelated, and dependent systems that are vulnerable to failures; they are easily damaged by extensive use or abuse. Ancillary components such as tape recorders, cassette tapes, and television monitors are all subject to breakdown.

Some educators who have tried to use microcomputers for individualized instruction report that the isolated and sometimes frustrating personal interaction with the machine encourages abuse and, thus, expensive repairs.

Microcomputer systems are relatively new. There is little long-term or unilateral information of life expectancy of the equipment or software or on probable maintenance costs under real-life operating conditions. As with modern color televisions, it is often less expensive and troublesome to simply discard malfunctioning microcomputer equipment and to replace it. In this sense, the equipment is consumable and thus very expensive as a throw-away medium.

Problems with Programming and Programs

"I am a very poor typist and, unfortunately, lack of anything short of superb accuracy in typing makes entering a program a nightmare" (Beder 1981: 5). This complaint, frequently voiced by those who undertake their own programming or even interaction with some typical courseware, may seem like a rather minor issue. In fact, it is a significant problem. Not only does poor typing or keyboarding hinder effective development or use of programs, but it also tends to create immense anxiety toward the machine system. Microcomputers absolutely require keyboarding skills at least at a minimal level. It is difficult, if not impossible, for a person who does not type to master programming. Non-typing users can, of course, respond, if slowly and often incorrectly, to commercially prepared courseware, but the "hunt and peck" approach to the keyboard is not efficient and delays short-term, shared use of the equipment. Too much time is lost in correcting typing errors even in elementary canned programs. For this reason, many potential users will avoid microcomputers; they will be left out of the "age of the microcomputer."

Some educators contend that microcomputers will soon be able to respond and interact with spoken idiomatic English, without resorting to a keyboard. But this breakthrough, which would greatly facilitate the use of the device, is far in the future, if it is possible at all. "Computers, on the other hand, have no knowledge of the world. As a result, except in limited cases, prodigious efforts by computer scientists to get machines to extract the meaning of ordinary written English sentences have been unsuccessful" (Dembert 1982: 1). And, this is for written English; spoken English with its many dialects, idioms, and supportive gestures is even more complex. "The language is simply too vast, there are too many meanings attributed to words and with those meanings go varieties of symbolic properties" (Dembert 1982: 1). The dream of language reactive microcomputers is just that—a dream. The likelihood of developing commercially available microcomputers with spoken language response capabilities is remote.

Learners must also possess fundamental and accurate reading competencies to use most instructional programs. While there have been some efforts to provide courseware for non-readers, in the main, such specialized programs do not exist. This is true for the young as well as for the adult non-reader; except in the case of specific reading and bilingual courses it is also true for the speaker of a language other than English. Most other curriculum areas have been neglected.

Human psychomotor and intellectual skills are also required

for adequate use of the medium. The machine cannot compensate for the lack of human skills or for errors. Such compensatory programs would be costly and limited in teachable content. All the program data would be devoted to keeping the user on-track rather than to providing new knowledge or skills.

Microcomputer programs have very limited capabilities to teach motor skills. The computer shares the limitation of almost all instructional media in that, with the possible exception of simulators such as driver-training or pilot-training devices, it lacks the ability to successfully teach hands-on skills. It is unlikely that a microcomputer could ever teach a learner to tune a piano or fix a car. Microcomputer programs and equipment are generally limited to intellectual and highly logical instruction. Few programs are able to convey affective learning objectives or to encourage intuitive or serendipitous learning.

As suggested in the preface to this book, recent research on the use of computers for learning has indicated that perhaps as much as one half of the population has the sort of cognitive structure that resists acquisition of knowledge from the highly linear and orderly process of the computer. These learners are extroverts and rely on random, often intuitive learning; they gain far more in a typical classroom situation than when forced to sit in front of a video screen for extended periods of time (Hopmeier 1981). Additional research to support the argument that microcomputer instruction will not be the best means of instruction for a large portion of young or adult learners will undoubtedly be undertaken. Adults will fare even less well than youngsters in a microcomputer environment since they do not have extensive life experiences conducive to lengthy exchanges with microcomputers. Adults simply do not spend large amounts of time at a console, in front of a video screen, at a keyboard interacting with a machine. The young, who may be developing attitudes and abilities to spend time thus engaged, may fare better in the future electronic would. Many, but not all, have logged numerous hours playing video games—a kindred experience. Most adults, however, and many children will simply be eliminated from effective use of the microcomputer for lack of preparation in dealing with this highly demanding and time-stealing medium.

As noted previously, comprehensive elementary, secondary, and adult curricula are not typically available on microcomputer programs. Beder observed that "there are programs to do this, and programs to do that, programs to do about anything—

except what you want to do" (Beder 1982: 5). Many entertainment programs exist, but teaching programs are still in short supply.

It is also necessary to consider the fact that existing instructional programs are often difficult to understand and use. "At present, complexity and cumbersomeness bedevil the software industry, creating an obstacle to even greater acceptance of microcomputers. Everybody is saying their software is easy to use, but it isn't" (*Time* 1981: 69). Conscientious learners and teachers inevitably consider programming their own instruction projects. But, this approach is also fraught with complexities. Programming, even BASIC, can be difficult to learn and is easily forgotten if not constantly used. Programming requires knowledge of the subject area, typing skills, a logical mind, patience, considerable time, sufficient expertise in a programming language, and operable and available equipment. To comply with all these demands makes programming a dreadful chore. Learners and teachers seldom write their own textbooks; it is unlikely that they will write their own programs.

It may be incorrect to assume that the current extensive use of microcomputer/video games or exemplary instructional applications of microcomputers will necessarily translate to widespread individual or personal production of teaching materials for the medium; after all, watching television or videotaping programs does not automatically lead to the production of television shows. Just as commercial television has continued to cater to the entertainment demands of viewers, software producers for home telecommunications-computer centers will probably provide mass entertainment materials rather than quality instructional ones. It has been predicted that the software industry of the 1980s will be a commercial industry of some one billion dollars.

Reluctance to Use Microcomputers Justified

As noted earlier, educational administrators have not been aggressive in their acquisition of microcomputers as a primary means of delivery of instruction. These leaders have been slow to promote the use of the medium if willing to buy and support one or two systems as evidence of their concern for modernity. Money for instruction is dedicated, for numerous practical, political, pedagogical, and human reasons, to teachers and to traditional audiovisual equipment. It is not without some previous experience in enthusiastic moves to innovative media like television and teaching machines that today's decision makers are reluctant to invest in as yet untested technologies. This caution is transferred to the public, potential users who are still waiting to determine if this medium is more valuable than earlier glamorous teaching devices.

> TRS - 80 MICROCOMPUTER WITH 16 K MEMORY, HAS BEEN SITTING ON DESK FOR LAST SIX MONTHS
>
> (Daily Chronicle 1981: 18)

This classified ad for a microcomputer suggests the frustration many buyers have experienced. The promises of easy learning, entertainment, and business-management support have just not materialized. The potential of self-directed learning or teacher-produced programs has not been realized. The barriers to the production and use of programs are many. Breakthroughs in equipment that can be easily used and programmed, language-activated computers, better instructional programs, appropriate typing and specific computer interaction skills, and a general positive attitude toward sitting in front of a machine for long periods of time are far in the future.

Home telecommunications-computer centers will emerge, but they will not find the pervasive role suggested by equipment possibilities alone. The medium is beset with numerous technical problems, the lack of programs of a useful nature, and difficulties for users and programmers.

It is probable that more buyers will join the ranks of the disillusioned. The home telecommunications-computer centers will be neglected or misused in many homes. Experiences with television serve as proofs of the probable directions of this new medium: entertainment, overuse for trivial purposes, regimented mass delivery of low quality programming, and passive noninteraction with the medium.

Adult Educator Responsibility

Many adult educators are becoming increasingly interested in and supportive of remote delivery of lifelong schooling, what has sometimes been called the "super school" (Gueulette 1972).

The "super school" is a centralized organization that may be governmentally controlled and that produces or acquires and distributes television programming, films, audio materials, and/or computer programs. This organization could use computers to manage or actually provide instruction with interactive responses from those tied into the system. Via existing and expanded cable television networks or current satellite facilities, this central television/computer school could be piped into all homes in America that have television receivers and microcomputers. With such an arrangement, the home telecommunication center would provide "schools for everyone forever."

The latest generations of computers, with their speed and facility for many simultaneous transactions, invite network sharing of computer-assisted instruction (CAI) among thousands of users, thereby decreasing per-unit (per-person or -terminal) cost of instruction. The high cost of original capital equipment for the computer demands centralization of program development and delivery. The costs of developing courseware for the instructional computer are excessive and the best way to cover the high expense is to create and implement wide-scale and unified programs for many users.

Computers can provide CAI to local receivers with microcomputers through television cable, satellite networks, or telephone lines. Adult educators need to recognize the problems associated with a powerful, centralized, computer-controlled education. It would be all but impossible to legislate the morality, humanity, or selflessness of purpose that could make the computer-dominated "super school" effective yet supportive of the best interests of the majority or the many diverse, yet important, minorities. Safety lies in the maintenance of many different educational ideals and practices rather than in attempts to control or unify people through the "super school."

The rapid and unplanned aggrandizement of the electronic monolith, most evident in the amazingly rushed development and distribution of seemingly magical gadgets such as videodisks with laser decoding; digital audio recording equipment; half-inch cassette video recording and playback machines; microcomputers that can play games, store inventories, solve mathematical problems, teach spelling, and carry out a host of other information management duties; holographic (three-dimensional) photos and even moving films; and an array of other exotic devices, presents a definite risk. Current interest in home videocassette recorders, cable television, and microcomputers that can access the cable system indicates that the "super school" may be much closer than anyone could have foreseen several years ago. If one ties this technological nightmare to other awesome possibilities such as uniform federal support and control, daycare for the very young and the elderly, mandatory certification requirements, businesses contracting for schooling services, and increased interest in accountability, the future appears bleak indeed, susceptible to complete management.

While the content or curriculum of the "super school" may reflect highly desirable objectives and activities such as liberal and vocational education programs as specified by learners' requests, it is the mode of delivery, unified instructional programming, and participant dependence on the electronic device with its cadre of technical experts that present the greatest concern. The best-intentioned educational programs could be reduced to highly controlled behavioral management strategies that would enslave the users and that would also be vulnerable to mismanagement by political or economic interests. For example, it might be tempting to the managers to make vocational training for worker preparation and suppression the main thrust of the curriculum at the expense of other important objectives such as education for art, literature, peace, civil rights, or protection of the environment.

The problem of the "super school" is not one of possibility, for it could be used judiciously and democratically, but rather of probability—probability that it will become a tool of the government or of special-interest groups that would attempt to manage behavior on a large scale.

It would be wonderful to report that this exciting new technology is opening up interactive learning possibilities and new, useful educational programs, thus furthering a wider perspective. But there is little evidence of this. The new wired school seems to be little more than a wired business catering to the consumer demands of a selectively tasteless clientele.

References

Parts of this article originally appeared as "Home Computers: Teaching Machines Born Again," in *The Learning Connection,* Vol. 1, No. 3, Summer 1980 and as "The Wired Nation: The Wired School," in *The Learning Connection,* Vol. 2, No. 2, Spring 1981. *The Learning Connection* is published by Learning Resources Network, 1221 Thurston, Manhattan, KS, 66502.

Beder, H. 1981. In-home educational technology—what is the future? *Lifelong Learning: The Adult Years.* 5(4): 4–5, 30.

Daily Chronicle. 1982. Classified Ads. DeKalb, IL, p. 18.

Dembert, L. 1982. Computers as writers: bad reviews. *Los Angeles Times.* January 1, p. 1.

Gueulette, D. G. 1972. Is there school after death? *Adult Leadership.* 21(3): 92.

Hopmeier, G. 1981. New study says CAI may favor introverts. *Electronic Education.* 1(1): 16–17.

Kruse, N. 1980. Hands-on experience highlights microcomputer session. *ECT.* June, p. 6.

Miller, J. L. 1979. Potentials and perils: interactive cable television as an instructional medium. *Media Adult Learning.* 49: 3–6.

Shostak, A. B. 1981. The coming systems break: technology and schools of the future. *Phi Delta Kappan.* January, p. 358.

Skinner, B. F. 1968. *The technology of teaching.* Englewood Cliffs, NJ: Prentice-Hall.

Time. 1981. Portents of future learning. 118(13): 65.

Time. 1981. Software for the masses. 118(14): 69.

Alan B. Salisbury

Fundamentals of Microcomputer Hardware and Software

For many years educators have recognized the computer as an exceptionally promising educational tool. Major experiments and demonstration projects, generally funded by the federal government, have clearly demonstrated that the computer can be a powerful educational tool. Until recently, however, the reality has eluded the promise because of one simple factor: economics. The large mainframe computers used in most of the projects were—and still are—totally unaffordable for the vast majority of public elementary and secondary schools and adult education centers. Even minicomputers are generally beyond the budget range of these institutions.

The arrival on the scene of the microcomputer has rapidly changed the economics of computers in education to the point where they are almost becoming commonplace in the school. At prices starting at well under $1,000, schools are finding that microcomputers are not only affordable, but that they can be bought in quantity to outfit entire classrooms.

The applications of microcomputers in the classroom are many, as discussed in other articles in this book. This article will focus on the microcomputer itself. The purpose is to acquaint the reader (the educator) with the fundamentals of microcomputers and to provide a working knowledge of the vocabulary of microcomputer "buzzwords." Educators who understand the capabilities (and limitations) of computers, as well as the implications of the various aspects of computer hardware and software to be examined, will be better equipped to deal with planning for, selecting, and implementing microcomputers in the classroom.

Micros, Minis, and Mainframes

We have already used the terms *mainframe, minicomputer,* and *microcomputer* without defining them. The distinction between these computers has to do with the relative speeds with which they can process data and the amounts of memory they can directly access. These concepts will be clarified later. For the moment, it is important to understand that, regardless of the size of the computers, there is no inherent difference in their capabilities. A microcomputer can do anything that a mainframe computer can do; it will, however, take significantly longer to do the same job. The concepts presented in this article apply equally to all classes of computers.

Figure 1 shows the functional units of a typical computer. To understand these units, think of the familiar four-function calculator. The keys of the calculator are its "input" unit, used to enter information. The display is its "output" unit. Within the four-function calculator, lies a large-scale integrated circuit ("LSI Chip") that performs the functions of addition, subtraction, multiplication, and division. This chip is the "Arithmetic Unit" and +, −, ×, and ÷ are its "instruction set." More sophisticated calculators have larger instruction sets and may also have "memory" units to store and recall intermediate results. Finally, the so-called "programmable calculator" uses its memory to store not only data, but also "program steps"—the equivalent of pushing the function keys on the keyboard of a computer. When the program steps are stored in memory, the "control unit" reads them sequentially and causes the other functional units to respond to them, or "execute" them. When pre-stored in memory, program steps can be executed at electronic speeds; for a calculator this means that hundreds of thousands of steps (instructions) can be executed in a single second.

The block diagram shown in Figure 1 applies not only to the hand-held, programmable calculator, but also to the vast majority of microcomputers, minicomputers, and mainframe computers. The control unit and arithmetic and logic unit together are generally referred to as the Central Processing Unit (CPU) of the computer (see Figure 1).

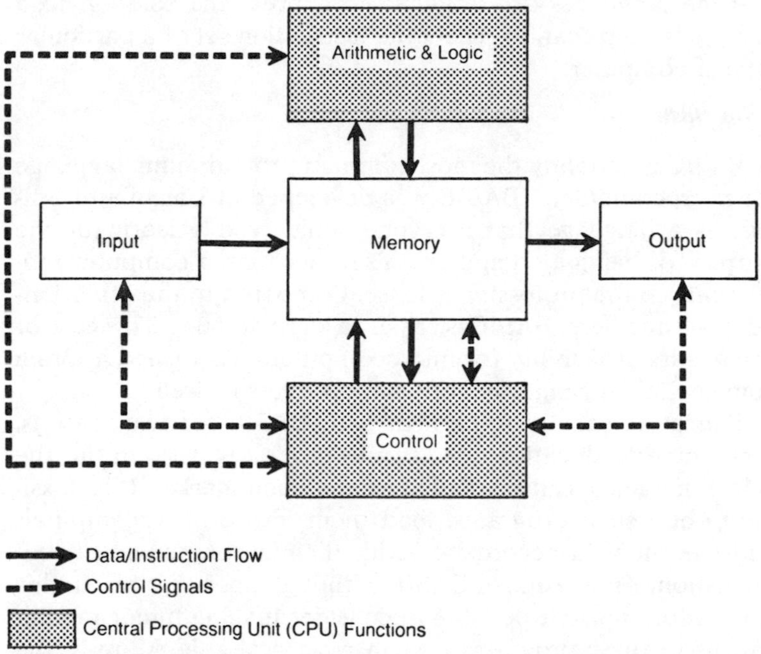

Figure 1. Functional Block Diagram of a Typical Computer. (Copyright 1977, Creative Computing. Reprinted by permission.)

Programming and Software

A "program" is a series of "instructions" that, when executed by a general-purpose computer of any size, causes it to solve a particular problem or to perform a particular task. Programs are called "software" to differentiate them from the physical hardware of the computer itself. The instructions that make up a program must be understandable by the hardware; they must be compatible with the system being used. Ultimately, the CPU of a computer can only execute programs written in the instruction set (machine) language of the computer. Programs are generally written in a "Higher Order Language" (HOL), however, which is both easier to write and understand.

Many higher level languages are available for computers. Examples include BASIC (Beginners All-purpose Symbolic Instruction Code), PL/1, PASCAL, FORTRAN, and COBOL (Common Business Oriented Language). These languages are problem-oriented and machine-independent; this means that the languages are designed to express the solution to a problem rather than to reflect the instruction set of a particular type of computer.

Using Basic

BASIC is certainly the most common programming language for microcomputers. BASIC was developed at Dartmouth College as a language that everyone could readily learn for the purpose of being a computer *user* rather than a computer *programmer* in the professional sense. Compared to the other languages listed here, BASIC is easier to learn and use. This ease of use and its availability for microcomputers has turned it into a commercial language for software products as well.

Educators should be familiar with BASIC for two reasons. First, many educational software programs written in the BASIC language can be bought on the open market. It is possible to buy such programs, load them into a microcomputer, and use them in accordance with their accompanying documentation. Knowledge of BASIC, although not necessary in this case, would make it possible to consider making minor modifications to these programs if such were desirable. More to the point, educators who are not satisfied with commercially available software can open the door to far greater potential use of the microcomputer in education if they develop a capability to write programs of their own. BASIC can be used to write teaching programs; support programs, such as those used for laboratory data reduction; and administrative programs for recordkeeping or grading.

Although it is not within the scope of this article to teach the reader BASIC, a few of the elements of BASIC will be presented in order to acquaint the reader with the language. This may help the reader overcome any fear factor that may exist regarding the difficulties of learning to program. To accomplish this, we will consider a sample BASIC program (Fig. 2).

Figure 2 presents a program written in BASIC that could be used to compute the average student grade (for up to 100 students) on a test. This program could be entered into the computer by typing it in from the keyboard, or alternatively, by loading it in from a cassette tape or a disk if it had previously been saved on one of these. Once the program is in the computer, the user would enter the command "RUN" to cause the program to execute.

```
10  REM GRADE AVERAGING PROGRAM
20  X = O
30  FOR I = 1 TO 100
40  INPUT Y
50  IF Y = 999 THEN GOTO 80
60  X = X + Y
70  NEXT I
80  AVG = X / (I - 1)
90  PRINT "AVERAGE = " ; AVG
100  END
```

Figure 2. An Example Program in the BASIC Language.

This program would run as follows: The computer would display a question mark ("?") on the screen and wait for the user to enter a grade. The grade would be entered from the keyboard followed by the "RETURN" key. The computer would accept the grade and then display another "?" and wait for another grade to be entered. This process would continue until the last grade had been entered. Once again, the computer would display the "?". This time, the user would enter "999" (obviously not a grade) followed by a "RETURN" to indicate to the computer that the last grade had already been entered. The computer would then display on its screen "AVERAGE=" followed by the computed average of the grades entered.

No knowledge of BASIC is required to use this program, even if entered by hand from the keyboard. A simple set of instructions could have been included with the program to explain how to load and use it for the complete novice unfamiliar with the computer.

A line-by-line review of the program in Figure 2 will aquaint the reader with the nature of the BASIC language.

The first thing to notice is that each line of the program begins with a "line number." BASIC uses line numbers for two reasons: first, the computer will automatically keep the lines (program "statements") in numerical sequence. If one wanted to add a new statement between lines 20 and 30, for example, one could assign it line number 25 and the computer would automatically insert it in the correct place. Line numbers, which can generally be up to four digits long, are chosen arbitrarily by the programmer. In the example, intervals of 10 were used to facilitate adding new lines if necessary. Second, line numbers permit identification of particular lines as destinations for GOTO statements, as in line number 50. This will be explained further later.

Line 10 is a "Remark" that begins with "REM." Remarks are used simply to permit the programmer to add comments to a program as a form of documentation or explanation. Except that they are stored as part of the program, these remarks are ignored by the computer.

Line 20 is an "assignment statement." X is the name of a "variable." This simply means that the computer will maintain within its memory a numerical piece of information that can be called by the programmer by referring to the name "X." Line 20 initializes this memory location's contents to the value "0."

Lines 20 and 70 together form a "FOR-NEXT loop." This kind of loop is used to cause the computer to repeat the same part of the program a given number of times. In this case, up to 100 repetitions will occur as controlled by the variable "I," which is used as a counter. When line 30 is executed the first time, it will cause I to be initialized to the value 1. Lines 40, 50, and 60 will then be executed. Line 70 ("NEXT I") will increment the value of I by 1 and compare it to the limit (in this case 100 as specified in line 30); if the new value of I is less than or equal to 100, the computer will execute the intervening lines 40, 50, and 60 again, and so on until line 70 increments I to a value greater than the limit (e.g., 101). When the limit value is exceeded, the computer will move from line 70 to line 80. The FOR-NEXT loop provides a powerful means of causing the computer to repeat parts of a program a controlled number of times.

Line 40 is an INPUT statement used to permit keyboard entry of data into the computer under program control. When this line is executed, the computer will stop and display a "?" on the screen. After a number is entered, pressing the "RETURN" or "ENTER" key will cause the computer to resume processing. In this case, the number entered will be stored as the value of a variable named "Y."

Line 50 demonstrates two features of BASIC. The "IF-THEN" statement provides for conditional execution. If the condition specified following "IF" is true, the portion of the statement following "THEN" will be executed. Otherwise it will be ignored. "GOTO" causes the program to automatically skip to line number 80 as the next statement to be executed. In this case, if Y has the value 999, the computer will skip to line 80 as the next statement to be executed. Alternatively, if Y has any value other than 999, the program will go to line 60. This program, therefore, uses the number 999 as a signal that the last grade has been entered. (The number 999 was chosen by the programmer for this purpose; any number obviously not a grade could have been selected.)

Line 60 computes a new value of X by adding the value of Y (the new grade just entered) to the old value of X (the total of all previous grades). If X was 650 and the grade just entered at line 40 is a 75, the new value of X computed by line 60 would be 725. Note that line 60 is not an "equation," but a statement of how to compute the value of X.

Line 80 is another computation (arithmetic) statement. The value of X will be divided ("/" sign) by the value I−1, and the result will be stored in a memory location named AVG. The total of all grades entered (X) is divided by the number of grades entered (I−1) to compute the average grade (AVG). Why I−1? If 25 grades were entered, the value 999 would be entered by the user when I=26. Hence, when line 80 is executed, the value of I will equal the number of grades plus one.

Line 90 is a "PRINT" statement that prints two items. The first item is the "string" of characters (letters, words, symbols) contained between the quotation marks that includes the word AVERAGE and the equal sign. The second item printed is the *value* of the variable "AVG." If the average of the 25 grades were 82.3, the computer would print AVERAGE=82.3 on the screen.

Finally, line 100 tells the computer that this is the end of the current program and that execution should cease.

To summarize, line 20 initializes the total of all grades at zero. Lines 30 through 70 permit entry of individual grades from the keyboard and add each grade to the running total. When the user signals that all grades have been entered by entering a 999 in lieu of a grade, line 80 will compute the average by dividing the total of all grades by the number of grades entered, and line 90 will print out the results.

In this short space, we have presented, through one example, a surprising amount of the BASIC language. The reader should mentally work through the sample program line by line to insure that he or she understands what the computer would be doing. While minor variations from microcomputer to microcomputer exist in the BASIC language (e.g., Apple BASIC vs Atari BASIC), the example presented in Figure 2 is generic. An understanding of this sample should convince the reader that BASIC is not a difficult programming language to learn.

Using PILOT

Another language of which educators should be aware is PILOT (Programmed Inquiry Learning or Teaching). PILOT is intended primarily for use by educators to create computer-assisted instruction (CAI) materials. It is a very simple language in content and structure, and even easier to learn than BASIC. A brief example will serve to illustrate the general characteristics of PILOT (Fig. 3).

Figure 3 is a partial PILOT program that could be used for a review lesson in American history. Once loaded into the computer's memory and "RUN," this program would execute in the following manner.

The computer would first print on the display screen

PLEASE ENTER YOUR NAME.

The student responds

BARBARA

followed by a "RETURN."

The computer then prints

HELLO, BARBARA, THIS LESSON WILL REVIEW
YOUR KNOWLEDGE OF AMERICAN HISTORY.
WHO WAS THE FIRST PRESIDENT OF THE
UNITED STATES?

If the student responds

WASHINGTON

the computer would print

THAT'S RIGHT! THE FIRST PRESIDENT WAS
INDEED GEORGE WASHINGTON.
NOW LET'S GO ON TO ANOTHER QUESTION.

•
•
•

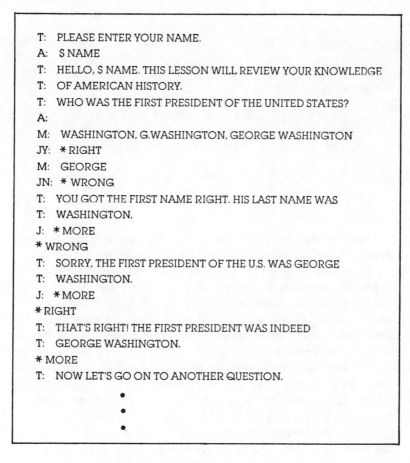

```
T:  PLEASE ENTER YOUR NAME.
A:  $ NAME
T:  HELLO, $ NAME. THIS LESSON WILL REVIEW YOUR KNOWLEDGE
T:  OF AMERICAN HISTORY.
T:  WHO WAS THE FIRST PRESIDENT OF THE UNITED STATES?
A:
M:  WASHINGTON, G.WASHINGTON, GEORGE WASHINGTON
JY: *RIGHT
M:  GEORGE
JN: * WRONG
T:  YOU GOT THE FIRST NAME RIGHT. HIS LAST NAME WAS
T:  WASHINGTON.
J:  *MORE
* WRONG
T:  SORRY, THE FIRST PRESIDENT OF THE U.S. WAS GEORGE
T:  WASHINGTON.
J:  *MORE
*RIGHT
T:  THAT'S RIGHT! THE FIRST PRESIDENT WAS INDEED
T:  GEORGE WASHINGTON.
* MORE
T:  NOW LET'S GO ON TO ANOTHER QUESTION.
          •
          •
          •
```

Figure 3. An Example Program in the PILOT Language. (Atari PILOT is used here.)

Alternately, if the student had responded

GEORGE

the computer would have printed

YOU GOT THE FIRST NAME RIGHT, HIS LAST
NAME WAS WASHINGTON.
NOW LET'S GO ON TO ANOTHER QUESTION.

•
•
•

As a final alternative, if the student had responded

DON'T KNOW

(or anything other than one of the pre-selected answers), the computer would print

SORRY, THE FIRST PRESIDENT OF THE U.S. WAS
GEORGE WASHINGTON.
NOW LET'S GO ON TO ANOTHER QUESTION.
•
•
•

Once again, it will be useful to review this program in some detail to gain an appreciation of the capabilities of PILOT.

"Commands" in the PILOT language are as simple as a single letter. The commands described here are for the Atari PILOT. Other implementations will vary somewhat. "T," "A," and "J" are examples of commands. Each of these commands is followed by a colon to separate it from the remainder of the instruction statement.

"T:" instructs the computer to "Type," which in microcomputer implementations actually prints on the video display screen. This command is used to present instructional material, to ask questions, and to put any message desired on the screen.

"A:" is the command to "Accept" an input from the user at the keyboard. If the user wishes the input to be saved so that he or she can refer to it later in this program, a "name" must be given to it, "$NAME" in the example. A name preceded by a "$" indicates a "string" variable (similar to a string in BASIC), which will be made up of characters (letters, symbols, etc.). A name preceeded by a "#" indicates a numeric variable. Note that in the second T statement of the example program, the name "$NAME" is imbedded in the type statement. When this statement is being executed by the computer, the actual name input by the student will be typed out in place of the variable name. This readily permits personalization of the lesson.

"M:" tells the computer to "Match" the last response to an Accept command with the possible responses listed on the right side of the statement. The first M statement of the example includes three equally acceptable answers; these answers are separated by commas.

"J" is the "Jump" command similar to the GOTO of BASIC. While BASIC causes execution to skip to the statement indicated by a line number following the GOTO, PILOT uses "labels" to indicate the destinations of Jump commands. Labels are names preceded by an asterisk (e.g., *RIGHT, *MORE).

"Y" or "N" following the J causes the Jump to be conditional. JY means "Jump if Yes, there is a match with *any* of the indicated possible matches," while JN means "Jump if No, there is no match." The labels *WRONG, *RIGHT, and *MORE are used to indicate Jump destinations.

The command JY: *RIGHT in the example causes execution to jump to the label *RIGHT if, and only if, the response to the question WHO WAS THE FIRST PRESIDENT OF THE UNITED STATES? is one of the three stated alternative answers: WASHINGTON, G. WASHINGTON, or GEORGE WASHINGTON. If none of these answers is given by the student, the computer will look to see if the student's answer was simply GEORGE. Here the JN command will cause execution to jump to *WRONG if anything *other* than GEORGE is the response. If the response was GEORGE, the computer will respond YOU GOT THE FIRST NAME RIGHT. . . .

Once again, the reader is encouraged to follow the flow of this program to achieve an understanding of its structure and hence of the PILOT language. Of course this short example does not display all of the features of PILOT, but it certainly illustrates the essentials. With just this limited set of commands, one could write CAI materials after very little study.

As in the case of BASIC, there are differences in implementations of PILOT. So-called "Common PILOT" is an attempt to standardize a useful but limited set of PILOT commands that can be used on a variety of computers. Most commercially available implementations go beyond Common PILOT to add more powerful capabilities such as graphics. Adding *too much* power increases the complexity of the language and begins to defeat its purpose—to provide a language by which non-programmer subject matter experts (teachers) can develop teaching materials for use on the computer.

Machine Language

As mentioned earlier, the CPU of a computer understands only a limited instruction set—its "machine language." Ultimately, programs written in BASIC or PILOT must be executed by the CPU executing a machine-language program. One way this could be accomplished is by directly translating HOL programs into machine-language programs.

Higher order languages would be of little value if the programmer were saddled with the job of doing the translation from BASIC, for instance, to machine language. Fortunately, this is the type of job that a computer can do very well; programs called "compilers" have been written to do the translation. A compiler takes as its "input" a higher order language program (called the "source program") and produces as its "output" a machine-language program (called the "object" program) ready to be run on the computer. We thus have a two-step process including a "compile" (translate) phase and an "execute" (run) phase.

We have mentioned machine language many times without really addressing how it differs from higher order languages. This difference can best be understood by looking once more at the familiar four-function calculator. This calculator can do four functions: add, subtract, multiply, and divide; this is, in effect, the vocabulary of "instructions" that the calculator understands. The four-function calculator can be used to solve any problem whose solution can be reduced to a series of steps (a "program") using the +, −, ×, and ÷ operations.

As an example, consider the BASIC statement

$$X = A + 5$$

This can be translated into a series of steps (using the calculator) such as the following:

Step	*Description*
Clear	Depress the clear key on the calculator
Enter A	Enter the numerical value of "A"
Depress +	Depress the "+" key
Enter 5	Enter the value "5" by depressing the 5 key
Depress +	Depress the "+" key
Read X	Read the value of "X" on the display

The vocabulary of the calculator above has been expanded to include the human actions—clear, enter, depress for input, and read for output. In the language of the machine/human team, this program is a translation of the BASIC statement. (The exact sequence will depend on the logic of the particular calculator. The sequence shown is typical.)

Moving from the four-function calculator to a microcomputer is not difficult. One major difference is that the vocabulary, or "instruction set," is greatly increased; a typical microcomputer may have 70 or more functional instructions that it understands, including the familiar add, subtract, multiply, and divide. New capabilities includc such things as "shifting" numbers left or right or "comparing" two numbers to determine if one is greater than, less than, or equal to the other.

Another significant difference is the amount of memory available. The calculator in the example did not include memory. Many calculators have one or more "memory" locations in which a number may be "stored" and later "recalled" by thc use of appropriate keys (which actually add to the instruction set vocabulary of the calculator). Each location in memory has a unique "address" that differentiates it from other memory locations. Computers generally have thousands of such memory locations that can be used to store not only numbers or "data," but that can also be used to store instructions so that the entire program can be stored within the computer.

It is this last fact—program storage—that makes the computer the powerful instrument it is. With the program stored inside the computer, the operator only needs to depress the "start" or "run" switch to execute the program at electronic speeds, typically in millions of instructions per second. Add to this the fact that the computer can make "decisions" (by using a "compare" instruction for example) and one has a good explanation of the power of the computer.

Returning to the previous example, a sequence of microcomputer-type instructions to perform the X = A + 5 function might be

```
CLA A
ADD Five
STO X
```

CLA, ADD, and STO are abbreviations (called "mnemonics") for the full instruction names. For example, CLA could be "Clear and Add," meaning "clear the accumulator register to zero and add to it the contents of the memory location indicated" (in this case, the location symbolically referred to as A). ADD would simply be "add to the accumulator register" without clearing beforehand, and STO would be "store" the contents of the accumulator register in the indicated memory location. Each of the many instructions of the computer has a similar detailed and precise meaning. ("Registers" referred to in this discussion are high-speed temporary working storage.)

To complete the picture, we have to now point out that even this three-instruction program sequence is not really in machine language. Computers don't normally understand letters and words such as CLA. In fact, everything within the machine must ultimately be in the form of binary numbers, consisting only of combinations of ones and zeros. This is the fundamental unit of information within the machine, known as the "bit" (for binary digit).

Binary Numbers

In the binary number system, only two symbols (digits) may be used: 0 (zero) and 1 (one). The decimal system, on the other hand, has ten symbols: 0 thru 9. In the binary system, just as in the decimal system, when counting causes us to run out of symbols in one column we carry 1 into the next column and start over. The difference is that a carry in the decimal system occurs for every count of ten, while it occurs for every count of two in the binary system. Thus, "place values" in the binary system are powers of 2 (1, 2, 4, 8, 16, etc.) instead of powers of 10 (1, 10, 100, 1000, etc.).

Conversion from binary to decimal is a simple process requiring only that the place values corresponding to 1's in the binary number be added up. For example,

64's	32's	16's	8's	4's	2's	1's		
								32
								8
								4
0	1	0	1	1	0	1	=	1
								45

Memory locations and working registers within a computer generally contain a fixed number of bits. A bit is the "word" length of the computer. Microcomputers typically process 8 bits at a time. This quantity, 8 bits, is referred to as a "Byte." The largest number that can be stored in a byte is 11111111 (binary) = 255 (decimal). Larger numbers will require more than one byte. The real significance of word length, therefore, lies in the speed of the computer. A 16-bit computer can, for instance, add two 16-bit (2-byte) numbers in a single instruction execution cycle; an 8-bit computer would require two cycles to process the numbers one byte at a time.

We mentioned earlier that memory is used to store both data

and the program. Program instructions are stored in memory words according to precise formats. For example, a 16-bit instruction may be divided into 6 bits for an "operation code," which specifies the particular instruction to be performed, and 10 bits for a memory address, the location of the data to be used. The CLA A instruction could thus include a 6-bit code for CLA (it might be 001010) and a 10-bit binary address for the location we chose to call A (this could be 0000101101 if location 45 were used for A). The complete machine-language instruction would then be

001010 0000101101
Opcode Address

Assemblers

Once again we are faced with the problem of translating from the mnemonic (or symbolic) form of instruction into the numeric machine-language form. The computer comes to the rescue as before with a special translation program, available from the hardware manufacturer, that "assembles" machine-language programs from the symbolic instructions. The input for an "assembler" program is the symbolic Assembly-Language source program; the output is a binary machine-language object program ready for execution. Unlike higher order language programs, which are largely machine independent, Assembly-Language programs are very machine dependent since each CPU type has its own, generally unique, machine and Assembly Language.

In addition to relative machine dependence or independence, there are other considerations involved in understanding the differences between compilers and assemblers. The example showed that a single BASIC statement resulted in several assembly-language-type instructions. Each Assembly-Language instruction, on the other hand, usually causes a single binary machine-language instruction to be generated. It is not uncommon for a good Assembly-Language programmer to write a program requiring fewer machine instructions than one written in a higher order language and compiled into machine instructions. The Assembly-Language programmer's program may therefore require less memory and execute faster. The price paid for this possible bonus is usually the extra time (and training) required to do Assembly Language programming. As compilers become more efficient, this difference may come to disappear.

Data Representation

Now that we have seen that instructions within the computer are actually represented by 1's and 0's of the binary system, we should point out that *all* information within the computer, including instructions and data, is similarly encoded into binary. It is not difficult to see how numbers can be stored as their binary equivalent. It is important to note, though, that *letters* can also be stored in binary form. The American Standard Code for Information Interchange (ASCII) code assigns an 8-bit code to each letter (capitals separate from small letters), digit (0-9), punctuation mark, and other symbols. Each byte thus has the capability of storing one character. It is often useful to think of memory in terms of its capacity to store a given number of characters, rather than simply as being so many bytes in size.

Systems Software

Compilers and assemblers belong to a class of programs referred to as "systems software" and are usually written by the manufacturer's "systems programmers." The using programmer is, in contrast, referred to as an "applications programmer" and the "applications programs" are the programs written to solve the user's problem.

Starting with a program written in BASIC, many steps are required before the output is available when a compiler is used. First, a "loader" must be in the machine to enable it to load programs into its memory. Then the BASIC compiler can be loaded in, the source program read, and the translated object program produced as output. Now the object program is read in (again by a loader) and then executed producing the final results. Input/output utilities and math routines may well have been required and loaded in along with the object program.

The smallest mini- or microcomputers may be operated in just this fashion, with an operator handling many separate programs and manually controlling the sequences of loading and execution. This job, too, is one in which the computer can lend a hand. (And this is, fortunately, the case with most microcomputers).

Operating Systems

The most important of the "systems" programs is one called an "operating system"; sometimes it is called an "executive," "monitor," or "control" program. The operating system program takes over these tasks of scheduling, allocating space in memory, loading programs, calling other systems programs, etc. Most of today's popular microcomputers come equipped with a monitor-type program in permanent memory or with an operating system that can be loaded in from external memory. The result is that use of the computer is greatly simplified.

Interpreters

This brief tour of systems software has thus far omitted one important type of program, the "interpreter," which is particularly important to BASIC users. The use of a BASIC compiler to translate a BASIC program into machine language for later execution is one method that may be available for the BASIC user to execute his programs. Generally, however, a BASIC interpreter is used to execute BASIC programs.

An interpreter differs from a compiler in one major way: an interpreter does not translate the source program, but executes it directly. Each line of a BASIC program is examined by the interpreter to determine what actions will have to be executed or evaluated. The interpreter then performs those actions by immediately executing the appropriate portions of its *own* program, then it moves on to the next source BASIC statement. This is in contrast to the compiler process in which the entire BASIC program is translated into a unique set of machine-language instructions that are executed after the compiler has finished its job.

To illustrate the difference between the two systems, consider how each would process the BASIC statement

$$X = 2 + 3$$

A compiler would produce as its output a machine-language program consisting of several instructions, which, when executed later, would calculate the desired result and assign it to the variable *X*. An interpreter, on the other hand, would produce as its output the new value of *X*, which is 5; no instructions or new program would be produced by the interpreter.

What differences does a user see between a compiler and an interpreter? Not many. Both methods ultimately produce the same results. If the program is to be executed many times, there is a benefit to using the compiler method: it is possible to obtain a copy of the object program produced by the compiler, on disk or tape for instance. Then, when the user wants to execute the program again, he or she can simply load the object program (in machine language) and execute it without going through the time-consuming translation phase. Compilation therefore offers the potential of time-saving efficiency.

Interactive Systems

Interpreters offer an advantage of their own in that they are generally "interactive." This allows the programmer to sit at a keyboard with the interactive BASIC interpreter in control and to get immediate "feedback" from the interpreter as the BASIC statements are entered. Errors can be immediately identified by the interpreter and corrected by the programmer. Also, the results of executing each BASIC statement can be available immediately, thus making the system react to the user as if it were a sophisticated calculator. For a new program, it may therefore be possible to get an answer faster by using an interpreter rather than a compiler since the interpreter does not have to go through the separate translate and execute phases.

Text Editors

Other programs besides interpreters may be interactive. One of the most common is a "text editor" which can be used to help create a new program or "file." If a BASIC compiler were available through a time-sharing system, an interactive text editor could be used to build or create a BASIC program using an on-line terminal; the text editor would permit the programmer to make changes such as adding or deleting individual characters or whole lines. When the programmer is satisfied with a program, he or she could ask the system to compile it and execute it. The software performing the actual time-sharing operations serving many users simultaneously is essentially a more complex type of operating system as previously discussed.

Most popular microcomputers include a limited text-editor capability in the onboard monitor or operating system. This provides text editing capabilities for inserting or deleting lines or characters as the user works with a program displayed on the screen.

Software Summary

This completes a general introductory overview of systems software. The reader should now have a reasonable understanding of the various types of programs involved, the functions they perform, and how they relate to one another. The types of systems programs available and the functions they perform are summarized in Table 1 on the next page.

Many of the seeming complexities of software operations described in this section have been completely eliminated for today's popular microcomputers (Apple, Atari, Commodore, TRS-80). A built-in operating system (monitor) with limited text-editing capabilities and a simple user-oriented command structure takes care of most of the internal processing requirements. A companion BASIC interpreter makes it relatively easy to load and run BASIC programs.

Hardware Considerations

The distinction between a microprocessor and a microcomputer should be clearly understood. A microprocessor can be simply defined as a central processing unit on a single large-scale integrated circuit (LSI) chip. As was shown in Figure 1, the CPU consists of the arithmetic and logic unit (ALU), with its working registers, and the control unit of a computer. A microprocessor therefore does not include the main memory or the input/output units and interfaces.

To qualify as a microcomputer, the total hardware package must include a basic amount of memory and input/output circuits. In terms of today's hardware, a microprocessor may be available as a single LSI chip, while a microcomputer may be available on a card. This can be carried one step further and a complete microcomputer system can be defined as a microcomputer circuit card plus the required power supply, control panel (this may be as little as an on/off switch), chassis or cabinet, and some input/output devices.

With this perspective, one can appreciate that a $9.95 microprocessor is a long way from being a working computer. Still, within every microcomputer there beats a microprocessor heart that gives it its "personality." The implications of this are many; some will be discussed in this section.

A good example of a microprocessor is the popular Intel 8080 (Fig. 4). The 8080 is an 8-bit microprocessor with 78 different instructions, packaged in a single 40-pin package. Newer versions of the 8080 operate faster, require less external support, and may have expanded instruction capabilities. A prime example is the Z-80 processor included in the Radio Shack TRS-80

Table 1. A Table of Key "Systems" Programs*

Systems Program				
Name	**Function**	**Input(s)**	**Output(s)**	**Comments**
Compiler	Translates HOL program to machine-language program	HOL source program	Listing; machine-language object program	Object program may be punched out or loaded into memory
Assembler	Translates Assembly-Language program to machine-language program	Assembly-Language source program	Listing; machine-language object program	Object program may be punched out or loaded into memory
Interpreter	"Executes" HOL program	HOL source program	Problem solution	Output is only what the source program produces; interactive
Loader	Loads machine-language programs	Machine-language object program(s)	Machine-language programs ready to be executed	Loaded into memory
Text Editor	Creates or edits files	Source programs, data, etc.	Listing or copies of files when requested	Interactive
Operating System	Overall control of computer system and its resources	Job-control language or equivalent; all other inputs to computer	Responses to JCL commands; log of system status, error messages to operator, etc.	Schedules jobs, allocates memory, etc., to minimize need for operator

computers. Programming the 8080 or Z-80 involves machine- or Assembly-Language programming in detail as described earlier.

Another popular microprocess chip is the 6502. This chip is used as the CPU of the Apple II, Atari, and Commodore PET computers.

Memories

Two types of memories are used within microcomputers: "read/write" and "read-only." Read only memories (ROMs), as their name implies, may be read but not written (altered) under program control. The information stored in a ROM is permanent and will not be lost when power is turned off. ROMs may be used in microcomputer systems that are dedicated to a single application such as an industrial process controller. The program in this type of application normally remains constant. A small amount of separate read/write memory is often included for data that may be variable.

Key systems programs (monitors, interpreters, etc.) are normally provided by microcomputer manufacturers in ROM form to eliminate the necessity of having to read them into memory. Programs in ROM are often referred to as "firmware." Several of the popular personal computers use optional plug-in memory cartridges that contain firmware programs.

General-purpose microcomputers of interest to the educator require read/write memories for both programs and data. Read/write memory is usually called RAM in contrast to ROM, for "random access memory." When power is turned off, any information in RAM is lost.

A key factor concerning memories is capacity. Memory is usually available in increments of 1K (K = 1024 bytes). From the hardware standpoint, a system should be able to accommodate additional plug-in boards to expand memory (that is, physical space in the cabinet plus power) and the boards must electrically interface with the CPU. "Plug-compatible" memories have already been provided by independent companies for the more popular microcomputers. Typical minimum memories are 4K bytes expandable up to 48K or 64K bytes. Memory has become inexpensive enough so that one should procure the maximum size available for computers to be used in educational applications.

Connections between IC chips (CPU, memory, input/output interfaces, etc.) normally use "buses." A bus is simply a parallel set of conductors grouped together as a set; each line is

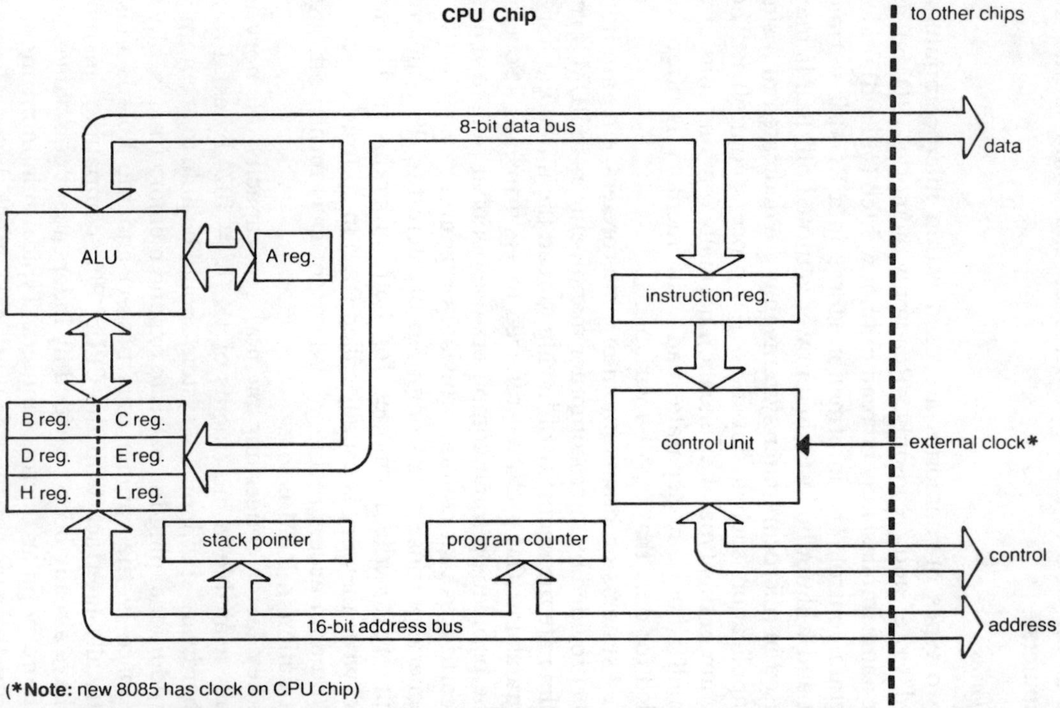

Figure 4. INTEL 8080 Central Processing Unit. (Copyright 1977, Creative Computing. Reprinted by permission.)

specified as to function. More than one device can be connected to a bus at the same time; addresses are used to select the desired device.

Input/Output and Peripherals

In order for the CPU to communicate with an Input or Output (I/O) device, it must connect to it through an "interface." An interface consists of a circuit board that plugs into the computer and, in some cases, software. Its function is two-fold: first, it provides for electrical connection to the external device. Different manufacturers use different voltage/current levels and these may require translation. The physical connector itself must be compatible. Second, the functional purpose of the individual wires must be common between the devices and "instructions" from the computer must be understandable by the I/O device. In short, unless the proper interface is used, equipment from different manufacturers cannot be interconnected.

Two general types of input/output (I/O) interface are available for microcomputers. Serial interfaces (one bit at a time, sequentially) are probably the most practical since they can be used with more common input/output devices. Parallel interfaces (multiple bits simultaneously, usually 8 to form a complete character) are more powerful (faster) but require greater equipment sophistication.

The most economical input device available is a simple alphanumeric keyboard. These are widely used, and most microcomputers have suitable interfaces either as a standard feature or as an option. A keyboard is ideal for interactive work such as working with short programs in BASIC. They can be quite frustrating, however, when used for loading long programs since they are limited in speed to the user's typing speed.

On the output side, video displays are both effective and practical. Their practicality stems from the fact that it is possible to use a normal home TV set without any modifications for this purpose. As many as 1024 characters can be displayed on the screen at any time. Again, this is a very effective output medium for interactive use. The disadvantage here lies not in speed, but in performance, since no "hard copy" (paper) is available. As with keyboards, interfaces for video output are generally available as options for microcomputers; in some cases they are standard.

When a standard TV set is used for display, the computer

must feed its output through an "RF modulator." This device is like a miniature TV broadcasting station that transmits to channel 3 or 4 or in some cases to a specified UHF TV channel. The TV set is then tuned to the designated channel to receive the display. Several of the popular microcomputers contain built in RF modulators; on some, it may be necessary to have a modulator installed at a modest cost.

The best image quality comes not from a TV set but from a "monitor." A display monitor is like a TV set but does not have a channel tuner. The video image is fed directly to a monitor without being broadcast at TV channel frequencies; hence, no RF modulator is required. Ironically, monitors cost more than TV sets, even though less electronic circuitry is required.

Low- and medium-speed printers are now available at reasonable prices. So-called "dot matrix" printers are the least expensive, but the visual quality of characters formed by dots may be unacceptable. For most educational applications, however, these printers should be adequate. The alternative "letter-quality" printers use selectric type mechanisms or daisy-wheel devices with fully formed characters. The cost of these is at least twice that of dot-matrix printers.

External Memory/Program Storage

Two external read/write memory devices commonly used for microcomputers are the cassette tape and the floppy disk. The first is inexpensive but comparatively slow and sometimes unreliable. The second provides significantly better performance, but at significantly greater cost. Serious use in an educational environment, however, demands the floppy disk.

A typical program stored on cassette tape may take 3 minutes to load into main memory, while the same program could load from disk in perhaps 10 seconds or less. Also, it frequently happens that a tape load will not be successful (due to bit errors) and that the tape must be rewound and loaded again.

Floppy disks look something like 45-rpm records but are made of a light, flexible plastic material coated magnetically. Information is recorded in parallel tracks on the disk. A single floppy disk may hold anywhere from 50 thousand bytes (characters) to 500 thousand characters depending on whether or not both sides of the disk are used and how densely bits are packed together on the disk. The disk is maintained in a paper sleeve that is inserted into the disk drive along with the disk itself. Since the disk spins at several hundred RPM, it takes a short period of time to read information from any location on the disk.

Outlook

The state-of-the-art in microcomputer technology is changing rapidly. Price and performance figures can be expected to change remarkably for the better as each year passes. There is no doubt, however, that systems are available today with a low enough cost and high enough performance to merit full-scale application by the educator.

About the Contributors

Cheryl Anderson is on the faculty of Instructional Technology, Department of Curriculum and Instruction, The University of Texas, Austin. Dr. Anderson has been involved in course development and instruction in the area of computer literacy. She set up a microcomputer laboratory in the College of Education Learning Resources Center and is an active member of the Association of Educational Communications and Technology (AECT).

Jerold W. Apps, a professor of adult education at the University of Wisconsin, Madison, has been widely published in the field. Dr. Apps is well known for his concern for humane and liberatory education for adults. He has served as president of both the Adult Education Association of Wisconsin and the National Commission of Professors of Adult Education. Many of his books are basic texts in the field. His recent interest in and use of microcomputers prompted him to provide the Foreword for this collection.

Hugh Garraway is with the Department of Computer Science and Statistics at The University of Southern Mississippi, Hattiesburg. Dr. Garraway has been involved in the development of programs to teach adults microcomputer programming and use. He is instrumental in the continuing building of a computer curriculum for the university. His articles in professional journals have dealt with the role of educators and microcomputers in the emerging instructional environment.

David G. Gueulette is at Northern Illinois University, DeKalb, on the faculty of Instructional Technology. He has been chairperson of the Media in Adult Learning Section of the Adult Education Association of the U.S.A. (AEA) and has edited its journal, *Media and Adult Learning.* Dr. Gueulette has been writing on the uses of media in adult learning for many years, focusing on such topics as television, instructional design, and computer-based learning. His interests and experience include educational programs with adults in developing countries.

Thomas Heaney is the Director of Community Services, Northern Illinois University, DeKalb. Dr. Heaney organized Basic Choices/Chicago, an educational resource center for neighborhood development and empowerment. He is a cofounder of the National Alliance for Voluntary Learning, which developed a comprehensive report on mandatory education for adults and its dangers. He has been involved in several community-based interactive media projects in the nation and has initiated an international network of resources and educators interested in participatory research.

John Hortin is in the Department of Media Education, Library Science, Communications and Technology at Kansas State University, Manhattan. He is the current editor of the Adult Education Association journal *Media and Adult Learning* and chairperson of the Media in Adult Learning Section of the organization. Dr. Hortin is the author of articles on the nature of brain functions and learning, visual literacy, and instructional technology research methods. He is an officer of the International Visual Literacy Association and active in AECT.

Dorothy Judd is on the faculty of the Department of Curriculum and Instruction, Northern Illinois University, DeKalb, and is a consultant specializing in the evaluation of instructional microcomputer programs. She is a contributing editor to *Educational Computer Magazine* and a resource person on microcomputers for the National Council for the Social Studies. Her research has been in microcomputer applications in reading and language arts. Dr. Judd has been active in the Association for Educational Data Systems and related professional organizations.

Carol Kasworm is on the faculty and is Project Director, Continuing and Higher Education, Department of Curriculum and Instruction, The University of Texas, Austin. Dr. Kasworm is an officer of the Adult Education Association of the U.S.A. and is chairperson of its Publications Committee. She is author of numerous publications regarding instructional environments and strategies for teaching adult learners, with particular emphasis on those returning to college and on older adult populations.

Wesley C. Meierhenry is chairperson of the Department of Adult and Continuing Education, Teachers College, The University of Nebraska, Lincoln. Dr. Meierhenry is a past president of the Department of Audiovisual Instruction of the National Education Association (now AECT). He received the AECT Distinguished Service Award in 1980. He is an author and consultant in media, technology, and adult education. He has recently been engaged in research in adult learning styles and brain functions.

George Mozes is the Coordinator of the National Medical Audiovisual Center and the Director of Library and Media Resources at Michael Reese Hospital and Medical Center, Chicago. For the last nine years, Dr. Mozes has been working in biomedical communications, information management, and faculty development. He has worked on the design and evaluation of audiovisual materials and served as a consultant in such media use for health professionals. He has developed computer simulations and made presentations on the use of microcomputers in education before such associations as AECT, the Association of American Medical Colleges, and the North American Simulations and Gaming Association.

Alan B. Salisbury is the Project Manager, Operations Tactical Data Systems, U.S. Army, Fort Monmouth, New Jersey. He is founder and vice president of Educmatics Corporation which conducts training seminars for the instructional uses of microcomputers and which is developing a national network of computer-learning centers as well as software programs for them. Colonel Salisbury is the author of numerous technical and management articles. His Ph.D. from Stanford University is in Computer Engineering and Computer Science.

Roger Sanders is Coordinator of Media Services for Community Unit School District Number Five, Sterling, Illinois. He selects district microcomputer equipment and learning programs. Sanders has established and led district in-service training programs for teachers who are preparing to use microcomputers. He also has designed extensive planning strategies for adopting new instructional media.

Peter C. West is the Assistant Director of the Learning Center, College of Education, Northern Illinois University, DeKalb. West has been responsible for the selection and acquisition of microcomputer hardware and courseware and has had the opportunity to examine and evaluate many of the available microcomputer teaching programs. He is particularly interested in alerting possible users of the technology to the vast array of software materials now on the market.

GLOSSARY OF TECHNICAL TERMS

A A command in the PILOT computer language that causes the computer to "Accept" an input from the keyboard.

access To obtain data from a peripheral unit or to retrieve data from storage.

accessibility Pertaining to access.

accumulator register A computer register in the arithmetic unit that may be used for intermediate storage, to form arithmetic sums, or for other intermediate operations. *Also see* register.

Add A typical mnemonic abbreviation for an Assembly Language computer instruction: "ADD to the accumulator register." Causes a number to be added to the current contents of the accumulator.

address **1.** A name, number, or label that identifies a register, location, or unit in memory or storage. **2.** The part of an instruction that specifically locates an operand. **3.** To put a specific piece of information into or to take it from the computer memory. **4.** The coded representation of the destination of a message or information.

algorithmic Pertaining to a well-defined set of rules for problem solving in a definite number of steps.

alphanumeric keyboard A typewriter-like keyboard with individual keys for letters (alpha), numbers (numeric), and special symbols such as punctuation marks.

American Standard Code for Information Interchange (ASCII) A code developed to achieve compatibility between computers. It uses 8 binary bits to represent characters (letters, numbers, symbols) internally within a computer and is used for communications between computers and other devices, e.g., over telephone lines.

ALU *See* arithmetic and logic unit.

Apple **1.** Apple Computer Corp., a manufacturer of microcomputers. Popular computer products include the Apple II Plus and the Apple III. **2.** A microcomputer manufactured by Apple Computer Corp.

APPLESOFT A language version (dialect) of the BASIC language developed for use with Apple computers. *Also see* Floating-point BASIC.

applications programmer A computer programmer who writes end-user–oriented programs that enable the computer to perform useful functions (applications) for the user. Education, business, and scientific functions are typical application areas.

arithmetic and logic unit (ALU) That portion of the central processing unit of a computer that executes the arithmetic and logical operations.

artificial intelligence Describes the use of computers in which they perform functions that are normally associated with human intelligence, i.e., analagous to the human learning and decision-making abilities.

ASCII *See* American Standard Code for Information Interchange.

assembler A computer program that translates a symbolic source program (using mnemonic instructions and symbolic address names) into a binary object program (machine language). One symbolic Assembly-Language instruction will be translated to one machine language instruction.

Atari **1.** Atari, Inc., a manufacturer of microcomputers. Popular computer products include the Atari 400 and Atari 800. **2.** A microcomputer manufactured by Atari, Inc.

authoring system A program or set of programs used to interact with the program in creating interactive modules. The system then organizes and stores the information entered by the author for later presentation to learners.

BASIC Acronym for Beginner's All-purpose Symbolic Instruction Code, a simplified higher-order computer language especially suited for time-sharing.

battery packs Electrical power source (DC) now available with some models of stand-alone microcomputer systems.

binary digit A number in the binary notation system; the digit can be either a 0 or 1. Computers use these numbers internally.

binary notation A notation system that shows position; used to represent numbers in the base 2.

bit **1.** A binary digit. **2.** A single unit of binary information; can take on one of only two values, a "1" or a "0."

Boolean logic The expression of logical relationships in algebraic notations, similar to expression of mathematical relationships using conventional algebra.

branch To depart from the normal sequence of executing instructions.

bus A conductor (e.g., a wire) over which data or power can be transmitted between hardware devices.

byte A group of 8 binary bits. The fundamental unit of storage (memory) in a microcomputer. Each byte can store one character (*see* ASCII) or a numeric value in the range 0–255. It is a sequence of adjacent binary digits constituting a unit representing either a subdivision of a word or a whole word.

cablecasting Broadcasting or transmitting television programs through a wired system.

CAI Computer-assisted or -aided instruction. A concept in education whereby a student interacts in a conversational mode with a computer that has a preprogrammed study plan. CAI has also been known as computer-based education (CBE), computer-assisted learning (CAL), and computer-based training (CBT).

CAL *See* CAI.

call up To retrieve data from the computer; to initiate a program or ask for a specific item in a computer memory.

CAT *See* computer-assisted testing.

CBBS Community Bulletin Board System; a centralized message communication system that enables users to leave or call up existing messages. Accessible by any terminal equipped with a modem.

CBE *See* CAI.

CBI Computer-based instruction; *see* CAI.

central data base A central point or location where several data bases may be housed or found.

central processing unit (CPU) The unit of a computer that contains the circuits that perform the execution of instructions; controls and activates all other units of the computer. Includes the arithmetic and logic unit, the control unit, and the memory unit.

Chat A form of electronic communication that enables a person to have a conversation at the computer with another user who is connected to THE SOURCE. *See* THE SOURCE.

chip A wafer slice of a semiconductor material, usually silicon, on which integrated circuits are imprinted.

circuit board A device for containing a collection of electronic elements; usually used to divert, amplify, or alter electronic signals. *Also see* IC.

CLA Mnemonic abbreviation for an Assembly-Language computer instruction: "clear the accumulator register and add to it." Causes the accumulator register to be cleared to zero and a number to be added to it.

clear To reset (a register or memory location) to zero.

clustered system A system whereby the computer may copy stored software from the mass storage device into its own memory; allows the user to interact with the program as if he or she were on a stand-alone system. Sometimes called a star network.

CMI Computer-managed instruction. A system with the capability of relieving the teacher of menial tasks associated with individual instruction; e.g., keeping records on learner programs or tabulating grade-point averages.

COBOL Acronym for Common Business Oriented Language; developed for general commercial use. COBOL is an internationally accepted programming language.

code A system of symbols for representing data.

coding The writing of an ordered list, in computer code, of instructions for a computer; part of the programming activity.

color table animation A special graphics gesture that permits the development and display of visuals in color; the visuals can be manipulated to show various aspects of the visual object.

command An electronic pulse or signal to start, stop, or continue a computer operation.

Commodore Commodore Business Machines, a manufacturer of microcomputers. Popular computer products include the PET and CBM personal and small-business computers.

Commodore PET *See* PET.

Community Bulletin Board System *See* CBBS.

compiler A computer program that translates a higher-order-language (e.g., BASIC or FORTRAN) source program into a binary-object program (machine language). One higher order language instruction will usually be translated to several machine language instructions. *Also see* Higher Order Language.

computer A device that can accept and process data; usually consists of five parts—input, output, storage, arithmetic and logical unit, and control units/devices. Computers may accept information, apply prescribed processes to the information, and supply the results of these processes.

computer-assisted instruction *See* CAI.

computer-assisted learning *See* CAI.

computer-assisted testing (CAT) Tests administered by a computer and appropriate for certain subject disciplines.

computer banks A collection of mainframe computers connected in series or parallel to provide increased capacity for information storage and retrieval.

computer literacy Being knowledgeable about computers, their applications and functions. Includes experience in computer use and programming skills as well as an awareness of the computer's impact on society.

computer-managed instruction *See* CMI.

CONDUIT An organization that distributes, documents, and evaluates software production of individuals and institutes of higher learning. CONDUIT sells curriculum programs for computers or microcomputers for university and general education applications.

console The unit of a computer that may be used to control the machine manually, correct errors, determine the contents of storage, etc., either through a typewriter or through display lamps.

control program A minimal operating system for a microcomputer. In the Apple II, for instance, the control program selects between BASIC and machine language according to control characters entered by the user from the keyboard.

control unit That portion of a computer that directs the automatic operation of the computer, interprets computer instructions, and initiates the proper signals to other computer circuits to execute instructions.

courseware Refers to the actual instruction involving both content and technique used in a CAI system; not to be confused with software, the actual program that directs a computer's operation.

CPU *See* central processing unit.

CRT Cathode Ray Tube. A TV-like display used to show information retrieved; takes the form of an electronic vacuum tube in which an electronic lens can direct and control a beam of electrons producing a visible display of information on the surface of the tube or to store data in the form of an energized portion of the tube's surface.

curriculum designer One who creates the plan, content, or method of delivery for an instructional event or entire course.

daisy wheel device A print-head mechanism for a computer printer in which individual letters/symbols are arranged at the ends of spokes radiating from a central hub. In operation, the daisy wheel is rotated to bring the proper character into position to be printed.

data analysis Interpretation of facts, figures, etc., in making statistical inferences and in drawing conclusions.

data base A large collection of well-organized data that are continuously updated; abstracts, information, or references on a particular subject or subjects that can be retrieved by a computer.

data processing The performance of operations on data so as to achieve order or to obtain information among files.

dialect Version of a computer language. For example, Integer Basic is a dialect of BASIC.

Dialog A computer command language developed by the University of London for computer simulations on the PET microcomputer; designed to provide experiences in searching the Lockheed data bases.

dialogue Interaction between user and computer or computer and computer.

dial-up To initiate and effect telephone calls through a dial telephone to access a computer.

digital audio recording Disk recordings that differ from conventional phonograph records in the manner in which the audio information is reproduced for subsequent impression on the vinyl. A computer is used to code the audio using a mathematical system. The code is then physically transferred to the disk for playback.

digital computer A computer operating by using numbers to express all the quantities and variables of a problem.

disk Flat circular metal plates with magnetic surfaces used as storage devices. Each surface contains a number of tracks onto which data are written or from which they are read by means of one or more read/write heads. *Also see* magnetic disk.

disk drive A peripheral unit used to run programs of floppy disks.

disk magnetic record A storage device. *Also see* disk.

diskette A recording medium of the computer also known as floppy disk. *Also see* disk.

display device Used to present information in visible form; the most common are CRTs and printed paper.

dot matrix A scheme for printing individual characters as a pattern of dots. A typical matrix is 9 dots high by 7 dots wide. Characters are printed by selecting specific dots in the matrix to be printed.

drill and practice Takes the form of stimulus-response-feedback interaction between user/learner and computer.

electric pen A pen-like instrument with an electronic stylus used with a CRT for inputs to the computer. The stylus signals the computer with an electronic pulse and the appropriate response is made.

Enter A special key on a computer keyboard used to signal the computer that the user has completed typing input for a single entry or line and that this information is now to be "entered" into the computer. Sometimes labeled "RETURN."

executive program *See* operating system *and* control program.

Exits The final instructions of a program; usually deviates from the routine to another portion of the program or to a control routine.

external memory Computer memory external to the CPU; cassette tapes and floppy disks may be considered as external memory. Information must be transferred from external memory into main memory (within the CPU) before it can be processed.

feedback The use of information produced at one stage of output as input at another stage.

file Any collection of information in organized form. May be subdivided into "records" and then further subdivided into "fields" within records.

Floating-point Basic Also known as APPLESOFT; dialect of BASIC.

floppy disk *See* diskette.

For-Next Loop A control mechanism within BASIC; used to control multiple executions of the same lines of a computer program.

Forth A programming-language system readily implemented on microcomputers. Expressions of solutions to a wide range of problems are offered by this language on a high level form.

FORTRAN Acronym for Formula Translator. A programming language developed by IBM Corp. originally used on scientific problems. Has now also been extensively applied to most commercial problems.

Genis I A microcomputer developed by Bell and Howell Corporation; uses English as a command language. It can provide statistics for learner scores and tests and can retrieve information on video or audio cassette tapes.

global edit A function of some text-editing programs that allows the user to locate multiple occurrences of a word or string of words throughout an entire text and to make changes or corrections automatically. *Also see* text editor.

GOTO A control instruction in BASIC. Used to cause the computer to "go to" a particular line number for the next instruction.

graphic plotter An instrument that automatically draws a graph.

hardware The physical components of a computer system as opposed to the programs (software).

Higher Order Language (HOL) A computer language in which instructions are written in a problem-oriented form without regard to the machine language of the computer on which they will be executed. Languages such as BASIC and FORTRAN are "higher order" than machine language since *one* BASIC or FORTRAN instruction will require *many* machine-language instructions in order to be executed.

high-resolution graphics The capability of reproducing and displaying visual information on a CRT or television screen with a high degree of fidelity or sharpness. Also very dense and well-defined graphics.

holographic A three-dimensional photographic laser process that records and displays a seemingly solid object. The object recorded with lasers and chemicals or glass or film can be projected or illuminated with laser light.

hook up To make connections between various computer units or parts.

HOL *See* Higher Order Language.

host computer The device that supervises the accessibility of the other computers in a cluster configuration to mass storage and peripheral devices. The host is linked to the mass storage device of other shared peripherals.

IC Integrated Circuit. A circuit in which the equivalent of various electronic components are all produced on a single monolithic piece of silicon together with the interconnecting wires. Many identical integrated circuits are produced on a single thin wafer of silicon and then cut into individual "chips," which are then packaged into cases with the necessary conducting heads for installation on circuit boards.

information management Management of information by the computer, whereby it maintains and manipulates data files, e.g., in budgeting, inventory, record-keeping, and scheduling.

information retrieval systems A system whereby certain documents or graphic records may be located and selected from a file upon demand, e.g., classification, indexing, and machine-searching systems.

Input The process of transfer of data or program instruction from a peripheral unit into the memory unit of the computer. May also signify the data itself.

instruction set The total set ("vocabulary") of machine-language instructions (operations) executable by a particular CPU. The instruction set of each CPU type is unique and defined by the manufacturer. *Also see* central processing unit.

Integer Basic A dialect of BASIC.

integrated circuit *See* IC.

Intel 8080 The 8080 is the nomenclature of a CPU microprocessor originated by Intel (a semiconductor manufacturer).

interactive instruction The capability of each party in an instructional activity to learn from the other. In computer usage it reflects the ability of some computer programs to learn basic facts about the user and to incorporate this data into a subsequent instruction.

interactive videodisk systems The combination of videodisks and microcomputers, resulting in an interactive learning device that has the advantages of CAL and instructional television.

interface A device (usually on a circuit board) that enables two different pieces of equipment to communicate with one another; for example, a printer interface is necessary between a CPU and a printer. Generally refers to the connection between any two units, but can also refer to the channels providing the connection between peripheral units and the CPU.

interpreter A computer program that directly executes programs written in a specified language; generally written in the machine language of the computer on which it is designed to run.

I/O Input/Output. An I/O device is any device that can be used to input information into the computer and/or accept output information from the computer; e.g. printer.

J A command in PILOT that causes the computer to "jump" to a specified part of the program and resume execution; similar to GOTO in BASIC.

JN or JY Computer command similar to GOTO in BASIC followed by a label N or Y; JN means no match of data, JY means a data match or alternative match. *Also see* GOTO.

K Abbreviation for kilo. In computer terminology, K indicates 1024, the power of 2 closest to 1000; a 16K memory contains 16,384 bytes (16 times 1024).

key in To use the keyboard to enter data into a computer system.

keyboard The set of keys on an input device used for encoding characters by the depression of keys, as in a typewriter.

language, computer A definite structure for computer programs as understood by the user and the computer following certain rules of syntax thus providing the computer with a set of instructions.

large-scale integrated circuit "Large-scale" pertains to the number of equivalent transistors on a single chip (several thousand). Medium-scale chips contain hundreds of transistor equivalents, while small-scale chips contain tens. Abbreviated LSI, MSI, SSI respectively. *Also see* IC.

laser decoding The process of using laser devices to read light codes imprinted on disks for reproducing audio or video information. The basis for several videodisc player systems.

line number **1.** In BASIC, a number associated with each line of the program (at the beginning) is used to keep lines properly sequenced (numerical order) and to provide a unique identification of each line. **2.** Numbers designated to lines seen on the display screen of the computer.

linear type A type of highly sequential computer program whereby the computer presents a concept, followed by a question requiring recall, judgment, or inference, and in which the answer may be made in the user's own words.

LISP List processing. An interpretative language used to manipulate symbolic strings of recursive data; primarily designed to process data consisting of lists.

loader A program (may be included in the operating system) that performs all necessary functions to load a program from external memory into the computer's main memory within the CPU.

LSI chips *See* IC.

M A command in PILOT language. It causes the computer to attempt to "Match" a response from the keyboard (entered by the user) with an anticipated response contained within the program. Other commands can then be executed conditionally, depending on whether or not a match was found.

magnetic disk A storage device containing a number of flat circular plates; both sides of the plates have been coated with a magnetizable substance. Several tracks are present on each surface and data is written to or read from these tracks by means of read/write heads. Several heads may be available to each surface with a particular head being assigned to a specific area on the disk.

MAIL An electronic communication system whereby a user can type a message at the terminal and have it transmitted to an individual by providing the individual's identification (ID) number.

mailbox A group of locations in a common RAM storage area, an area reserved for data addressed to certain peripheral devices as well as other microprocessors. *Also see* RAM.

mainframe computer The major part of the computer, housing the central processing unit. *See also* central processing unit.

memory, computer The circuitry and devices holding the binary 1's and 0's that can be accessed by the computer, e.g., cassette tape and floppy disk.

microcomputer Somewhat similar to a minicomputer in terms of function and structure; major differences are in price, size, speed of execution, and computing power. The microcomputer main processing blocks are made of semiconductor integrated circuits and the hardware is made of a microprocessing unit usually assembled on a printed circuit board with memory and auxiliary circuits.

microelectronics The field dealing in production techniques of miniature circuits, e.g., integrated circuits.

micronet Electronic communication system that provides information retrieval services for microcomputers or terminals. On-line computerized data base that allows accurate and fast retrieval of information. A commercial enterprise providing services such as person-to-person mail, classified ads, and similar services. *Also see* MAIL.

microprocessor One of the principal components of the microcomputer, the semiconductor central processing unit (CPU). Microprocessor elements are usually contained on a single chip or within the same package although they can, at times, be distributed over several separate chips. The microprocessor of a microcomputer with a fixed instruction set consists of the arithmetic logic unit and the control logic unit, whereas, it features an additional control memory unit in a microcomputer with a microprogrammed instruction set. *Also see* central processing unit.

minicomputer Compared to microcomputers or programmable calculators, minicomputers contain units which are characterized by higher performance, richer instruction sets, higher price, and an abundance of high-level languages, operating systems and networking methodologies.

mini-floppy disk The smaller 5¼-inch (diameter) floppy disk. *Also see* disk.

mnemonic A meaningful notation or abbreviation for a computer instruction; used to aid in human understanding and recall.

Modem Modulator/Demodulator. A device that enables the computer terminal to be linked to the computer by a telephone line.

modules A set of learning experiences to be presented in achieving a group of related objectives; generally constituting instruction of several hours to several weeks.

monitor A TV set-like display without a channel tuner. Input is from a "video" signal rather than a radio frequency broadcast TV signal. Provides the best visual image quality.

monitor program *See* operating system *and* control program.

MUMPS Massachusetts General Hospital Utility Multiprogramming System. A computer language.

natural language Refers to a language with rules describing and reflecting current usage instead of prescribed usage.

network, computer An interlinked system of computers and/or terminals whose components may be physically apart; are often connected by telephone lines.

object program A machine-language program produced by translation from a higher-order-language (HOL) program (i.e., by a compiler) or by translation from an Assembly-Language program (i.e., by an assembler).

on-line Describes a system and peripheral equipment in which the operation of such equipment is under the control of the central processing unit.

Opcode *See* operation code.

operating system A collection of systems programs that make the computer easier to use; directs the sequencing of programs, performs loading operations, assists in input/output operations, and performs related service functions.

operation code The part of an instruction (machine or Assembly Language) that designates the particular operation to be performed.

parallel interface An interface that transmits all 8 bits of a character simultaneously. Faster than serial. *Also see* serial interface.

PASCAL A language developed to enable teaching of programming as a systematic discipline and to do systems programming; named after the seventeenth-century French mathematician Blaise Pascal.

Pass A new computer language developed by Bell and Howell Corporation; designed to be used by teachers to create curriculum materials through self-tutoring and self-authoring.

peripheral devices Various types of equipment that are not physically part of the computer but that operate in combination or conjunction with a computer. Peripheral devices consist of input and output devices and storage devices.

permanent memory Memory that cannot be altered during program execution and that remains unaltered when power is turned off.

personal computer Refers to the low-cost microcomputers (in comparison to mini and standard computer systems) that are structured from tiny microcomputer chips; have such features as portability, facility of use, and personal control.

PET A microcomputer manufactured by Commodore Business Machines.

photomicroscopy The process of creating photographically magnified images of small objects; for example, a human cell can be photographed using electronic magnification techniques for display in a much larger aspect.

PILOT A dialect of BASIC.

PL/1 Programming Language One. Developed during the mid-1960s as a higher-order language for both scientific and business-computing applications.

Plasma display terminal Terminal used in PLATO instruction that is capable of retaining its own images and responding directly to digital signals from the computer.

PLATO Programmed Logic for Automatic Teaching Operations. The most sophisticated computer-based education system developed to date; developed at the University of Illinois.

plug-compatible Interchangeable; while the design of two devices may not be identical, if one is functionally identical to the other and may be plugged in in its place, the two may be said to be plug-compatible.

plug-in boards Circuit boards with external connectors that permit plugging in (connecting) to a larger circuit board or cabinet.

printer An output device that prints computer results as numbers, words, or symbols; devices may range from electric typewriters to high speed printers.

printout The printed output from a printer.

problem solving The process of applying rules and general practices in order to solve a problem.

program A series of computer instructions, which, when executed, cause a general purpose computer to perform a desired function.

program driver A computer program that assists a curriculum specialist or teacher to develop CAI without specific knowledge of a program language. The computer prompts the user on how to develop the instructional program.

program statement A single line or instruction of a computer program.

programmed instruction A sequence of specific instructions for the teaching of a certain subject; not to be confused with computer programming.

programming Process of producing instructions for a computer to perform specified tasks.

prompts Messages submitted to an operator by an operating system or computer.

QUBE A two-way interactive cable system installed by Warner Amex Cable in Columbus, Ohio; it allows students and instructors to communicate in a limited manner during a college course broadcast.

QUEST Program derived from MUMPS. *Also see* MUMPS.

Radio Shack A manufacturer of microcomputers, a subsidiary of Tandy Corp. Popular computer products include the TRS-80 Model II, Model III, and Color Computer.

RAM Random Access Memory. Technically, "random access" means that any one location is accessible in the same amount of time as any other location; popularly, RAM is used to describe the read/write memory available for user programs.

Random Access Memory *See* RAM.

Read Only Memory *See* ROM.

real-time simulation An operation of a simulation program or simulator in which the occurrence of most basic incidents in the simulator occur at similar times as they would in the system being simulated.

register A high-speed memory device capable of storing a fixed number of binary bits of information; generally 8, 16, or 32 bits long. *See* bit.

REM Abbreviation for REMARK in BASIC programs. Used to insert remarks in the program that have no effect on the program (are not executed) but that permit notes to be included for clarity.

REMARK *See* REM.

remote delivery The transmission and reception of communication over an extended geographic distance; often describes the transmission of instructional courses through broadcast television or telephone.

retrieval The act of finding stored data from a file or files by looking for specified keys or labels found in records stored on file. *See also* file.

Return *See* Enter.

RF Modulator A mini-TV broadcasting transmitter; accepts a video signal as input and produces a TV broadcast signal as its output, ready to be connected to the antenna terminals of a standard TV set.

ROM Read Only Memory. A form of permanent memory used to store programs and data; information is retained even when power is turned off. Cannot be altered by program execution (i.e., no "write" capability).

serial interface An interface in which one bit is transmitted at a time; separate bit transmission times are required to complete transmission of a single character. Slower than parallel. *Also see* parallel interface *and* bit.

signal An electrical impulse, event, or phenomenon that transmits information between two points.

silicon chip A chip made of silicon containing the microcomputer's central processing unit; it is the size of a small fingernail.

simulations Depictions of phenomena and physical systems by computers.

software Programs for the computer or microcomputer. The content of the program written in a language that a computer can understand and transmit to the user.

source program A computer program in a form other than machine language. HOL or Assembly-Language programs may be source programs for compilers or assemblers which translate them into machine-language programs (object programs).

speech recognition The ability of the computer to recognize human speech.

speech synthesis The capability of computers to reproduce sounds that approximate human speech; words can be verbalized by the computer by stringing together machine-produced syllables.

stand-alone computer A computer that can operate independently; does not require any other piece of equipment for completion of its own operation.

star network *See* clustered system.

stereoscopic computer graphics The process of displaying three-dimensional images on a video screen as provided by a computer; relies on an optical instrument with two lenses to help the observer combine two pictures taken from points of view a little apart, thus creating the effect of solidity or depth.

STO Mnemonic abbreviation for an Assembly-Language computer instruction: "Store the accumulator register." Causes the contents of the accumulator register to be stored in a specified location in memory.

storage device A device where data and program instructions may be stored, retained, and then retrieved for future use. *See also* disk.

systems program A program used to assist in computer unique functions, in contrast to applications programs, which perform end user functions. Example systems programs are compilers, interpreters, assemblers and operating systems.

systems programmer A programmer who writes systems programs.

systems software *See* systems program.

T A command in PILOT; causes the computer to "Type" a message on the screen.

tachistiscope A device that exposes for a very brief period of time (e.g., 1/10,000 second) a word or picture.

task environment exercise (TEE) An instrument (computer program) that assists physicians in decisions regarding diagnostic problem-solving. The program asks questions that provide a context for a clinical problem and requests and records step-by-step decisions and activities in diagnosing and treating the patient.

TEE *See* task environment exercise.

Tektronix 4051 A microcomputer produced by Tektronix Inc.

telecommunication The transmission or reception of signals by wire, radio, light beam, or other electromagnetic system.

telecourses Instructional courses developed for and delivered by television.

telelecture A setting that enables a teacher or lecturer to be heard by the class/audience via regular telephone lines. The speaker is able to interact with one or more classes at different locations.

Telemail/IBS Electronic communication system that provides information retrieval services for microcomputers or terminals. On-line computerized data base that allows accurate and fast retrieval of information. A commercial enterprise providing services such as person-to-person mail, classified ads, and similar services. *Also see* MAIL.

telematics *See* telematique.

telematique An expression from French that describes the intercommunications between computer and telecommunications systems or devices such as satellites, videodiscs, broadcast or cable television, or telephone networks.

terminal, computer A point where data becomes input to or output from the computer system. Usually with a console and/or CRT.

text editor A computer program that facilitates editing of text with the computer; typical editing functions include insertion and deletion of characters or whole lines of text, and replacement of one character or word by another character or word. *Also see* global edit.

THE SOURCE An electronic communication system to which users may subscribe; enables the user to "mail" and "chat." Two parties can communicate with one another if connected to THE SOURCE. *Also see* MAIL *and* Chat.

time-sharing The use of a particular device for two or more concurrent operations. Typically, the device momentarily operates to accomplish one purpose then another, returns to the first, and so on in succession until all operations are fulfilled.

track The path along which information is recorded on a storage device such as a floppy disk; a typical floppy disk surface is divided into 40 concentric tracks. *Also see* disk.

transistor A small solid-state semiconductor made by attaching one or more wires to a tiny wafer of semiconducting material; usually constructed of germanium or silicon. Transistors are small and light and have very quick switching speeds.

TRS-80 A popular microcomputer manufactured by Radio Shack, a division of Tandy Corporation.

TSC/Mail Electronic communications system that provides information retrieval services for microcomputers or terminals. On-line computerized data base that allows accurate and fast retrieval of information. A commercial enterprise providing services such as person-to-person mail, classified ads, and similar services. *Also see* MAIL.

tutorial A process of instruction whereby a tutor conducts a question-and-answer dialogue with a small number of individuals in the pursuit of knowledge in a certain discipline.

videocassette recorder A device that records television images and sound on a tape cassette and that can play back the tape cassette for later viewing on a television monitor or receiver.

videodisc A disc (usually plastic) on which recordings of video and/or audio signals are imprinted; can be played back and viewed on a television monitor.

Votrax A voice synthesizer produced by Federal Screw Works. *Also see* speech synthesis.

word processing Operations associated with word processing include interactive information, retrieval systems, management information systems, text editing, translation, and typesetting.

Z-80 An 8-bit microprocessor; a more powerful version of the Intel 8080.